BARRON'S

HOW TO PREPARE FOR THE

CAHSEE-
ENGLISH-LANGUAGE ARTS

CALIFORNIA HIGH SCHOOL EXIT EXAM

BARRON'S

HOW TO PREPARE FOR THE

CAHSEE-
ENGLISH-LANGUAGE ARTS

CALIFORNIA HIGH SCHOOL EXIT EXAM

Christina Lacie

BARRON'S

All inquiries should be addressed to:
Barron's Educational Series, Inc.
250 Wireless Boulevard
Hauppauge, New York 11788
http://www.barronseduc.com

Library of Congress Catalog Card No. 2002038365

International Standard Book No. 0-7641-2292-4

Library of Congress Cataloging-in-Publication Data

Lacie, Christina.
     How to prepare for the CAHSEE-English language arts : California High School Exit Exam /
Christina Lacie.
          p.   cm.
Includes index.
     ISBN 0-7641-2292-4
     1. Language arts (Secondary)—California—Examinations, questions, etc.—Study guides.   2. High schools—California—Graduation requirements—Study guides.   3. Educational tests and measurements—California—Study guides.   I. Title.

LB1631.5 .L33 2003
373.126′2—dc21   2002038365

PRINTED IN THE UNITED STATES OF AMERICA
9 8 7 6 5 4 3 2

Contents

Preface

Introduction to the CAHSEE

The California High School Exit Exam is a test that needs to be taken seriously. The purpose of the exam, adopted by the California Department of Education, is to make certain that students graduating from California high schools are competent in reading, writing, and mathematics. It's all about accountability. Teachers need to teach and students need to learn. The exam concept originated with a state law (Senate Bill 2) that was passed in 1999 and authorized the development of the exam (ETS or Educational Testing Service is the company that designed the exam). This basically means that all students in California public schools beginning with the graduating class of 2004 will have to pass the exam to receive a high school diploma.

The exam has two sections; one section is language arts and the other is mathematics. The language arts section (the focus of this study guide) contains two "sessions." Both language-arts sessions consist of both multiple-choice questions and a writing task. Over the course of three years, you will take the exam until you pass all portions of it; however, if you pass one section and not the other, you will retake only the portion(s) that you did not pass.

The scoring of the exams is scaled. This means that statistical measures or concepts—using statistical jargon: Standard Error of Measurement, Conditional Standard Error of Measurement, Raw Score to Scale Score Conversion, Weighting of Examination Portions—are used to ensure that a more precise measurement of your achievement is actually achieved. This also ensures that tests given at different times of the year are comparable. What all that boils down to is how it is all made fair in the end. The scoring range of the exam is 250–450. To pass the exam, you must score a minimum of 350 in both sections (language arts *and* mathematics). To pass the writing tasks, you must score a 3 or 4. The two writing tasks account for 30% of your English language arts scaled score. The multiple-choice scores are totaled and then weighted to account for the remaining 70% of the scaled score. By the way, each paper is read by two different readers who are specially trained to do so. To make certain that the readers are consistent, the papers are "back-read" by yet another person who then formally records the scores.

Those are the basics—the ins and outs of the exam. If you have any more questions, please check the California Department of Education's web site devoted to the exam at: *http://cahsee.cde.ca.gov*. You can also look into the ETS (the makers of the exam) web site as well. It is linked from the state's exit exam site listed above.

Content Standards—Defined and Aligned to the Exam

The California High School Exit Exam is aligned to the English-Language Arts Content Standards for California Public Schools. The content standards are a list of skills that need to be taught in each grade level and in each subject. Teachers are required to teach the standards and students are required to master them and that's what this test is all about—making sure that everyone is doing their job. These standards were adopted in 1997 by the State of California.

The exit exam covers the content standards for English and language arts for the ninth and tenth grades and very few from the eighth-grade standards. These standards are listed below. They cover very specific things such as: Reading—Word Analysis, Fluency, and Systematic Vocabulary Development; Reading Comprehension; Literary Response, and Analysis; Writing Strategies; Writing Applications (Genres and Their Characteristics); Written and Oral English Language Conventions—Grammar and Mechanics, Listening and Speaking Skills, and Speaking Applications (Genres and Their Characteristics). If you look carefully at the list of standards, you will see how specific and thorough they are in identifying the skills you need to learn at each level. This list, remember, is only for English—Language Arts and only for the ninth and tenth grades. There is a list like this for each subject at every grade level.

To be more specific about what is covered on the exam from the standards, the following is a list of what was included on the first exam given in 2000 and how these questions were aligned to the standards:

- Word Analysis, Fluency, and Systematic Vocabulary Development—**10** multiple-choice items/questions
- Reading Comprehension (Focus on Informational Materials)—**24** multiple-choice items/questions
- Literary Response and Analysis—**24** multiple-choice items/questions
- Writing Strategies—**11** multiple-choice items/questions
- Writing Applications—Genres and Their Characteristics—**2** written essays
- Written and Oral Language Conventions—Grammar and Mechanics—**13** multiple-choice items/questions

It would be impossible to predict what the exam will contain each year, but if you are mastering the skills that are presented in the standards in your English classes, you have a head start on the exam.

English—Language Arts Content Standards for California Public Schools Grades Nine and Ten

Reading

1.0 Word Analysis, Fluency, and Systematic Vocabulary Development

Students apply their knowledge of word origins to determine the meaning of new words encountered in reading materials and use those words accurately.

Vocabulary and Concept Development

1.1 Identify and use the literal and figurative meanings of words and understand word derivations.
1.2 Distinguish between the denotative and connotative meanings of words and interpret the connotative power of words.
1.3 Identify Greek, Roman, and Norse mythology and use the knowledge to understand the origin and meaning of new words (e.g., the word *narcissistic* drawn from the myth of Narcissus and Echo).

2.0 Reading Comprehension (Focus on Informational Materials)

Students read and understand grade-level-appropriate material. They analyze the organizational patterns, arguments, and positions advanced. The selections in *Recommended Literature, Grades Nine Through Twelve* (1990) illustrate the quality and complexity of the materials to be read by students. In addition, by grade twelve, students read two million words annually on their own, including a wide variety of classic and contemporary literature, magazines, newspapers, and on-line information. In grades nine and ten, students make substantial progress toward this goal.

Structural Features of Informational Materials

2.1 Analyze the structure and format of functional workplace documents, including the graphics and headers, and explain how authors use the features to achieve their purposes.
2.2 Prepare a bibliography of reference materials for a report using a variety of consumer, workplace, and public documents.

Comprehension and Analysis of Grade-Level-Appropriate Text

2.3 Generate relevant questions about readings on issues that can be researched.
2.4 Synthesize the content from several sources or works by a single author dealing with a single issue; paraphrase the ideas and connect them to other sources and related topics to demonstrate comprehension.
2.5 Extend ideas presented in primary or secondary sources through original analysis, evaluation, and elaboration.
2.6 Demonstrate use of sophisticated learning tools by following technical directions (e.g., those found with graphic calculators and specialized software programs and in access guides to World Wide Web sites on the Internet).

Expository Critique

2.7 Critique the logic of functional documents by examining the sequence of information and procedures in anticipation of possible reader misunderstandings.

2.8 Evaluate the credibility of an author's argument or defense of a claim by critiquing the relationship between generalizations and evidence, the comprehensiveness of evidence, and the way in which the author's intent affects the structure and tone of the text (e.g., in professional journals, editorials, political speeches, primary source material).

3.0 Literary Response and Analysis

Students read and respond to historically or culturally significant works of literature that reflect and enhance their studies of history and social science. They conduct in-depth analyses of recurrent patterns and themes. The selections in *Recommended Literature, Grades Nine Through Twelve* illustrate the quality and complexity of the materials to be read by students.

Structural Features of Literature

3.1 Articulate the relationship between the expressed purposes and the characteristics of different forms of dramatic literature (e.g., comedy, tragedy, drama, dramatic monologue).
3.2 Compare and contrast the presentation of a similar theme or topic across genres to explain how the selection of genre shapes the theme or topic.

Narrative Analysis of Grade-Level-Appropriate Text

3.3 Analyze interactions between main and subordinate characters in a literary text (e.g., internal and external conflicts, motivations, relationships, influences) and explain the way those interactions affect the plot.
3.4 Determine characters' traits by what the characters say about themselves in narration, dialogue, dramatic monologue, and soliloquy.
3.5 Compare works that express a universal theme and provide evidence to support the ideas expressed in each work.
3.6 Analyze and trace an author's development of time and sequence, including the use of complex literary devices (e.g., foreshadowing, flashbacks).
3.7 Recognize and understand the significance of various literary devices, including figurative language, imagery, allegory, and symbolism, and explain their appeal.
3.8 Interpret and evaluate the impact of ambiguities, subtleties, contradictions, ironies, and incongruities in a text.
3.9 Explain how voice, persona, and the choice of a narrator affect characterization and the tone, plot, and credibility of a text.
3.10 Identify and describe the function of dialogue, scene designs, soliloquies, asides, and character foils in dramatic literature.

Literary Criticism

3.11 Evaluate the aesthetic qualities of style, including the impact of diction and figurative language on tone, mood, and theme, using the terminology of literary criticism. (Aesthetic approach)
3.12 Analyze the way in which a work of literature is related to the themes and issues of its historical period. (Historical approach)

Writing

1.0 Writing Strategies

Students write coherent and focused essays that convey a well-defined perspective and tightly reasoned argument. The writing demonstrates students' awareness of the audience and purpose. Students progress through the stages of the writing process as needed.

Organization and Focus

1.1 Establish a controlling impression or coherent thesis that conveys a clear and distinctive perspective on the subject and maintain a consistent tone and focus throughout the piece of writing.

1.2 Use precise language, action verbs, sensory details, appropriate modifiers, and the active rather than the passive voice.

Research and Technology

1.3 Use clear research questions and suitable research methods (e.g., library, electronic media, personal interview) to elicit and present evidence from primary and secondary sources.

1.4 Develop the main ideas within the body of the composition through supporting evidence (e.g., scenarios, commonly held beliefs, hypotheses, and definitions).

1.5 Synthesize information from multiple sources and identify complexities and discrepancies in the information and the different perspectives found in each medium (e.g., almanacs, microfiche, news sources, in-depth field studies, speeches, journals, technical documents).

1.6 Integrate quotations and citations into a written text while maintaining the flow of ideas.

1.7 Use appropriate conventions for documentation in the text, notes, and bibliographies by adhering to those in style manuals (e.g., *Modern Language Association Handbook*, *The Chicago Manual of Style*).

1.8 Design and publish documents by using advanced publishing software and graphic programs.

Evaluation and Revision

1.9 Revise writing to improve the logic and coherence of the organization and controlling perspective, the precision of word choice, and the tone by taking into consideration the audience, purpose, and formality of the context.

2.0 Writing Applications (Genres and Their Characteristics)

Students combine the rhetorical strategies of narration, exposition, persuasion, and description to produce texts of at least 1,500 words each. Student writing demonstrates a command of standard American English and the research, organizational, and drafting strategies outlined in Writing Standard 1.0.

Using the writing strategies of grades nine and ten outlined in Writing Standard 1.0, students:

2.1 Write biographical or autobiographical narratives or short stories:

a. Relate a sequence of events and communicate the significance of the events to the audience.

b. Locate scenes and incidents in specific places.

c. Describe with concrete sensory details the sights, sounds, and smells of a scene and the specific actions, movements, gestures, and feelings of the characters; use interior monologue to depict the characters' feelings.

d. Pace the presentation of actions to accommodate changes in time and mood.

e. Make effective use of descriptions of appearance, images, shifting perspectives, and sensory details.

2.2 Write responses to literature:

a. Demonstrate a comprehensive grasp of the significant ideas of literary works.

b. Support important ideas and viewpoints through accurate and detailed references to the text or to other works.

c. Demonstrate awareness of the author's use of stylistic devices and an appreciation of the effects created.

d. Identify and assess the impact of perceived ambiguities, nuances, and complexities within the text.

2.3 Write expository compositions, including analytical essays and research reports:

a. Marshal evidence in support of a thesis and related claims, including information on all relevant perspectives.

b. Convey information and ideas from primary and secondary sources accurately and coherently.

c. Make distinctions between the relative value and significance of specific data, facts, and ideas.

d. Include visual aids by employing appropriate technology to organize and record information on charts, maps, and graphs.

e. Anticipate and address readers' potential misunderstandings, biases, and expectations.

f. Use technical terms and notations accurately.

2.4 Write persuasive compositions:

a. Structure ideas and arguments in a sustained and logical fashion.

b. Use specific rhetorical devices to support assertions (e.g., appeal to logic through reasoning; appeal to emotion or ethical belief; relate a personal anecdote, case study, or analogy).

c. Clarify and defend positions with precise and relevant evidence, including facts, expert opinions, quotations, and expressions of commonly accepted beliefs and logical reasoning.

d. Address readers' concerns, counterclaims, biases, and expectations.

2.5 Write business letters:

a. Provide clear and purposeful information and address the intended audience appropriately.

b. Use appropriate vocabulary, tone, and style to take into account the nature of the relationship with, and the knowledge and interests of, the recipients.

c. Highlight central ideas or images.

d. Follow a conventional style with page formats, fonts, and spacing that contribute to the documents' readability and impact.

2.6 Write technical documents (e.g., a manual on rules of behavior for conflict resolution, procedures for conducting a meeting, minutes of a meeting):

a. Report information and convey ideas logically and correctly.

b. Offer detailed and accurate specifications.

c. Include scenarios, definitions, and examples to aid comprehension (e.g., troubleshooting guide).

d. Anticipate readers' problems, mistakes, and misunderstandings.

Written and Oral English Language Conventions

The standards for written and oral English language conventions have been placed between those for writing and for listening and speaking because these conventions are essential to both sets of skills.

1.0 Written and Oral English Language Conventions

Students write and speak with a command of standard English conventions.

Grammar and Mechanics of Writing

1.1 Identify and correctly use clauses (e.g., main and subordinate), phrases (e.g., gerund, infinitive, and participial), and mechanics of punctuation (e.g., semicolons, colons, ellipses, hyphens).

1.2 Understand sentence construction (e.g., parallel structure, subordination, proper placement of modifiers) and proper English usage (e.g., consistency of verb tenses).

1.3 Demonstrate an understanding of proper English usage and control of grammar, paragraph and sentence structure, diction, and syntax.

Manuscript Form

1.4 Produce legible work that shows accurate spelling and correct use of the conventions of punctuation and capitalization.

1.5 Reflect appropriate manuscript requirements, including title page presentation, pagination, spacing and margins, and integration of source and support material (e.g., in-text citation, use of direct quotations, paraphrasing) with appropriate citations.

Listening and Speaking

1.0 Listening and Speaking Strategies

Students formulate adroit judgments about oral communication. They deliver focused and coherent presentations of their own that convey clear and distinct perspectives and solid reasoning. They use gestures, tone, and vocabulary tailored to the audience and purpose.

Comprehension

1.1 Formulate judgments about the ideas under discussion and support those judgments with convincing evidence.
1.2 Compare and contrast the ways in which media genres (e.g., televised news, news magazines, documentaries, on-line information) cover the same event.

Organization and Delivery of Oral Communication

1.3 Choose logical patterns of organization (e.g., chronological, topical, cause and effect) to inform and to persuade, by soliciting agreement or action, or to unite audiences behind a common belief or cause.
1.4 Choose appropriate techniques for developing the introduction and conclusion (e.g., by using literary quotations, anecdotes, references to authoritative sources).
1.5 Recognize and use elements of classical speech forms (e.g., introduction, first and second transitions, body, conclusion) in formulating rational arguments and applying the art of persuasion and debate.
1.6 Present and advance a clear thesis statement and choose appropriate types of proof (e.g., statistics, testimony, specific instances) that meet standard tests for evidence, including credibility, validity, and relevance.
1.7 Use props, visual aids, graphs, and electronic media to enhance the appeal and accuracy of presentations.
1.8 Produce concise notes for extemporaneous delivery.
1.9 Analyze the occasion and the interests of the audience and choose effective verbal and nonverbal techniques (e.g., voice, gestures, eye contact) for presentations.

Analysis and Evaluation of Oral and Media Communications

1.10 Analyze historically significant speeches (e.g., Abraham Lincoln's "Gettysburg Address," Martin Luther King, Jr.'s "I Have a Dream") to find the rhetorical devices and features that make them memorable.
1.11 Assess how language and delivery affect the mood and tone of the oral communication and make an impact on the audience.
1.12 Evaluate the clarity, quality, effectiveness, and general coherence of a speaker's important points, arguments, evidence, organization of ideas, delivery, diction, and syntax.
1.13 Analyze the types of arguments used by the speaker, including argument by causation, analogy, authority, emotion, and logic.
1.14 Identify the aesthetic effects of a media presentation and evaluate the techniques used to create them (e.g., compare Shakespeare's *Henry V* with Kenneth Branagh's 1990 film version).

2.0 Speaking Applications (Genres and Their Characteristics)

Students deliver polished formal and extemporaneous presentations that combine the traditional rhetorical strategies of narration, exposition, persuasion, and description. Student speaking demonstrates a command of standard American English and the organizational and delivery strategies outlined in Listening and Speaking Standard 1.0. Using the speaking strategies of grades nine and ten outlined in Listening and Speaking Standard 1.0, students:
2.1 Deliver narrative presentations:
a. Narrate a sequence of events and communicate their significance to the audience.
b. Locate scenes and incidents in specific places.
c. Describe with concrete sensory details the sights, sounds, and smells of a scene and the specific actions, movements, gestures, and feelings of characters.
d. Pace the presentation of actions to accommodate time or mood changes.
2.2 Deliver expository presentations:
a. Marshal evidence in support of a thesis and related claims, including information on all relevant perspectives.
b. Convey information and ideas from primary and secondary sources accurately and coherently.

c. Make distinctions between the relative value and significance of specific data, facts, and ideas.

d. Include visual aids by employing appropriate technology to organize and display information on charts, maps, and graphs.

e. Anticipate and address the listener's potential misunderstandings, biases, and expectations.

f. Use technical terms and notations accurately.

2.3 Apply appropriate interviewing techniques:

a. Prepare and ask relevant questions.

b. Make notes of responses.

c. Use language that conveys maturity, sensitivity, and respect.

d. Respond correctly and effectively to questions.

e. Demonstrate knowledge of the subject or organization.

f. Compile and report responses.

g. Evaluate the effectiveness of the interview.

2.4 Deliver oral responses to literature:

a. Advance a judgment demonstrating a comprehensive grasp of the significant ideas of works or passages (i.e., make and support warranted assertions about the text).

b. Support important ideas and viewpoints through accurate and detailed references to the text or to other works.

c. Demonstrate awareness of the author's use of stylistic devices and an appreciation of the effects created.

d. Identify and assess the impact of perceived ambiguities, nuances, and complexities within the text.

2.5 Deliver persuasive arguments (including evaluation and analysis of problems and solutions and causes and effects):

a. Structure ideas and arguments in a coherent, logical fashion.

b. Use rhetorical devices to support assertions (e.g., by appeal to logic through reasoning; by appeal to emotion or ethical belief; by use of personal anecdote, case study, or analogy).

c. Clarify and defend positions with precise and relevant evidence, including facts, expert opinions, quotations, expressions of commonly accepted beliefs, and logical reasoning.

d. Anticipate and address the listener's concerns and counterarguments.

2.6 Deliver descriptive presentations:

a. Establish clearly the speaker's point of view on the subject of the presentation.

b. Establish clearly the speaker's relationship with that subject (e.g., dispassionate observation, personal involvement).

c. Use effective, factual descriptions of appearance, concrete images, shifting perspectives and vantage points, and sensory details.

How to Use This Book

The most important thing to remember in using this book, is that it is for review purposes. It is a guide and aligned to the California English-Language Arts Content Standards, but it is not a substitute for what you are learning for nine months of the year in your English classroom—that can be done only in an English classroom. The more you read, study vocabulary, write and work on grammar and mechanics during the course of the school year, the better prepared you will be. But this guide should help remind you of what you have learned throughout the course of the year in English, especially ninth and tenth grades.

Look at each of the chapters and take an honest look at your weaknesses and strengths. For instance, if you read and comprehend well, but struggle with writing, focus more on the writing chapters. Whatever it is that you feel you need to review, spend more time, *quality time*, reviewing those areas.

Good luck in taking the test—be calm, think positively and, most importantly, take it seriously. Always do your best.

Section I

Reading

Chapter 1

Word Analysis, Fluency, and Systematic Vocabulary Development—Part I

The California High School Exit Exam is directly tied to the California Content Standards. The content standards are basically (and very simply defined) the specific skills that you are learning in the classroom every year according to the state's education department. At the top of the list—rated number one in importance is READING. Reading is a lot more than just reading! Understanding the *words* that you are reading and making sense of them is vital to improving your overall skills as a reader. In this chapter, we will be looking at **words** and how they are used in sentences. On the exam, there are times when you need to be able to choose an actual or **literal** definition. There will be other times when you will need to select the **figurative**, **denotative**, or **connotative** meaning of the word or to know what an **idiom** is. You're asking yourself, "and just what does all that mean?" Read on.

CHAPTER FOCUS:　　*Literal—meanings of words*

　　　　　　　　　　　　Figurative—meanings of words

　　　　　　　　　　　　Denotative—meanings of words

　　　　　　　　　　　　Connotative—meanings of words

　　　　　　　　　　　　Idioms—mean something different than what is actually said

　　　　　　　　　　　　Vocabulary words

Literal Meanings

　　　Choosing the literal meaning of a word from a list of answers is a frequent occurrence on the CAHSEE. The test makers don't come right out and say "choose the literal meaning of this word" in their questions, but when they want to know if you can choose the correct definition, that is *really* what they mean. The literal meaning of a word is simply the *actual* or *exact* definition of the word as it is used in the sentence. That's it—nothing more! No need to add or infer meanings that aren't there. A car is a car (something that carries people and moves on four wheels), a fish is a fish (something that swims and breathes in water), and a dog is a dog (a four-legged animal that barks). Not a black Mercedes with leather interior, or a fabulous Ford, or a tiny Toyota. Not a rainbow trout, Atlantic salmon, or mahi mahi. Not a poodle, Labrador retriever, or dachshund. Just a car, a fish, and a dog!

Reading Vocabulary Review I

　　　Before true understanding can take place, you must be able to identify the meanings of the words that you are reading. Without understanding, the words run together and don't make sense *at all*. Before looking at example test questions for literal meanings, we will look at some of the words used in the short readings of the test. Review these words and their definitions. If you are unfamiliar with them, become familiar! To learn new words, some people prefer to make note cards, others read the words over and over (at least three to five times), and others complete vocabulary foursquares (see the example below and the page that can be copied at the end of the book), which is a very visual way of learning words. This will help you lock the definition information into your brain where it will be ready to use when you need it. The definitions provided, by the way, are the literal or actual definitions of the words as they are used in the sentences of the short readings. At the end of the chapter, there will be a short quiz to test your understanding of the test vocabulary.

Word	Definition
foundation _____	a basis upon which something is built
stationary _____	fixed, unchanging, immobile
propel _____	to drive forward or onward
experimenting _____	trying a new procedure, idea, or activity
required _____	demanded as necessary
inquisitive _____	inclined to ask questions, curious
mounted _____	attached to a support
intelligent _____	having a high degree of mental capacity
curious _____	marked by a desire to investigate and learn
curiosity _____	desire to know
tinker _____	to fool around with, to putter with
darning _____	mending or repairing with a needle
intended _____	planned or designed for a specific use
immigrant _____	a person who comes to a country to live permanently
mechanical _____	relating to machinery or tools
journey _____	an act of traveling from one place to another
variety _____	having different forms or types
carriage _____	a wheeled vehicle, especially horse-drawn, used to carry people or things
protest _____	to object or to disapprove
impressed _____	deeply influenced
incentive _____	something that promotes determination or action
encouraged _____	spurred on, inspired to continue
operable _____	to be able to use
commonplace _____	ordinary, commonly found
genius _____	extraordinary intellectual power or aptitude
dramatic _____	striking in appearance or effect

Reminder—Study the Words by Using Any of These Techniques:
- Reading the words again and again and again
- Making note cards
- Completing vocabulary foursquares

Vocabulary Foursquare

Complete one for each word you need to learn!

Write the word here	Draw a picture of the word
Write the definition here	Write synonyms here / Write antonyms here

Synonyms—words that have the *same* or *similar* meanings.

Antonyms—words that mean the *opposite* of the defined word.

Example:

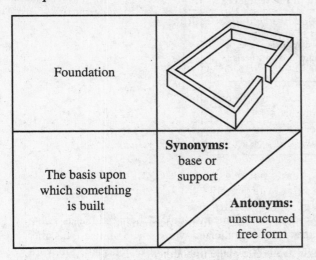

Foundation	
The basis upon which something is built	**Synonyms:** base or support **Antonyms:** unstructured free form

Pictures—Drawing pictures of the words can be challenging. But it forces you to visualize the word. Some words are easier to draw than others. Sometimes you really have to use your imagination.

Test Samples

On the exam, you will be asked to read a short essay followed by questions asking for the meaning of the word(s) used in the essay. Although the word **literal** will not be used specifically in the question, you will know by the phrasing of the question itself. Look at the two samples below. Both are asking for literal meanings.

1. **What do the words *inquisitive boy* mean in the sentence below taken from the essay?**

   Experimenting with household objects can often get young people in trouble, but for one intelligent, inquisitive boy, it created the foundation of his future.

   A one who doesn't understand
   B one who gets confused
   C one who knows a lot of information
   D one who asks many questions

Your Answer:

A ❑   **B** ❑   **C** ❑   **D** ❑

Analysis: Looking carefully at the answer choices, you will see that there are two that can be eliminated almost immediately as the weakest links! We are looking for an answer that tells us that what this young man experimented with "created the foundation of his future." Answers **A** and **B** refer to someone who is perhaps not particularly bright. Answer **C** is closer, but it refers to actual intelligence. Therefore, **D is the correct answer.** An *inquisitive boy* is someone who asks way too many questions—but in a good way. That's the literal meaning of the word.

> **2. What do the words *remain stationary* mean in the sentence below from the essay?**
>
> > This marvelous engine was used for sawing wood and other tasks that required it to remain stationary, but it was mounted on wheels to propel itself from one location to another.
>
> **A** move from one place to another
> **B** stays in one place and does not move
> **C** move in two directions
> **D** stay in more than one place

Your Answer:

A ❑   **B** ❑   **C** ❑   **D** ❑

Analysis: If you are not certain what the word *stationary* means, look at the word that is italicized just before it. *Remain*—stays in one place. The two italicized words mean almost the same thing. Now look at the answers. Answers **A** and **C** move around, but **B** and **D** both have the word "stay." Look again at **D**: "Stay in more than one place?" that's a little weird. Therefore, logically we must conclude that Answer **B** is used correctly.

Figurative Meanings

If someone were to make the comment to you that "two heads are better than one," you might think about this statement in two ways. One, the literal meaning would have you thinking "Wow, there are times when I really could use another head on my shoulders, especially on nights when I have a lot of homework—one could do math and the other English." The second way to consider the comment is figuratively. Thinking of this figuratively, the meaning of the statement changes completely. "Two heads are better than one" means that two people, each with one head (meaning brain), thinking together or brainstorming about something is better than just one person with one head. Why? Because. With two heads, you can bounce ideas off each other and come up with twice the number of solutions. So, two heads **are** better than one—figuratively speaking.

In other words, figurative meanings go beyond literal meanings. Writers use this device to make their word images stronger and more colorful—their writing becomes less boring. Poets are especially fond of using figurative language in their poems. **Simile, metaphor,** and **personification** are examples of figurative language—let's take a closer look at them.

Similes (Pronounced sim-i-lees)

Similes are everywhere and they are easy to spot. When a writer compares two different things using the words *as* or *like*, you will know that it is a simile or a **figure of speech**—hence, **figurative** language.

> Love is *like* a rose.
> I feel *like* a sitting duck out of water.
> His temper is *as* explosive *as* a volcano.
> Clouds are *as* white *as* puffy marshmallows.
> His brain is like a sponge.

Metaphors

These are used to compare two different things, but without using *as* or *like* in the comparison. With metaphors, the thing actually becomes what it is being compared to. In fact, the word *is* (or other form of *is* such as *are* for plural or *am* for first person singular) *is* often found in metaphors!

> Love *is* a rose.
> His brain is a sponge.
> I ***am*** a rock.
> Clouds *are* white puffy marshmallows.

Notice the difference between **similes** and **metaphors?** Similes are *like* something else and metaphors *are* or *become* something else. In other words, metaphors make bold, strong, dynamic (*am* or *is*) comparisons, while similes make less bold and rather soft or gentle (*like* or *as*) comparisons.

Personification

This describes something (an *inanimate* object, to be precise) that is not really a person, such as an animal, an idea, or an object, that is given traits of a human to make it appear as if it were almost human. Sometimes, these objects will hear, talk, feel, or do other things that seem rather strange, but at the same time it seems rather poetic. Writers use personification to make their work come alive!

> The moon is content as he glides across the midnight sky.
> The trees bend with stiff backs as the wind blows through their branches.
> The cheerful flowers shout their joy to the glorious sun.
> The acrobatic surf rolls and tumbles into the shore.

To test your knowledge of figurative language/meanings, the test makers will ask you to read a poem or a short, very colorful passage of prose (paragraph writing). The questions will follow. Let's see how well you understand figurative language. Read the following poem and then answer the questions. This will test your understanding of **similes, metaphors,** and **personification.**

---

3. Which line in this stanza does NOT have a simile?

From *The Night before Christmas* by Clement C. Moore

His eyes how they twinkled! His dimples how merry!   (1)
His cheeks were like roses, his nose like a cherry!   (2)
His droll little mouth was drawn up like a bow,   (3)
And the beard on his chin was as white as the snow;   (4)

A lines 4 and 3
B line 2
C line 1
D lines 1 and 2

Your Answer:

A ❑   **B** ❑   **C** ❑   **D** ❑

Analysis: The question is asking for the line that does *not* have a simile. The key words to look for in finding a simile are *as* and *like*. In this example, there is only one line that does not have *like* or *as*, and that line is 1. Therefore, **C** is the correct answer!

NOTE: *First of all, read the question very carefully and closely. Sometimes the questions are worded almost the opposite of what you're used to reading.*

4. The metaphor in this poem by Emily Dickinson is stated in which line?

Hope is the thing with feathers	(1)
That perches in the soul,	(2)
And sings the tune without the words,	(3)
And never stops at all,	(4)
And sweetest in the gale is heard,	(5)
And sore must be the storm	(6)
That could abash that little bird	(7)
That kept so many warm.	(8)
I've heard it in the chillest land,	(9)
And on the strangest sea;	(10)
Yet, never, in extremity,	(11)
It asked a crumb of me.	(12)

A line 12
B line 2
C line 7
D line 1

Your Answer:

A ❑   **B** ❑   **C** ❑   **D** ❑

Analysis: A **metaphor** is a comparison of two unlike things. Frequently, you will see the word *is* or *am* included, but not all the time, so beware! In this poem, we see the metaphor in the very first line! *Hope is the thing with feathers*—the poet is comparing **hope** to a **bird** that sings and *never stops at all!* The correct answer is **D**.

5. There are two things being personified in this poem by Carl Sandburg. Name them.

"Summer Grass" by Carl Sandburg	
Summer grass aches and whispers.	(1)
It wants something; it calls and sings; it pours	(2)
out wishes to the overhead stars.	(3)
The rain hears; the rain answers; the rain is slow	(4)
coming; the rain wets the face of the grass.	(5)

A grass and rain
B grass and stars
C stars and rain
D whispers and wishes

Your Answer:

A ❑   **B** ❑   **C** ❑   **D** ❑

Analysis: Carefully look at the poem. Remember, **personification** transforms or *morphs* inanimate objects by adding human characteristics or traits. Immediately, we see that the grass *aches* and *whispers* and *calls* and *sings* and *pours* out wishes (lines 1–3). That's personification. But, check out line 4! The rain *hears* and *answers!* **A** is the correct answer. It is the only one that mentions grass and rain together.

Reading Vocabulary Review II

Study the list of the following testing words. Become familiar with those you are unfamiliar with through the methods mentioned in the vocabulary review section I.

Word	Definition
falconry _____	the art of training hawks to hunt
ancient _____	having had an existence for many years, or relating to a remote period in time
medieval _____	relating to or characteristic of the Middle Ages
royalty _____	privileged class, of royal status or power
jousting _____	fighting on horseback as knights used to do
enthusiast _____	a person who is extremely excited or interested in something, (enthusiastic)
predatory _____	inclined to injure or exploit others for personal gain
establish _____	to bring into existence
coax _____	to persuade, or gently influence
bond _____	to hold together
horizon _____	the apparent junction or joining of the earth and sky
patience _____	not hasty, bearing pain or problems calmly
populated _____	inhabited, wherever people are
polluted _____	making physically impure or unclean
deplete _____	to use up, exhaust a resource
cumulative _____	made up of additional parts, adding up to
environmental _____	having to do with complex physical surroundings—climate, soil, living things
counter _____	having the opposite effect
impose _____	to bring about by force
exhaust _____	to use up, deplete
regulate _____	to govern according to rule
monitor _____	to watch
generate _____	to bring into existence, to cause
efficient _____	producing desired effects easily
conversely _____	reversing the order of
aerodynamic _____	moving easily without wind resistance
drag _____	something that slows motion
maintenance _____	the upkeep of property or equipment
rebate _____	to return money to consumer for reward
preserve _____	to keep safe from injury or harm

Idioms

These are common, everyday expressions that really don't mean what they say literally. They reflect the way people talk in normal conversations—and people use them all the time! The basic idea of **idioms** fits nicely in this area of review. They are actually entertaining to look at both literally and figuratively. There are hundreds of idioms, but here are a few examples to play around with. The figurative meanings are given. In the neighboring box, draw a picture of the literal meaning of the idiom; it will help you to remember them. P.S. Idioms are very strange to people who are learning English for the first time; after looking at them, you will see why!

BREAK THE ICE—to say or do something that will reduce the social awkwardness or coldness at a meeting or social event (a party).

ONCE IN A BLUE MOON—something that happens very seldom or rarely.

SECONDHAND—information from somewhere other than the original source.

PICK SOMEONE'S BRAIN—to get information from someone who is more knowledgeable than you are about something.

FOLLOW YOUR NOSE—Instead of following guidelines or rules, to follow your instincts or intuition.

CATCH SOMEONE'S EYE—to attract someone's attention, such as a waiter or waitress, or someone cute at a party.

I'LL EAT MY HAT—expression to emphasize that the probability of something actually happening is not likely.

PUT A SOCK IN IT—to keep quiet or stop talking!

THE LION'S SHARE—the best or largest part of something.

BIRDS OF A FEATHER FLOCK TOGETHER—people with the same or similar interests or traits seem to stick together.

Reading Vocabulary Review III

More words to study! Some of them may be familiar; others not so familiar. Remember to learn the words that you don't know. These are words that are found in the readings on the exam. Study on!

Word	Definition
frost	frozen covering of tiny ice crystals
liberty	the state of being free
hubbub	noise, excitement, an increase in activity
dismantled	taken apart
eager	excited, anxious
deliberately	intentionally, on purpose
slink	to slither away quietly without being noticed
dense	thick, difficult to see through
thicket	a dense growth of shrubbery or bushes
intermittently	off and on, not constant
aroused	awakened from sleep, or stimulated
tremble	to shake nervously
impulse	a sudden spontaneous inclination to do something without thinking
undertaking	setting about to do something
perturbed	annoyed
lurking	lying in wait or hiding in the shadows for evil purposes
ominous	feeling that something bad will happen
perilous	dangerous
shrill	high piercing noise, sharp
gruff	rough, surly
inedible	cannot be eaten
bondage	state of being tied to something forcefully
idle	without activity
impending	something about to happen, hovering threateningly
colossal	giant, extremely large
whimper	a quiet cry or whine
suppressed	held in, not let it out
seized	taken possession of

Denotative—or Denotations

Denotative word meanings are just like literal meanings.

Denotative (or denotation) is another word for the exact meaning or definition of a word. The denotation of the word *cake* for instance is simply that it is a baked mixture of flour, eggs, and sugar. The denotation is usually serious and straightforward. However, writers often use denotation hand-in-hand with:

Connotative—or Connotations

The **connotative** meanings bring word definitions to a more emotional level. They are meanings that go beyond the literal or denotative meanings. Connotative meanings are the meanings that the reader attaches or associates with the word. As in the example above, *cake* may mean a baked mixture of flour, sugar, and eggs denotatively, but **connotatively** you might think of a beautifully decorated birthday cake, a wedding cake, or any other holiday cake. Connotations usually cause us to react emotionally to a word. Take a look at the lists of words that follow. One list demonstrates the denotative meaning and the other the connotative meaning. Think about what comes to your mind when you review both lists.

Denotation	Connotation
skinny	slender
statesman	politician
parch	evaporate
beggar	degenerate
filth	contamination
shout	announce
dog	cur
goofy	insane
cook	chef
long	extensive
fastidious	fussy
cocky	arrogant
small	cramped

DIRECTIONS: *After reading the next list of words, write your immediate connotative reaction to them in the column on the right. Your reaction may be positive or negative.*

Word	Your Connotative Reaction
antique	
old	
odor	
aroma	
bland	
mild	
ornate	
gaudy	
snake	
dentist	
demanded	
requested	
stingy	
thrifty	

As you can see, connotative meanings and denotative meanings are different and alike in a way. Denotative meanings are just as they are—simple definitions—while connotative meanings touch something in your brain, your heart, or your soul—and that is what writers do intentionally. The words may in fact be synonyms, but the emotional response to the word is what separates the two dramatically.

Reading Vocabulary Review IV

Yet another set of words for you to review. Take your time with them. Be aware that any of these words could possibly appear on your CAHSEE. So, study!!!

Word	Definition
majestic _____	stately, grand
pastoral _____	pleasingly peaceful, innocent
diverse _____	differing from one another, unlike
intensifies _____	strengthens, increases in density
enlivens_____	gives life or action to
intercultural _____	between cultures
eccentricities _____	odd or whimsical mannerisms
hordes _____	a large crowd or swarm
oblivious _____	lacking conscious knowledge or memory
stamina _____	strength, endurance
precipice _____	a hazardous place
mimicked _____	imitated
propelled _____	driven as the force or speed of a jet or airplane
contaminate _____	to soil, stain, or corrupt
graciously _____	with kindness and courtesy
promptly _____	quickly, right away
ensure _____	to make sure or certain, to guarantee
drape _____	to hang something (usually cloth) over
foyer _____	an entry into a building, a lobby
applicant _____	someone who applies for a position
distress _____	a situation causing danger, worry, or suffering
prominently _____	standing out above/beyond, noticeable
perimeter _____	the outer limits of a designated area
aggressive _____	driving forceful energy
dominate _____	to rule over others with commanding preeminence
receptionist _____	a person hired to greet customers, patients, telephone callers, etc.
pronounce _____	to declare authoritatively or as an opinion
protruding _____	jutting out, causing to project
iridescent _____	a lustrous or attractive quality, rainbowlike (soap bubbles, oil on water)

Now let's move on to the review on the next few pages. Don't be afraid to look back at the chapter before you attempt the quizzes.

Chapter Review and Quick Quizzes

Now, let's review what you have learned so far—from the beginning. These quizzes are not simulations of the actual test. They are intended for review only. The actual test will be in a multiple-choice format like the tests at the end of the book. The answers will be found in the appendix in the back of the book.

Definition Review Quiz

In the following sentences, use one of the words from the word bank below to complete the definition.

> **Word Bank:** literal, denotative, connotative, idiom, figurative, simile, metaphor, personification. Some words might be used more than once.

1. The _____ meanings of words come straight from the dictionary without adding any other meaning to it.
2. *To kill two birds with one stone* is called an _____.
3. _____ meanings of words tend to make you think or feel something specific about the word itself. In other words, you add your own definition or response to it.
4. *Taking the bull by the horns* is also an _____.
5. *School is like a dream* is an example of a _____, which is a part of _____ language.
6. _____ meanings go beyond literal meanings; they add color and personality to writing.
7. *Clouds tiptoe across the sky;* is an example of _____. Poets use this device a lot!
8. _____ and _____ meanings are very similar.
9. *I am a rock!* is a _____.
10. *His droll little mouth was drawn up like a bow* is an example of a _____.

Reading Vocabulary Review Quizzes

DIRECTIONS: Write the letter of the matching definition in the box to the left of the number.

VOCABULARY REVIEW I-A

ANSWER	WORD	DEFINITION
_____	1. dramatic	a. basis upon which something is built
_____	2. foundation	b. ordinary, commonly found
_____	3. genius	c. to be able to use
_____	4. propel	d. to spur on, to inspire to continue
_____	5. commonplace	e. striking in appearance or effect
_____	6. experimenting	f. to attach to a support
_____	7. operable	g. extraordinary intellectual power
_____	8. stationary	h. fixed, unchanging, immobile
_____	9. encourage	i. to drive forward or onward
_____	10. mounted	j. trying a new procedure, idea, or activity

DIRECTIONS: Fill in the blanks with the word that best completes the sentence.

Word Bank: curious, curiosity, tinker, darning, intended, immigrants, mechanical, journey, variety, carriage, protest, impressed, incentive

VOCABULARY REVIEW I-B

1. Henry Ford was a very _____ person. He asked a lot of questions.
2. Getting an allowance is an _____ for me to do my chores.
3. My grandfather liked to _____ around in the garage with all of his tools.
4. Sometimes they say that "_____ killed the cat."
5. The teacher was _____ with the results on the test. Everyone earned an A.
6. Not many people these days are found _____ their socks. They just buy new ones.
7. The students held a very loud and boisterous _____ against wearing school uniforms.
8. The new uniform policy was _____ to discourage certain behavior, but no one thought it would work.
9. Before the car was invented, people moved around with horse-drawn _____.
10. America attracts many _____. It is a land of opportunity.
11. The ice cream store had a large _____ of ice cream available.
12. The dog, tired of being ordered around, took a _____ far away from his master.
13. Soda Pop, the character in *The Outsiders* was a very _____ person. He loved to work on cars.

DIRECTIONS: Write the letter of the matching definition in the space to the left of the number.

VOCABULARY REVIEW II-A

ANSWER	WORD	DEFINITION
_____	1. patience	a. to hold together
_____	2. falconry	b. to persuade or gently influence
_____	3. horizon	c. having had an existence for many years
_____	4. ancient	d. not hasty, bearing pain or problems calmly
_____	5. bond	e. relating to or characteristic of the Middle Ages
_____	6. coax	f. privileged class, of royal status or power
_____	7. royalty	g. the apparent junction or joining of the earth and sky
_____	8. predatory	h. to fight on horseback
_____	9. establish	i. a person extremely excited or interested in something
_____	10. jousting	j. inclined to injure or exploit others for personal gain
_____	11. enthusiast	k. the art of training hawks to hunt
_____	12. medieval	l. to bring into existence

DIRECTIONS: *Choose the correct definition for the listed word and write the letter in the space on the left.*

VOCABULARY REVIEW II-B

ANSWER	WORD	DEFINITION
_____	**1.** preserve	**a.** to slow motion **b.** to upkeep property or equipment **c.** to return money to consumer for reward **d.** to keep safe from injury or harm
_____	**2.** rebate	**a.** to move easily without wind resistance **b.** to return money to consumer for reward **c.** to watch **d.** to keep safe from injury or harm
_____	**3.** maintenance	**a.** the upkeep of property or equipment **b.** to soil, to make impure **c.** having the opposite effect **d.** to bring about by force
_____	**4.** drag	**a.** to keep safe from injury **b.** to use up, deplete **c.** to slow motion **d.** to enter from the side
_____	**5.** aerodynamic	**a.** something that slows motion **b.** describing upkeep on property or equipment **c.** institution of new policies **d.** the ability to move easily without wind resistance
_____	**6.** conversely	**a.** holding together **b.** the reverse order of **c.** efficient **d.** thick growth of shrubbery
_____	**7.** efficient	**a.** producing the desired effects easily **b.** desperate to live **c.** submerged **d.** professionalism in the workplace
_____	**8.** generate	**a.** to persuade **b.** a very thickset person **c.** to bring into existence, to cause **d.** very angry, tempestuous
_____	**9.** monitor	**a.** sharp, cutting edge **b.** to watch **c.** chest of drawers **d.** to reverse the order of
_____	**10.** regulate	**a.** to govern according to rule **b.** gleaming with anticipation **c.** to tunnel into the earth **d.** to break into a home
_____	**11.** exhaust	**a.** secretive, keeping to oneself **b.** polite and courteous **c.** to contain, reserve **d.** to use up, deplete
_____	**12.** populate	**a.** loud, brassy, bold **b.** to inhabit, wherever people are **c.** an undercover assignment **d.** sparse, unpopulated

_____ 13. pollute
    a. pure, without disease
    b. to fight or brawl
    c. to make physically impure or unclean
    d. first-class, excellent

_____ 14. deplete
    a. to use up to exhaust a resource
    b. an article used as a weapon
    c. to increase in amount
    d. to arrange in a group

_____ 15. cumulative
    a. made up of additional parts, adding up to
    b. to pounce upon, to jump
    c. circumference
    d. small amount, ineffective

_____ 16. environmental
    a. lenient, not withholding privileges
    b. divided into separate areas
    c. having to do with physical surroundings
    d. perceptive, not needing assistance

_____ 17. counter
    a. considerate, polite
    b. blind, the inability to see
    c. synonymous, one and the same
    d. having the opposite effect

_____ 18. impose
    a. abandon, ignore
    b. to bring about by force
    c. a loud, incessant noise
    d. to move swiftly

DIRECTIONS: Fill in the blanks with the word that completes the sentence best.

Word Bank: frost, liberty, hubbub, dismantled, eager, deliberately, slink, dense, thicket, intermittently, aroused, trembled, impulse, undertaking

VOCABULARY REVIEW III-A

1. When the explorer set out upon his journey, it was an _____ no other man had ever attempted.
2. When the _____ arrives in the fall, the harvesters must work fast or lose their crops.
3. The school bell was not functioning properly; it rang _____ on and off all day.
4. Sometimes when she goes shopping she suddenly has an urge to buy something she doesn't need. She is the perfect _____ shopper.
5. The schoolchildren were _____ to leave for summer vacation.
6. The _____ and freedom of the world is at risk during troubled times.
7. During the holidays, the _____, excitement, and activities increase every day.
8. The mechanic _____ the car in order to repair it.
9. On the edge of the forest, there is a dense _____ of brush that is very difficult to get through.
10. When the reindeer landed on the roof, the father was _____ from his sleep.
11. The fog was so _____ it was the cause of a seventy-car pileup on the freeway.
12. The Slitherins in the novel *Harry Potter* seem to _____ like snakes.
13. He _____ ran ahead of us so that he would get the best seat.
14. The students _____ with excitement when the contest winners were announced.

DIRECTIONS: Write the letter of the correct definition in the space to the left of the word.

VOCABULARY REVIEW III-B

ANSWER	WORD	DEFINITION
_____	1. shrill	a. annoyed
_____	2. perturbed	b. took possession of
_____	3. seized	c. a quiet cry or whine
_____	4. gruff	d. to hold in, not to let it out
_____	5. whimper	e. dangerous
_____	6. inedible	f. lying in wait or hiding in the shadows for evil purposes
_____	7. colossal	g. feeling that something bad will happen
_____	8. lurking	h. without activity
_____	9. perilous	i. high piercing noise, sharp
_____	10. impending	j. rough, surly
_____	11. ominous	k. giant, extremely large
_____	12. idle	l. something about to happen, to hover threateningly
_____	13. suppress	m. cannot be eaten
_____	14. bondage	n. tied to something forcefully

DIRECTIONS: Choose the correct definition and write the letter in the space on the left.

VOCABULARY REVIEW IV-A

ANSWER	WORD	DEFINITION
_____	1. propelled	a. driven as the force or speed of a jet or airplane b. strength or endurance c. to simplify, to unburden d. to share in expenses
_____	2. contaminate	a. a childlike toy b. desperate, in great need or desire c. to soil, stain, or corrupt d. sarcastic, insulting
_____	3. mimic	a. virtuous and moral b. to teach or instruct c. in addition to d. to imitate
_____	4. majestic	a. nonsensical gibberish b. stately, grand c. theatrical, always on stage d. the wasteland, the moor
_____	5. pastoral	a. pleasingly peaceful, innocent b. urban dwellers c. the largest portions, giant-sized d. to humiliate and insult
_____	6. intercultural	a. laden with guilt b. a particle used in the construction of an alloy c. between cultures d. maternal affection

_____   **7.** enliven
- **a.** a guaranty or a warranty
- **b.** somber, sullenness
- **c.** retarded, imbecile
- **d.** to give life or action to

_____   **8.** diverse
- **a.** at daybreak, dawn
- **b.** a small mouthful, bite
- **c.** differing from one another
- **d.** to fail, to bungle up

_____   **9.** eccentricities
- **a.** odd or whimsical mannerisms
- **b.** to wrap or envelop
- **c.** to tinker, or play around with
- **d.** many-sided, complex

_____   **10.** hordes
- **a.** to amplify, to make much of
- **b.** a large crowd or swarm
- **c.** approximately, nearly
- **d.** a very minute amount

_____   **11.** oblivious
- **a.** abundant, plentiful
- **b.** lacking conscious knowledge or memory
- **c.** the outer limits or perimeter
- **d.** multicolored, polychromatic

_____   **12.** precipice
- **a.** a hazardous place
- **b.** stubborn, obstinate
- **c.** caught, without a way out
- **d.** to confuse or mix up

_____   **13.** stamina
- **a.** changeable, variable
- **b.** informal, casual in appearance
- **c.** strength, endurance
- **d.** performer, accompanist

_____   **14.** intensifies
- **a.** to assemble, to gather together
- **b.** genteel, quiet in demeanor
- **c.** brawny, very muscular
- **d.** strengthens, increases in density

DIRECTIONS: Fill in the blanks with the word that best completes the sentence.

Word Bank: iridescent, protruding, pronounced, receptionist, dominate, aggressive, perimeter, prominently, distress, applicant, foyer, draped, ensure, promptly, graciously

---

VOCABULARY REVIEW IV-B

1. The _____ glass shimmered in the bright sunlight and its many colors glistened.
2. The next _____ to arrive for his interview must complete the application form immediately.
3. The man's coat was _____ over his chair and the waiter almost tripped on it.
4. If you study for the exam, you will _____ your success.
5. Do not leave the _____ of the playing field or you will be suspended.
6. The statue stood _____ in the square among all of the fountains.
7. It is always exciting to see which team will _____ over the other in the basketball game.
8. When the storm hit, the small fishing vessel was in much _____, but the captain seemed to handle the waves appropriately.
9. The _____ and main lobby of the new hotel was decorated in a style similar to those in Italy.
10. The doctor's office relies heavily upon the _____ who greets patients, answers the phones, and schedules appointments.
11. With ease, the queen _____ accepted the award for her country.
12. If treated _____, the disease will not spread.
13. Many football players seem to be _____ on the playing field.
14. The jogger didn't see the limb of the tree _____ in the path and tripped on it.
15. The winner of the election was _____ with much enthusiasm.

Chapter 2

Word Analysis, Fluency, and Systematic Vocabulary Development—Part II

In this chapter, we will focus on words from the root up because the basis of word development through history is truly from the ground up—it's called **etymology**. Many words begin with or contain a part of a word that is the same as another word and that is called a **root word**. With the knowledge of root words, understanding the basic background and meaning of many other words is made much easier. For instance, take the root word "<u>sol</u>," which means the sun. If you add endings (called suffixes) to the root word "sol," you'll get these words that all have to do with the sun—*solar*, *solstice*, and *solarium*. In keeping with learning vocabulary from the ground up, many of our words arrived via Greek, Roman, and Norse mythology (such as *echo* and *narcissistic*). The stories behind the words are interesting and will help you to better understand the words.

CHAPTER FOCUS: *Root words*

Words from Mythology

Chapter Review and Quizzes

Root Words: Learning Vocabulary from the Ground Up

Learning **root words** will allow you to understand the meanings of words with similar roots without using the dictionary. Again, *your* learning style is unique to you. How you learn them is always the challenge. Some people learn better by hearing, others by seeing, and still others by doing both. Read them aloud. Write them on cards. Do what you have to do to remember them. They are important! NOTE: The **root** is in **bold** type and its meaning is in parentheses ( ).

- **a (without)** agnostic, amoral, atrophy, atypical
- **ab/abs (off, away from, apart, down)** abnormal, abduct, abhor, abstract
- **ac/acr (sharp/bitter)** acerbate, acidity, acute, acrid, exacerbate
- **act/ag (to do, to drive, to force, to lead)** act, agent, agile
- **ad/al (to, toward, near)** adapt, addict, advice, allure, alloy
- **al/ali/alter (other, another)** alias, alibi, alien, alienation, altruist, allegory
- **am (love)** amateur, amorous, enamored, amity, paramour, amiable, amicable
- **amb (to go, to walk)** ambitious, amble, preamble, ambulance
- **amb/amph (around)** amphitheater, ambience
- **amb/amph (both, more than one)** ambiguous amphibian, ambivalent
- **anim (life, mind, soul, spirit)** animosity, unanimous, equanimity
- **ante (before)** ante, anterior, antecedent, antedate, antebellum
- **anthro/andr (man, human)** anthropology, android, misanthrope, philanthropy, anthropomorphic
- **annu/enni (year)** annual, anniversary, biannual, biennial, centennial
- **anti (against)** antidote, antiseptic, antipathy
- **apo (away)** apology, apostle, apocalypse
- **apt/ept (skill, fitness, ability)** adapt, aptitude, apt, inept, adept
- **arch/archi (chief, principal)** architect, archetype, archipelago
- **archy (ruler)** anarchy, hierarchy, monarchy, matriarchy, patriarchy
- **art (skill, craft)** artisan, artifact, artful, artless, artifice, art, artificial
- **auc/aug/aux (to increase)** augment, auction, auxiliary
- **auto (self)** automobile, automatic, autopsy, autocrat, autonomy

---

In the following sentence, what does the word *monarchy* mean?

> The British *monarchy* is under attack by the foreign press for blatant misconduct.

A a colorful butterfly
B any monetary unit
C a form of government ruled by a king or queen
D a country in Europe

Your Answer:

A ☐   B ☐   C ☐   D ☐

Analysis: Don't get confused. Read the sentence carefully. **The correct answer is C.** However, if you were in a hurry and didn't read carefully, answer **A** might have caught your eye because, after all, there *is* a monarch butterfly. But, the sentence mentioned that the monarchy was under attack by the foreign press; what are the chances that a monarch would behave poorly, which misconduct means? Fat chance! Answers **B** and **D** are there to throw you off, especially if you are not paying attention.

- **be (to be, to have a certain quality)** beguile, bequeath, belittle, bemoan, befriend, bewilder
- **bel/bell (war)** belligerent, antebellum, rebel
- **ben/bon (good)** benefit, benefactor, benign, bonus, bona fide
- **bi (twice, doubly)** biplane, biannual, binoculars, bilingual
- **bio (life)** biology, biotic, biosphere, biopsy
- **bri/brev (brief, short)** brevity, brief, abbreviate, abridge

---

What does *antebellum* mean in the following sentence?

> The *antebellum* South was a land of aristocratic landowners and their indentured servants.

A after the war
B the area just above the South
C before the war
D during the Civil War

Your Answer:

A ☐   B ☐   C ☐   D ☐

Analysis: Two roots, two roots, two roots in one! From the last section we have the root **ante,** which means **before.** Add to that, **bellum. Bel** means **war.** Put them together and you have **before the war. The correct answer is C.** The other answers are confusing if you are unfamiliar with what went on in the United States before, during, and after the Civil War. It pays to know your roots!

- **cad/cid (to fall, to happen by chance)** cascade, coincidence, cadence, recidivism, decadent
- **cand (to burn)** candle, incandescent
- **cant/cent/chant (to sing)** chant, enchant, accent, recant
- **cap/cip/cept (to take, to get)** capture, recipient, emancipate, anticipate
- **cap/capit/cipit (head, headlong)** captain, principal, capitulate, caption
- **card/cord/cour (heart)** cardiac, cordial, accord, encourage
- **carn (flesh)** carnivorous, carnal, carnage, reincarnation
- **cast/chast (cut)** caste, castigate, chastise, chaste
- **caust (to burn)** caustic, holocaust

- **ced/ceed/cess (to go, to yield, to stop)** cessation, incessant, abscess, recede, antecedent, access, concede, recess, exceed, precede
- **centr (center)** central, concentrate, eccentric, egocentric
- **cern/cert/cret/crim/crit (to separate, to judge, to distinguish, to decide)** discern, criterion, discrete, secret, concern
- **chron (time)** chronicle, chronology, chronic, synchronize
- **circu (around, on all sides)** circumscribe, circumvent, circuit, circumference
- **cis (to cut)** incision, concise, scissors, precise, excise
- **cit (to set in motion)** incite, solicit, excite
- **cla/clo/clu (shut, close)** seclude, cloister, foreclose, recluse, enclose, closet
- **claim/clam (to shout, to cry out)** reclaim, clamor, acclaim, exclaim
- **cli (to lean toward)** recline, decline, climax
- **co/col/com/con (with, together)** conjugal, coalesce, coalition, connect, confide, cohesive, commiserate
- **crat/cracy (to govern)** democracy, aristocracy, bureaucracy, autocracy
- **cre/cresc/cret (to grow)** crescendo, increment, accrue, creation, increase
- **cred (to believe, to trust)** credible, credo, credence, incredulous, incredible, credentials
- **cryp (hidden)** cryptic, crypt, cryptography
- **cub/cumb (to lie down)** succumb, incumbent, recumbent, cubicle
- **culp (blame)** culpable, exculpate, inculpate, mea culpa, culprit
- **cour/cur (running, a course)** courier, occur, recur, current, incur

---

What does *secluded* mean in the following sentence?

> The pioneers built their cabins in the *secluded* wilderness, but they were often close to a river.

A screened or sheltered from view
B in the city
C above the forest
D clearly in view

Your Answer:

A ☐   B ☐   C ☐   D ☐

Analysis: Thinking back to the roots, what comes to mind? **cla/clo/clu** means **to be shut off from** or **closed in**. Looking at the answers there is only one that clearly is correct. **A is the correct answer.**

- **de (away, off, down, completely, reversal)** descend, defame, delineate, defile, deface, decipher
- **dem (people)** demographics, democracy, epidemic
- **di/dia (apart, through)** dialectic, diagnose, dialogue
- **dic/dict/dit (to say, to tell, to use words)** dictate, dictionary, predict, verdict, indicted, diction
- **dign (worth)** dignitary, dignify, indignant, dignity
- **dis/dif (away from, apart, reversal, not)** diffuse, dissipate, disperse, disseminate, dissuade
- **dac/doc (to teach)** doctrine, didactic, doctor
- **dog/dox (opinion)** dogma, dogmatic, paradox, orthodox
- **dol (suffer, pain)** doldrums, doleful, dolorous
- **don/dot/dow (to give)** dowry, donate, donor, pardon, antidote
- **dub (doubt)** dubious, indubitable
- **duc/duct (to lead)** duct, conduct, abduct, conducive, seduce, induct
- **dur (hard)** durable, endure, duress
- **dys (faulty)** dyslexia, dysfunctional, dystrophy

In the following sentence, what does the word *doctrine* mean?

> All religions have a unique set of *doctrines* that are followed by their members.

A a set of tablets
B a healing person
C principles and beliefs
D a briefcase full of documents

Your Answer:

A ❑   **B** ❑   **C** ❑   **D** ❑

Analysis: Doc means **to teach.** So, looking at the answers logically, there could be some confusion with these answers. A healing person is a doctor, but that is not the correct **doc** word; therefore **B** is **not correct.** The other two answers refer to writings, but still not the correct answers. There is one answer left—**C**, "principles and beliefs" **is the correct answer.** *Doctrines* is a word that is often connected with religious groups.

- **epi (upon)** epitaph, epidermis, epidemic, epilogue
- **equ (equal, even)** equitable, equivocal, equilibrium, equation
- **err (to wander)** error, aberrant, errant, erroneous
- **esce (becoming)** incandescent, effervescent, adolescent, convalesce
- **eu (good, well)** euphoria, euthanasia, euphemism, eulogy
- **e/ef/ex (out, out of, from, former, completely)** exalt, expire, extricate, exonerate, exclude, evade, exult, effervesce
- **extra (outside of, beyond)** extraneous, extrasensory, extraordinary

---

In the following sentence, what does the word *extricate* mean?

> The determined animal managed to *extricate* himself from the hunter's trap.

A a newspaper
B unusual circumstances
C to add meaning to
D to release or disentangle from

Your Answer:

A ❑   **B** ❑   **C** ❑   **D** ❑

Analysis: ex means **out of.** Reading the sentence carefully, key words such as **determined** and **trap** help key you into the answer. **A** is one of those nonsense answers. **B** could be confusing if the sentence was read too quickly because it sounds like this is an unusual circumstance, and **C** really doesn't make sense, therefore **D** is the correct answer.

- **fab (to speak)** fabulous, fable, affable
- **fac (to do, to make)** facsimile, benefactor, factory
- **fer (to bring, to carry, to bear)** offer, transfer, proliferate
- **ferv (to boil, to bubble, to burn)** fervor, fervid
- **fid (faith, trust)** confident, fidelity, perfidy, infidel, bona fide
- **fin (end)** final, finale, definitive
- **flam (to burn)** flame, flamboyant, inflammatory
- **flect/flex (to bend)** flexible, genuflect
- **flict (to strike)** conflict, inflict, afflict
- **fore (before)** foreshadow, forgo, forebear

- **frac (break)** fraction, fracture, infraction
- **fund/found (bottom)** foundation, fundamental, founder
- **fus (pour)** transfusion, profuse, infusion

In the following sentence, what does the word *transfusion* mean?

During life-threatening surgery, a blood *transfusion* is often necessary.

A injection of blood into a person or animal
B to send out of the country
C a simple diagram
D taken away

Your Answer:

A ❑   **B** ❑   **C** ❑   **D** ❑

Analysis: **Fus** means **to pour.** Immediately, Answer **C** can be eliminated. **B** and **D** might be food for thought because the word "transfer" might come to mind. But, we are talking about a transfusion—a pouring of blood into a person or animal—and therefore **A is the only logical answer.**

- **gen (birth, creation, kind, race)** generate, genetics, homogeneous, genealogy, gender, genre, congenital
- **grand (big)** grandiose, grandeur
- **grat (pleasing)** grateful, gratuity, gratuitous
- **grad/gress (to step)** graduate, progress, gradual, digress

---

In the following sentence, what does the word *congenital* mean?

Because of recent scientific discoveries in the field of genetics, *congenital* birth defects are declining.

A a gathering of people
B rejection of faith
C existing at birth
D happiness

Your Answer:

A ❑   **B** ❑   **C** ❑   **D** ❑

Analysis: **Gen** means **birth, creation, race, kind.** Answers **D** and **B** are the two obvious wrong answers. Answer **A** might possibly cause confusion because congregation and congenital begin with the same prefix. But, **C is the correct answer.** A congenital defect exists at birth.

- **her/hes (to stick)** coherent, adherent, cohesive, adhesive
- **hetero (different)** heterosexual, heterogenous
- **hom (same)** homogenous, homonym, homosexual
- **hyper (over, excessive)** hyperactive, hyperbole
- **id (one's own)** idiot, idiom, idiosyncrasy
- **inter (between, among)** interstate, interim, intermittent
- **intra (within)** intramural, intrastate, intravenous
- **ject (to throw, to throw down)** eject, inject, dejected
- **join/junct (to meet, to join)** joint, junction,
- **jur (to swear)** perjury, jury

In the following sentence, what does the word *junction* mean?

> There was an accident at the *junction* of the 405 and the 110 freeways and traffic was delayed.

A a junkyard
B a place where two things join or cross
C a grammatical error
D a syncopated rhythm in a song

Your Answer:

A ☐   B ☐   C ☐   D ☐

Analysis: junct/join means to meet or to join. Answers **C** and **D** really make no sense at all. Answer **A** might possibly be confusing because of its similar sounding beginning. However, **B** is the obvious answer knowing that the root means **to meet or join.**

- **lect (to choose)** elect, select, collect
- **lev (life, rise)** levitate, elevator, alleviate
- **loc/log/loqu (word, speech)** soliloquy, colloquial, dialogue, prologue, epilogue
- **luc/lum/lus (light)** lucid, luminous, illustrate
- **mag/maj/max (big)** magnify, major, majestic, maximum
- **mal/male (bad, ill, evil, wrong)** malodorous, malicious, malaise, malevolent
- **man (hand)** manual, manufacture
- **mater/matr (woman, mother)** maternal, maternity, matriarch
- **min (small)** minutiae, miniature, diminish
- **mis/mit (to send)** remit, remission, transmit, emissary
- **mon/monit (to warn)** summons, admonish, monitor, monument
- **morph (shape)** anthropomorphic, metamorphosis
- **mort (death)** immortal, morgue, morbid
- **mut (change)** mutation, mutant, commute

In the following sentence, what does the word *metamorphosis* mean?

> The *metamorphosis* of the butterfly from its original state as a caterpillar is remarkable to witness.

A a mechanical being
B a change of shape or form
C figurative language
D a numbering system from ancient civilizations

Your Answer:

A ☐   B ☐   C ☐   D ☐

Analysis: Answers **A, C,** and **D** make the least sense when you look carefully at the sentence. **B is the correct answer.** Knowing now that *morph* means **shape,** the answer is easier to detect.

- **nom (rule, order)** astronomy, economy, gastronomy, taxonomy
- **nat (to be born)** natural, native, cognate
- **nox (harm, death)** noxious, obnoxious
- **nom/nym (name)** synonym, anonymous, nominate, acronym, homonym, nom de plume
- **nov/neo/nou (new)** novice, novelty, renovate, neophyte, nouveau riche
- **omni (all)** omnipresent, omniscient, omnipotent
- **pac/peac (peace)** peace, pacify, appease

- **pan (all, everywhere)** panorama, pandemic, panacea, pantheon
- **par (equal)** par, parity, disparity, apartheid
- **para (next to, beside)** parallel, paraphrase, paradox, parable, paralegal
- **path (feeling, suffering, disease)** apathy, sympathy, empathy, pathology, psychopath, sociopath
- **pater/part (father, support)** paternal, patriarch, patron, patronize
- **ped (child, education)** encyclopedia, pedagogue, pediatrician
- **ped/pod (foot)** pedal, pedestal, podiatrist, podium
- **pen/pun (to pay, to compensate)** penalty, punitive, repent
- **pend/pens (to hang, to weigh, to pay)** depend, expend, stipend, spend, expenditure, compensate, pendulum
- **peri (around)** perimeter, periscope, peripheral
- **phone (sound)** symphony, telephone, megaphone, cacophony
- **plac (to please)** placid, placebo, placate
- **port (to carry)** import, portable, deport, export
- **post (after)** posterior, posterity, posthumous
- **pre (before)** prelude, premonition, presume, preempt, premeditate
- **pro (much, for, a lot)** profuse, prodigal, proliferate, prodigy, prolific
- **prob (to test, to prove)** probe, reprobate
- **pug (to fight)** pugnacious, impugn, repugnant

In the following sentence, what does the word *noxious* mean?

> The fumes emitting from the factory pipes were *noxious* and the neighboring houses were evacuated.

A pleasing to the senses
B a nonspecific virus
C nothing to worry about
D unpleasant and harmful

Your Answer:

A ❑   B ❑   C ❑   D ❑

Analysis: Read the sentence carefully and think about what it is stating. Fumes that were bad enough to force a neighborhood to be evacuated would certainly be unpleasant and harmful. Therefore, **D is the correct answer.**

- **que/quis (to seek)** acquire, acquisition, request, inquisitive, query
- **qui (quiet)** quiet, tranquil, disquiet
- **sacr/sanct/secr (sacred)** sacred, sanctuary, sanctify, sacrament, sacrilege
- **sci (to know)** conscious, science, omniscient
- **scribe/scrip (to write)** scrip, scribble, inscribe, scripture, transcript
- **se (apart)** seclude, secede, sequester, segregate
- **sec/sequ (to follow)** sequel, sequence, consequence, second
- **sens/sent (to feel, to be aware)** sensory, sense, resent, consent, dissent
- **sol (sun)** solar, solstice, solarium
- **sol (to loosen, to free)** absolve, dissolve, soluble, resolve, solvent
- **spec (to look, to see)** spectator, perspective, aspect, spectacles, circumspect, retrospective
- **sta/sti (to stand, to be in place)** stationary, obstinate, obstacle, stagnant
- **sub/sup (below)** subordinate, sublime, subversive, suppress, subsidiary
- **super/sur (above)** superlative, surmount, surveillance, surpass

> **In the following sentence, what does the word *sequestered* mean?**
>
> > The jury was *sequestered* by the judge because he did not want them to hear the publicity given to the case by the news media.
>
> A secretive
> B an adventure
> C punitive measures
> D kept apart from, secluded

Your Answer:

A ☐   B ☐   C ☐   D ☐

Analysis: After reading the sentence carefully, **B** is an obvious wrong answer because why would a judge send a jury out on an adventure? **C** is incorrect for the same reason—why would a judge punish the jury? **A** might be troublesome if you did not know the root to the word *sequestered*. **The correct answer is D.** A jury is kept away from the news media in particularly sensitive cases that receive a lot of attention from the press.

- **tain (to hold)** contain, detain, pertain, sustain
- **theo (god)** theology, theocracy
- **tract (to drag, pull, draw)** attract, contract, detract, tractor
- **trans (across)** transport, transfer, transaction, transition
- **ven/vent (to come, move, toward)** convene, adventure, event, avenue, circumvent
- **ver (truth)** verify, verdict
- **vers/vert (to turn)** aversion, controversy, divert, cover, avert, revert
- **vi (life)** viable, vivacity, vivid
- **vid/vis (to see)** evident, television, vision, provident, vista
- **voc/vok (to call)** advocate, convoke, equivocate, vocal, vocabulary
- **vol (to wish)** benevolent, malevolent, voluntary

> **In the following sentence, what does the word *convene* mean?**
>
> > The meeting of the Snowboarding Club will *convene* at the normal time on Wednesday.
>
> A to come together
> B a conversation
> C enter a contest
> D inner portion of a circle

Your Answer:

A ☐   B ☐   C ☐   D ☐

Analysis: After reading the sentence carefully and then looking at all of the answers available, there is one that stands out knowing the root of the word *convene*. **The correct answer is A.** Answers **B** and **C** both have **con** words in them, which could confuse some people, but of course are incorrect. Answer **D** makes no sense at all considering the sentence.

Words from Mythology

Occasionally in your readings, you will encounter a word that originated from mythology. Writers often refer to or name certain gods, goddesses, or other mythological beings in poetry, drama (especially Shakespeare and other classically trained writers), novels, and occasionally in the newspaper (certain politicians are compared to a wide variety of mythological beings—and not always complementary!). Below is a list of some of the more common words that are derived from mythology. In *Webster's International Dictionary* alone, of the 166,724 words, 41,214 are Greek in origin, many mythologically derived. Become familiar with them.

Reminder: It is difficult to predict which of these words will surface on the exam but it will pay off to have them logged into your mind and ready to be called upon when needed.

- **Achates (faithful)** A companion and friend through thick and thin. This man fled the burning city of Troy with Aeneas.
- **Achilles' heel (a vulnerable spot)** His mother dipped him in the river Styx in an effort to make him immortal, but she held onto one of his heels. Later, in a battle, he was struck by a poisoned arrow in the heel and died.
- **Adonis (handsome man)** A youth who was so handsome that he managed to capture the heart of the goddess of love herself, Aphrodite.
- **Aeolian/aeolistic (giving a moaning or sighing sound, like the wind)** Created by Zeus, Aeolus the god of the winds was to keep the winds from sweeping away the sea and the earth. This association with the wind was so strong that two adjectives were created from it: *Aeolian* the windlike sound or anything carried or produced by the wind, and *aeolistic*, meaning a long-winded speech.
- **amazon (a large, strong, masculine woman)** One of group of fierce, female warriors who lived in Scythia, in Asia Minor.
- **Antaean/antaean (having superhuman strength)** The word is from Antaeus who was a Greek giant, the son of Poseidon (Sea) and Gaia (Earth). He was invincible as long as he remained in contact with his mother the Earth, who continually renewed his strength.
- **Apollonian (harmonious, balanced, ordered)** The Greek god Apollo, the son of intellect, of the arts, and of healing. He personified order and rationality, which was considered the bright side of the universe and of man.
- **arachnid (spiders, scorpions, mites, and ticks)** Named after Arachne, a Greek maiden who challenged the goddess Athena to a weaving contest.
- **Argonaut (an adventurer engaged in a quest)** The crew of the ship *Argo* that the goddess Athena helped the Greeks to build from Zeus's sacred talking oak. The crew was called the Argonauts and they were bold and brave adventurers.
- **Argus-eyed (dedicatedly observant)** Argus had one hundred eyes. He was asked by Hera, Zeus's wife, to guard the maiden Io so that Zeus would not resume his affair with her.
- **atlas (one who carries a heavy burden; a bound book of maps)** Atlas, a Greek Titan who was condemned to carry the weight of the world on his shoulders after helping Cronus fight against the Olympians. Although most of the Titans were banished, Atlas received the worst punishment: He was to bear the weight of the heavens on his shoulders forever.
- **aurora (dawn; a beginning; an early period)** Dawn was personified by the Greeks as the goddess Eos, but the Romans named her Aurora. She would ride across the sky with her brother, the Sun, in his chariot, spreading light from east to west. The dew that covers the earth in the mornings is said to be the tears of Aurora, crying over the death of her son Memnon who was killed by Achilles during the Trojan War.

In the following sentence, what does the word *arachnophobia* mean?

> The world is filled with people who have *arachnophobia* and shout out the minute they see one.

A breathing
B two arms and two legs
C fear of spiders
D reach for the stars

Your Answer:

A ☐   B ☐   C ☐   D ☐

Analysis: Reading the sentence carefully, there is one answer that appears to be correct right away especially if you know the mythological word **arachnid**. Arachnid has to do with spiders. The suffix *phobia* is added which means fear. **C is the correct answer.** Arachnophobia means fear of spiders.

- **bacchanal (a wild party; an orgy)** Bacchus was another name for Dionysus, the Greek god of vegetation, fertility, and of course, wine. Those who were devoted to Bacchus believed they were closer to God after drinking wine. Naturally, things got a little out of hand with these groups of devotees over the years and they were finally outlawed by the Roman Senate in 186 B.C.

- **berserk (irrational; reckless; frenzied)** Berserkrs were warriors who wore bearskin coats, according to Norse myths. They were so brave and confident that no one could hurt them that they refused to wear the traditional coat and went to battle wearing only the fur.

- **caduceus (symbol of the medical profession, a winged staff with serpents entwined around it)** In Greek mythology, the god Hermes was selected to be Zeus's messenger. Hermes was given a special cap, a pair of winged sandals, and a wooden kerykeion (a staff) from which white ribbons fluttered. How the ribbons became serpents is the real story behind the symbol.

- **cereal (commonly a breakfast food, a grain product)** Named after the Roman goddess of grain and agriculture, Ceres. Ceres assured fertile crops and a good harvest.

- **chaos (disorder and confusion)** The creation of earth is from Chaos who then bore the sky, Uranus. According to ancient Greeks, the god of all things rose from Chaos and separated earth from the heavens.

- **chimera (an illusion or fabrication of the mind)** In Greek mythology, the chimera was a fire-breathing she-monster. She had the body of a goat and the tail of a serpent. Today we call the products of an overactive imagination, *chimeras*.

- **circean (dangerously bewitching)** An enchantress, Circe lured Odysseus' crew into a castle. The men were fed a magic potion and then turned into pigs. Circe is the personification of evil pretending to be the delight of all earth. Odysseus, by the way, came to their rescue and forced Circe to turn them back into humans.

- **cornucopia (horn of plenty—symbolic of abundance, a bountiful harvest)** We think of Pilgrims when we see this horn-shaped basket, but the word really originated in Greek mythology. Zeus was nursed as an infant by a goat belonging to the nymph Amalthea. To show his appreciation, he broke off one of the goat's horns and gave it to his nanny. From that time on, it was constantly full of whatever food or drink was wished for.

- **cosmos (harmony and order; the orderly universe)** Because the Greeks believed that the original state of the world was Chaos, order was imposed gradually when the sky and earth were formed and then the sun, moon, plants, animals, and man.

- **Cupid's arrow (lovestruck)** The Roman goddess Venus had a son named Cupid. For entertainment, he would fly around shooting arrows into the hearts of gods and men. Cupid was often portrayed as blind which demonstrated the unpredictable nature of love. You've heard the term "love is blind"; now you know from whence it came.

- **cyclopean (huge, massive)** A giant with one circular eye who was extremely powerful. The three Cyclops (Brontes, Steropes, and Arges) were offspring of Uranus (Sky) and Gaea (Earth)

- **Daedalian (ingenious, intricate)** A master ironsmith, who is given credit for inventing the ax, the awl, the level, and the labyrinth. But Daedalus had no sense of right or wrong and managed to get into some tight fixes because of it.

- **demon (an evil spirit; a person with great drive)** Demon comes from the Greek word Daimon, which was a generalized term for a supernatural being, such as the spirits of the dead and the spirit that Zeus assigned to each human being at his birth. Not all demons, however, were considered evil.

- **Dionysian (opposite of Apollonian [above] unrestrained, disorderly)** Knowing that Dionysus is the Greek god of wine gives away the meaning of this word. He was also worshipped as the god of fertility, vegetation, woodlands, and wilderness. Think of it this way: Dionysian = wild and crazy; Apollonian = order and rational thinking.

- **dwarf (a small person or smaller-than-normal variety of plant or animal)** From Norse mythology, dwarfs arrived from the lowly maggot, if you can believe that. Evidently, Eddas (Norse myths) state that the world was made out of the slain giant Ymir who was being eaten by the maggots. He condemned them to eternal darkness and to their own underground realm.

What does the word *bacchanal* mean in the following sentence?

> It seems as though the Greeks had one *bacchanal* party after another.

A bachelor
B meeting of intellectuals
C gardening
D a wild party or orgy

Your Answer:

A ❑   B ❑   C ❑   D ❑

Analysis: Right away, not knowing the word *bacchanal*, you might be thrown off by the first answer, **A**. Bacchanal/bachelor are pretty close; therefore, reading the rest of the answers carefully and rereading the sentence might help. Answer **B, meeting of intellectuals,** could also throw you off if you confuse it with baccalaureate, which is a ceremony for graduates. **C** is an unlikely answer. Answer **D** makes the most sense. Bacchanal means a wild party or orgy, therefore, **answer D is correct.**

- **echo (repetition of a sound)** As a punishment by Hera to the mountain nymph Echo for her incessant chattering, Hera took away her power to begin a conversation; all she could do is repeat what others said. She unfortunately fell in love with Narcissus, but her love was unrequited. She hid in the mountains, caves, and forest and refused to eat or sleep. All that remains of her is the endlessly repeating words of those who venture into her lonely haunts.
- **Electra complex (excessive attachment of a girl to her father with hostility toward her mother)** Clytemnestra murdered her husband Agamemnon on the day he returned from the Trojan War. Electra, their daughter, believed the killing to be unjust and hated her mother for it. Electra wanted nothing more than to avenge her father's death. Years later she encouraged her brother Orestes to kill the mother, which he did; he was then punished by the Furies (winds) for it until the gods absolved him of his crime.
- **elf (a diminutive person, a small, lively creature)** From Norse mythology, there were two kinds of elves: dark elves and bright elves. The dark elves lived underground and the bright elves lived in a kingdom between heaven and earth. Most of us think of the bright elves—the ones who help Santa every year.
- **Elysian Fields (paradise, a place of peace and bliss)** Sounds great, doesn't it? The words come from early Greek mythology. Elysian Fields were located on earth and it is the place at the world's end where those who are favored by the gods are sent when they die.
- **erotic (having to do with physical love, arousing desire)** The word arrives via Eros, the son of Aphrodite, the Greek version of the Roman Venus and Cupid. Same story, but this word developed a connotation that is far more passionate and sensual.
- **a face that could launch a thousand ships (a great beauty)** This statement refers to Helen of Troy who, according to the Greeks, was the most beautiful woman in the world. She was kidnapped from her husband Menelaus. Because of an oath to defend his honor, the Greek princes rallied behind Menelaus and "launched a thousand ships" to help find her.
- **fury (usually depicted as a woman—an angry, violent person)** In Greek mythology, the Furies existed to avenge violations of the natural order such as murder and other crimes. They were called the Erinyes and it is said that there were three of them. They

were depicted as hideous old women with bat wings and snake hair, and had eyes that dripped blood. The Furies barked like dogs, carried whips, and pursued their victims to their death.

- **giant (larger than normal being, larger than life)** Gaia and Uranus had several sets of beings before humans arrived. The Giants were the fourth set of beings. The Giants (24 of them) rose up against Zeus because he had banished their brothers the Titans to Tartarus. It is said that they were huge hairy monsters with serpent tails for feet and would hurl huge boulders at the Olympians. This rebellion was known as the Gigantomachy.

- **golden age (a period of great prosperity)** During Cronus's reign, mortal people who lived on earth lived very much like the gods. They never grew old, they knew no sorrow, hard work, or pain, and when death did come, they had no fear; they simply went to sleep. It is a time when people look back with nostalgia and longing.

- **beware of Greeks bearing gifts (watch out for people with hidden motives)** This term relates to the Trojans who were tricked by the Greeks with a large wooden horse left at their gates. Laocoon, a priest, forewarned his fellow Trojans that "I fear the Greeks even when they bear gifts," but his warnings were not heeded.

In the following sentence, what does the term *Elysian Fields* mean?

> We all dream of some day finding our own *Elysian Fields*, where we can live happily ever after, but that time has yet to come.

A strawberry patches
B a baseball park
C paradise, a peaceful place
D a shopping mall in the suburbs

Your Answer:

A ❑   **B** ❑   **C** ❑   **D** ❑

Analysis: This sentence has a major clue that gives evidence to its meaning. Look at the "live happily ever after" part. If you have no idea what *Elysian Fields* means, reading that clue and comparing it to the answers, you could easily guess that **C is the correct answer.**

- **hot as Hades (sweltering hot)** Unlike us, the Greeks and the Norse believed that Hades was a cold, dark place never penetrated by the sun. It was referred to as the Underworld. But, the change in temperature occurred in the Bible where the Hebrew words referred to the afterworld in which sinners would die in the flames of Hell.

- **halcyon days (days of perfect peace to be recalled with nostalgia)** Alcyone was the daughter of Aeolus, the keeper of the winds. Her husband Ceyx wanted to take a sea voyage to consult an oracle, but Alcyone begged him not to because she knew the winds were capable of great damage and destruction. He went anyway and was drowned the first day of the voyage. Alcyone waited patiently for him to return but she had a dream that he was dead and would never return. She rushed down to the water's edge and saw her husband's body just off shore. As she tried to reach him, the gods felt sorry for her and turned both of them into birds (kingfishers). Each winter for seven days before and after the winter solstice, the birds build their nests and raise their young on top of the waves. At this time of the year, there is no rain and there are no clouds covering the sky so that Alcyone and Ceyx can raise their young in peace and tranquility.

- **harpy (a shrewish or grasping person, especially a woman)** To call someone a harpy is quite insulting. In Greek mythology, Harpies were creatures with the head of a woman and the body of birds of prey and an incredible stench about them.

- **hector (bully; boastful person)** *Hector* is believed to come from the Trojan prince who walked around as though he were a god's and not a man's son. However, he was one of the bravest and noblest heroes who fought for Troy.
- **Herculean/herculean (extraordinary strength, or requiring such strength)** Heracles (Greek) Hercules (Roman), probably the best-known character of the Greek heroes, had enormous strength and was larger than most men; in fact, he was almost a giant. He was Zeus's illegitimate son (his mother slept with Zeus, believing him to be her husband Amphitryon), which explains his size and strength.
- **hermaphrodite (one with the characteristics of both sexes)** Hermaphroditus, the son of Hermes (associated with virility) and Aphrodite (the goddess of love) inherited his father's virility and his mother's beauty. The nymph Salmacis fell in love with him, but he rejected her advances. Pleading to the gods for help, she prayed to be united with him and her prayers were answered literally. Their bodies grew together and formed the first hermaphrodite.
- **hero (a person of great courage who performs noble deeds)** Our word *hero* comes from the Greek *heros*. Heroes from the myths were extremely strong and brave and were favored by the gods. Many were part god and part man, or demigods.
- **hydra-headed (hard to eliminate)** The term comes from Hydra, a creature who had the body of a dog and nine heads. When one of its heads was cut off, it grew two more in its place. Hydra's blood was poison, as was its breath. It was a challenge to destroy, but Heracles finally did.
- **hyperborean (very far north; frigid)** Boreas was the Greek god of the north wind. His icy breath was believed to bring the freezing cold weather to the northern countries.
- **Icarian (foolishly daring)** The son of Daedalus, Icarus and his father needed to escape from a small island and using a ship was not an option. Daedalus constructed two sets of wings held together with wax. They took off flying and Daedalus warned his son not to fly too close to the sun, but giddy with excitement, Icarus flew higher and higher. His father lost track of him and the next thing he knew, he looked down to see the feathers floating on the water.

In the following sentence, what does the word *Herculean* mean?

In times of crises, humans achieve sudden and unexpected *Herculean* strength that serves to aid victims in a variety of circumstances.

A a type of linoleum
B a weakling
C a wrestler's uniform
D extremely strong

Your Answer:

A ❑   B ❑   C ❑   D ❑

Analysis: Because of its familiarity, this would be one of those questions on a test that most people would love to see. Answers **A** and **C** are wrong. Answer **B** is the exact opposite, an antonym. The only answer that makes sense is **D**.

- **jovial (merry, jolly)** The word *jovial* relates in a roundabout way to Jupiter. Jupiter or Jove was the supreme god of Rome. Although he was thought to be a stern fellow, his name in Latin (*Jovialis*) relates to the planet. Jupiter the planet was thought to be a good planet to be born under as it was thought that those born under the planet were happy and cheerful people.
- **labyrinth (a maze, a complicated arrangement)** A twisted, turning, confusing maze that was originally constructed by Daedalus to contain the monster Minotaur that was half man and half bull.

- **laurels, *covered with* (to receive honors or recognition)** Military heroes and the winners of competitions were given wreaths for their heads made of laurel leaves.
- **lethargy (state of being lazy, sluggish)** The word *lethargy* evolved from Greek mythology's Underworld. There were five rivers that one had to cross, called Lethe. To cross the river causes one to forget all past life experiences.
- **lunatic (deranged person)** In both Greek and Roman mythology, the moon was personified as a goddess. She was believed to have been able to induce spells of madness in those who irritated her. *Lunaticus* was a person who was under her spell.
- **martial (having to do with war or fighting)** Related to the Roman god Mars, who was viewed as the protector of Rome.
- **mentor (a teacher or counselor)** In Homer's *Odyssey*, Mentor was a wise old friend who stayed behind in Ithaca. Odysseus left the entire household and the upbringing of his son Telemachus to Mentor.
- **mercurial (swift, changeable)** This word evolved from the Roman god who was the messenger of the gods. He was walking, talking, running, and flying the day after he was born. Mercury was fast and quick and spent most of his time flying through the heavens carrying messages.
- **Midas touch (able to be successful at anything)** Midas was the King of Phrygia. He was granted a wish by the god Dionysus for being kind to one of his followers. Being the selfish and greedy person that he was, he wished that everything he touched would turn to gold. The wish, backfired, however, because everything he touched literally turned to gold, including the food he ate. Eventually, he was cured and managed to gain a bit of wisdom from the experience.
- **muse (an inspiration)** Originally three in number (later nine) the Muses are said to be the daughters of Zeus and Mnemosyne (Memory). Each one is responsible for the inspiration of a specific area of the arts such as art, history, poetry, tragedy, dance, comedy, music, and astronomy.

In the following sentence, what does the word *mercurial* mean?

> Spiderman, Batman, Superwoman, and Superman all appear to have *mercurial* flying speed.

A slow, sluggish
B fast, quick
C humorous, funny
D masterful

Your Answer:

A ❑   **B** ❑   **C** ❑   **D** ❑

Analysis: If you are aware of pop culture, the answer to this question is obvious. It is **B**. Relating a word to something that is familiar is always a good way to remember it. This question may not appear on the exam, but you will most likely remember the word *mercurial*.

- **narcissistic (conceited, self-absorbed)** A very handsome young man whose mother was told by a seer or prophet that the boy would live to a great old age if he never got to know himself. He was so handsome that many young men and women attempted to make advances for him, but he rejected them all. When the nymph Echo was rejected by him she asked for help, and Narcissus was cursed to love someone unattainable, himself. This happened when he saw his reflection in a pool of water. Obviously incapable of reaching the reflection, he lay down and died. His body vanished and a flower stood in its place.
- **nectar/ambrosia (something extremely delicious)** From Greek mythology, *nectar* and *ambrosia* are something so delicious that they are considered the drink and food of the gods.

- **nemesis (an unconquerable enemy or stumbling block)** The Greeks believed that the goddess Nemesis was sent to punish others. It was she who punished Agamemnon for the pride in his victory and caused Narcissus to fall in love with himself. Today, a nemesis is someone or something that gets in the way of accomplishing what we set out to accomplish.

- **nepenthe (anything that produces euphoria)** Helen of Troy (the face that launched a thousand ships) overheard the sorrowful stories of the men who had fought in the Trojan War and was so moved that she slipped a drug that would lift their spirits and take away the pain, anger, and grief. Literally, the word means *ne* (not) *penthos* (sorrow).

- **nestor (a wise old man)** Nestor was the oldest, wisest, and most respected member of the Greek forces. He survived the Trojan War and is said to have lived to be three hundred years old.

- **dressed to the nines (dressed in one's finest clothes)** The nine Muses of Greek mythology were elegant and beautiful. They appeared to be perfect and that is what is meant when we hear the saying, "dressed to the nine,"—someone who is attempting to strive for the best.

- **nymph (a beautiful young woman)** Any female spirit who lived on earth according to the Greeks were called *Nymphs*. There were different types of nymphs, the forest variety, as well as the fountain, mountain, and river variety of nymph. Each had a unique personality—some were a little questionable.

- **ocean (body of salt water that covers two-thirds of the earth; an immense expanse or large quantity)** Oceanus was the realm of the Greek Titan named Oceanus. He was the son of Uranus (Sky) and Gaea (Earth). The difference between Oceanus and his brothers and sisters was that he did not side against Zeus and was not exiled to Tartarus. Instead, he continued to rule over his great river.

- **odyssey (a long journey)** The word evolves from the long journey taken by Odysseus, the mythical king of Ithaca. The first part of his nearly twenty-year journey was spent fighting the Trojans. The second half was spent trying to get home.

- **Oedipus complex (a male's excessive attachment to his mother/hostility to his father)** To make a long story short, this term comes from Greek mythology. A prophecy came true that Oedipus would kill his father and marry his mother. A shepherd adopted Oedipus and as an adult he killed a stranger in an argument (not knowing it was his real father). After arriving in the city of Thebes, he was given the widow of King Laius, whom he married. She was his mother. She bore him four children before they realized that their relationship was incestuous.

- **Olympian (godlike, majestic)** This word evolved from the Greeks. Both Mt. Olympus and the Olympians who lived there were obviously larger than life; hence the word *Olympian*.

- **oracle (a person who speaks with authority and wisdom)** The Greeks and Romans believed that the gods spoke to mortals through oracles, giving them advice and predicting the future.

- **orphean (charming; enchanting)** Orpheus was the son of one of the nine Muses, Calliope, and his father was the king of Thrace whose subjects were the most musical of the ancient Greeks. Some say that he was the son of Apollo from whom he inherited his lyre and his musical talent. Orpheus was able to stop arguments as well as entertain with his music. He moved Hades to tears and managed to get his wife Eurydice released from his grasp, but he was asked to not turn back and look at her until they reached the upper world, Orpheus could not resist the temptation and lost his wife forever.

In the following sentence, what does the word *nemesis* mean?

> Watching television and playing video games seem to be his *nemesis* and his grades are suffering because of it.

A an obstacle
B name calling
C a hobby
D an encouragement

Your Answer:

A ❏   **B** ❏   **C** ❏   **D** ❏

Analysis: Read the sentence carefully. What is preventing this person from improving his grades? Television and video games! Now, look at the answers. Which of the four fit into the meaning of the word? **D** is an antonym; **C** is way out there; and **B**? The only thing that might cause some concern is that they both begin with the same letter, but "name calling" doesn't make sense otherwise. **A is the correct answer.**

- **panacea (cure-all)** Panacea was the daughter of the Greek god of medicine. Her father was struck down by Zeus, but she was believed to be able to heal all mankind's illness and injuries. Today the term *panacea* is used as the answer to all our problems.
- **pander (cater to low tastes)** Named for the son of Lycaon, Pandarus fought on the side of Troy. Athena tricked him into shooting Menelaus, which broke the truce between the Trojans and the Greeks.
- **Pandora's box (a source of all sorts of trouble)** A beautiful woman created by Zeus to take revenge on men. She was given irresistible traits by the Olympians and delivered to Epimetheus (Prometheus' brother) who immediately fell in love with and married her. She brought with her a dowry that contained all the evils unknown to man. The only positive thing in the jar was Hope. Pandora was instructed to never touch the jar, but giving in to temptation, she opened the lid and all the ills that have since plagued mankind escaped—Old Age, Insanity, Jealousy, Sickness, Vice, etc. Even though it was originally a jar, it was translated to mean box in later years.
- **panic (feel sudden, irrational fear)** The sudden fear of the ancient Greeks when hearing the nocturnal revelry of **Pan** (the half man with horns and half goat) and his followers.
- **climb Parnassus (to begin a career in the arts)** The mount on which Apollo is said to have lived on earth. The god of poetry, music, and dance played on his lyre there and enchanted all who heard its strains.
- **patience of Penelope (endless patience)** Penelope was the wife of Odysseus. She was left behind when he went to fight in the Trojan War that lasted ten years. It took Odysseus ten more years to get back to Ithaca. When he returned, Penelope was still faithfully waiting.
- **mount Pegasus (to soar to heights, do inspired or creative work)** winged horse named Pegasus sprang forth from the body of the Gorgon Medusa when Perseus cut her head off. It is said that Pegasus became the pet of the Muses who are the goddesses of the arts.
- **phaeton (a light, horse-drawn carriage)** A young man who rode to his death in a carriage, Phaëthon, although not immortal, begged his father the sun god Helios to allow him to guide the chariot of the sun across the sky. Helios watched as Phaëthon rose into the sky. Without the weight of the master, the horses of the sun went wild, crashing into stars. Phaëthon dropped the reins and the chariot plunged to earth, setting the world on fire. Zeus knocked the chariot and its driver into the river below putting out the flame. Of course, Phaëthon did not survive.
- **rise from the ashes like a phoenix (to make an unexpected comeback)** A bird that, according to Herodotus, was the size and shape of an eagle with red and gold plumage.

It would sit on a nest of fragrant spices awaiting its death (some say the bird lived for 1,461 years). The sun ignited the nest and flames consumed the aged bird. A short time later a worm appeared in its ashes and the worm became the new Phoenix, who then made the trip to Heliopolis carrying its parent's ashes as an offering to the sun god.

- **Promethean (creative or daringly original)** Named for the Greek Titan who at first fought on the side of Zeus, but changed sides once man was created. Zeus tried to punish Prometheus by chaining him to a rock and setting a vulture on him. The vulture ate his liver out each day and at night the liver grew back. Prometheus is credited with having taught mankind to cultivate land, tame horses, navigate by the stars, and to forge metal into tools and weapons.
- **protean (versatile, always changing)** Proteus, a Greek sea god, who was able to change shape at will and could turn himself into any creature or object in order to slip away from his questioners.
- **psyche (the human soul, the self)** Odysseus meets his mother in the Underworld and she explains to him that when we die our life force leaves our body and our soul (psyche) slips away and flutters in the air.
- **pygmy (a dwarf plant, animal; small human)** The word comes from the Greek word for fist. It originally stood for a unit of measurement that was equal to the distance from a man's knuckles to his elbow, which is about thirteen inches. But, the word *pygmy* represented the mythical dwarfs or very small humans who lived on the shores of the river Oceanus.
- **Rx (symbol for prescriptions or treatment)** An ancient sign used by apothecaries in Rome, where it meant *recipere* (take this).

In the following sentence, what does the term *patience of Penelope* mean?

> Raising eight children alone must take the *patience of* three *Penelope*.

A prescription
B impatient
C endless patience
D chattering

Your Answer:

A ☐   B ☐   C ☐   D ☐

Analysis: Understanding words in context is not as difficult as it sounds. To know that raising eight children would be difficult, one would need a lot of patience and understanding. **The only logical answer of the four is C.**

- **saturnalia (period of unrestrained partying)** A kind of Mardi Gras atmosphere celebrated at the end of December marking the winter sowing season. Saturn was the Roman god of sowing and the harvest. The planet Saturn and Saturday are named after him.
- **satyr (a lecherous man)** Mythological forest deities, these were the followers of the god Pan who was half man and half goat. They were known for their devotion to the god of wine, had a reputation for unrestrained lust, and no woman was safe from their advances. The medical terms *satyromaniac* and *nymphomaniac* refer to the male and female conditions of insatiable sexual appetite.
- **between Scylla and Charybdis (having to choose between two undesirable choices)** In Greek mythology, this saying means to be between the two monsters that were actual navigational hazards. On one side, a large rock posed a threat to all ships that tried to pass through the narrow channel. To avoid it, the ship had to sail closer to the coast, which was in the range of a dangerous whirlpool. We continue to use expressions like

"between a rock and a hard place," and "between the devil and the deep blue sea," to convey images of a difficult situation, no matter what choice is made.

- **sibylline (prophetic; mysterious)** An ancient woman who goes into a trance and utters predictions.
- **siren (a temptress, a device that gives off a shrieking sound)** From Greek mythology, the Sirens were three water nymphs whose singing, while not unpleasant, was a dangerous thing to hear. Sailors hearing their alluring song would run their ships aground and never sail again.
- **Sisyphean labor (a never-ending task)** After angering the gods more than was acceptable, Sisyphus was given an extremely frustrating punishment. He was to roll a huge block of stone up a hill, only to have it topple back to the ground just before reaching the top.
- **sphinx (a mysterious, inscrutable person)** The Sphinx originated in Greek mythology. She was a bloodthirsty monster, said to have the face and breasts of a woman, the body of a lion, the wings of an eagle, and a serpent's tail. She was sent to Thebes by Hera to punish its people. She asked a riddle to those walking by: "What creature walks on four legs in the morning, two in the afternoon, and three in the evening?" When they couldn't answer, she strangled them and then ate them on the spot. When Oedipus answered the question, she leapt to her death.
- **stentorian (loud; booming)** Stentor's voice was thought to be as loud and booming as that of fifty men together as it echoed through the Greek camp during the Trojan War.
- **stygian (dark, gloomy)** The river Styx in the Underworld had to be crossed in order to get to the area of Hades that was the departed souls' destiny. Greek myths depict the area as dreary, and cheerless, a place where the sun never warms the air or lifts the shadows. The word **stygian** is used figuratively to describe an atmosphere of gloom and depression.
- **syrinx (a musical instrument/panpipe)** Pan was a lecherous satyr who attempted to rape a virtuous nymph named Syrinx. She called out to the gods for help and was turned into a bunch of reeds. Pan made the reeds into a mouth pipe and became renowned for the beautiful sounds he produced from it.

In the following sentence, what does the word *sibylline* mean?

We read a mystery in class last year whose protagonist seemed *sibylline*; she was very old and could see into the future.

A simple
B protean
C homeless
D prophetic

Your Answer:

A ☐ **B** ☐ **C** ☐ **D** ☐

Analysis: This sentence is not completely unusual. Often, when we look at words in context, the answer is right in front of us. The difficult part is in knowing the proper terms or synonyms that match the word in the answer. In this case, *sibylline* means an ancient woman who could tell the future. Someone who can predict the future is prophetic. The **correct answer is D. A** and **C** are completely wrong and **B** might only pose a problem because it is a mythological word, and because it begins with the same letter as "prophetic." This might cause you to stop and ponder, but thinking logically, there is only one answer.

- **tantalize (to tease, to invite but remain unattainable)** After having offended the gods, Tantalus was sent to Tartarus (the section of the Underworld where sinners are punished). He was sentenced to eternal frustration after having attempted to serve his son as dinner to the gods. Zeus restored the life of Tantalus' son, but forced Tantalus to stand in a pool of water up to his chin. When he leaned over to drink, the water would suddenly retreat, leaving mud. When Tantalus stood up again, the water flooded back. The cycle repeated.

- **thersitical (loudmouth, scurrilous)** The ugliest of all Greeks who had come to Troy, Thersites liked to fling vulgar insults at royal masters and was hated for it. Finally, Odysseus had enough and hit him with his staff. After mocking Achilles for being in love, Achilles hit Thersites so hard that his soul was sent to Tartarus.
- **thunder (sound associated with electrical storms; loud booming noise)** The Norse god of the sky was named Thor. He rode across the heavens in his chariot, hurling his magic hammer. The hammer was his lightning bolt and the chariot's rumbling was thunder.
- **titan (leader in one's field; someone of great ability or power)** Larger than life, the first Titans were the first and largest beings in the universe. There were twelve Titans who were the children of Gaea and Uranus (Earth and Sky). They lost the war with the Olympians and were banished to the Underworld.
- **Triton among minnows (one who stands out; a superior individual)** The Tritons were the demigods of the deep. Their job was to attend the supreme god of the sea Poseidon.
- **Trojan (someone with great perseverance and stamina)** The Trojans fought the Greeks for nearly ten years. They lost only when they were tricked by the wiliness of Odysseus and his Trojan horse (see below).
- **Trojan horse (someone or something that subverts from within; a deceptive scheme)** A very large wooden horse constructed with a trap door through which Odysseus and his men climbed. The horse was left outside the Gates of Troy and when the Trojans saw that the Greeks were gone, they rolled the horse inside and began to celebrate the end of the war—they thought. When the Trojans went to sleep, the Greeks crawled out and signaled for reinforcements. Then they began to sack the city of Troy, killing all the men and enslaving the women.
- **troll (an ugly person)** From Norse mythology, the troll is an ugly, weird-acting, malicious creature. Most of you will remember the troll under the bridge in the story "The Three Billy Goats Gruff."
- **typhoon (a violent cyclonic storm; a hurricane)** Named for Typhon, the mythical Greek monster who was the son of Earth and Tartarus. He was the largest of all monsters born with coiled snakes for legs and a serpent's head instead of hands. He terrorized the gods and wounded Zeus who eventually killed him by hurling a thunderbolt at him.

In the following sentence, what does the word *titans* mean?

Devoted scientists often appear to be *titans* in their respective fields.

A losers
B leaders in their fields
C insensitive to the needs of others
D tight

Your Answer:

A ❑   B ❑   C ❑   D ❑

Analysis: **D, A,** and **C** are wrong. Although **D** could possibly throw you if you were attempting alliteration, **B is the correct answer.**

- **unicorn (a mythical, one-horned beast that often symbolizes virility and supreme power)** Although the one-horned creature is seen in the myths of many different countries, Greek and Roman writers told outrageous tales of the beast, which tell of magical powers of the horn and for centuries were thought to have medicinal value. Finally, the

Apothecaries' Society of London removed the unicorn horn from its list of effective medications. What the citizenry believed to be unicorn powder was identified as being made from narwhal tusks.

- **Valhalla (a special place for persons worthy of honor)** From Norse mythology, Valhalla was a place reserved in the afterworld for those who died in battle. The Norsemen placed a high value on military might and fierce fighting so they were taken to "the hall of the slain" after dying in battle.
- **Venus (a beautiful woman)** The Roman goddess of love, she was identified with the Greek goddess Aphrodite who was believed to inspire love and lust in all living things. *Venereal, venom, venerate, and venerable* are words that evolved from *Venus*.
- **volcano (a vent in the earth's crust through which steam and molten rock issue)** Named after the god of fire Vulcanus, which is identified with Hephaestus the son of Zeus and Hera. He was a master in metalworking and it is said that he created Zeus's thunderbolt and Achilles' armor. The fire god's forges are the holes in the earth where the fire appeared.
- **werewolf (a man who occasionally turns into a wolf)** This word arrives via Greek and Scandinavian myths. Our word is from the Anglo-Saxon *were* (man) and *wulf* (wolf). However, *lycanthrope* the original Greek word, means *lykos* (wolf) and *anthropos* (man). Lycacon was a king of Arcadia. It is said that he served Zeus a meal of human flesh, which Zeus detected and this made Zeus unhappy. Zeus then killed Lycacon's son with a thunderbolt and turned Lycacon into a wolf.
- **wheel of fortune (symbol of luck or chance)** Named for the Roman goddess Fortuna who, it is said, could grant a mortal all his wishes or take everything away when she spun her wheel of fortune.
- **zephyr (gentle breeze)** The god of the west wind in ancient Greece was called Zephyrus. The west wind is the early sign of spring, replacing the cold north winds indicative of winter.
- ♀ **Greek symbol for female (the sign of Aphrodite, goddess of love)** The circle with the cross beneath it is thought to represent her hand mirror or looking glass.
- ♂ **Greek symbol for male (represents Ares, the god of war)** The circle and arrow stand for either the helmet and plume or the shield and spear worn by Greek warriors as they charged into battle.

In the following sentence, what does the word *zephyr* mean?

> The slow start of the annual sailing regatta was due to the faint *zephyrs* blowing this morning.

A gentle breezes
B hurricanes
C snow storm
D tsunami

Your Answer:

A ❑   B ❑   C ❑   D ❑

Analysis: If you absolutely did not know what the word *zephyrs* meant, the answers could be weeded out easily once the statement was read again. The first clue is "slow start," the second clue is "faint." Both indicate something amiss and it is not a hurricane, snowstorm, or a tsunami (fifty-foot waves). The logical answer and **the correct answer is A.** Zephyrs are gentle breezes.

Chapter Review and Quick Quizzes
Root Words

In order to check your understanding and to review the roots presented in the first part of this chapter, take the following quick quizzes. You will find the answers in the appendix at the end of the book.

DIRECTIONS: Match the root with its meaning. Write the letter of the correct answer in the space to the left of the word.

SECTION I

ANSWER	ROOT WORD	MEANING
_____	1. a	a. away
_____	2. ab/abs	b. to go, to walk
_____	3. ac/acr	c. to do, to drive, to force, to lead
_____	4. act/ag	d. skill, craft
_____	5. ad/al	e. against
_____	6. al/ali/alter	f. year
_____	7. am	g. man, human
_____	8. amb	h. to increase
_____	9. amb/amph	i. sharp/bitter
_____	10. amb/amph	j. around
_____	11. anim	k. both, more than one
_____	12. ante	l. self
_____	13. anthro/andr	m. off, away from, apart, down
_____	14. annu/enni	n. to, toward, near
_____	15. anti	o. before
_____	16. apo	p. life, mind, soul, spirit
_____	17. atp/ept	q. other, another
_____	18. arch/archi	r. ruler
_____	19. archy	s. chief, principal
_____	20. art	t. skill, fitness, ability
_____	21. auc/aug/aux	u. without
_____	22. auto	v. love

SECTION II

ANSWER	ROOT WORD	MEANING
_____	1. be	a. life
_____	2. bel/bell	b. war
_____	3. ben/bon	c. to be, to have a certain quality
_____	4. bi	d. brief, short
_____	5. bio	e. twice, doubly
_____	6. bri/brev	f. good

SECTION III

ANSWER	ROOT WORD	MEANING
_____	1. cad/cid	a. head, headlong
_____	2. cand	b. time
_____	3. cant/cent/chant	c. to fall, to happen by chance
_____	4. cap/cip/cept	d. hidden
_____	5. cap/capit/cipit	e. to separate, judge, distinguish, decide
_____	6. card/cord/cour	f. flesh
_____	7. carn	g. running a course
_____	8. cast/chast	h. to lean toward
_____	9. caust	i. shut, close
_____	10. ced/ceed/cess	j. to burn
_____	11. centr	k. to go, to yield, to stop
_____	12. cern/cert/cret/crim/crit	l. to believe, to trust
_____	13. chron	m. center
_____	14. circu	n. blame
_____	15. cis	o. around, on all sides
_____	16. cit	p. heart
_____	17. cla/clo/clu	q. with, together
_____	18. claim/clam	r. cut
_____	19. cli	s. to grow
_____	20. co/col/com/con	t. to cut
_____	21. crat/cracy	u. to burn
_____	22. cre/crese/cret	v. to set in motion
_____	23. cred	w. to govern
_____	24. cryp	x. to lie down
_____	25. cub/cumb	y. to sing
_____	26. culp	z. to take, to get
_____	27. cour/cur	aa. to shout, to cry out

SECTION IV

ANSWER	ROOT WORD	MEANING
_____	1. de	a. to give
_____	2. dem	b. worth
_____	3. di/dia	c. hard
_____	4. dic/dict/dit	d. away from, apart, reversal, not
_____	5. dign	e. suffer, pain
_____	6. dis/dif	f. to say to tell, to use words
_____	7. dac/doc	g. faulty
_____	8. dog/dox	h. apart, through
_____	9. dol	i. opinion
_____	10. don/dot/dow	j. doubt
_____	11. dub	k. people
_____	12. duc	l. to teach
_____	13. dur	m. away, off, down, completely, reversal
_____	14. dys	n. to lead

SECTION V

ANSWER	ROOT WORD	MEANING
_____	**1.** epi	**a.** good, well
_____	**2.** equ	**b.** upon
_____	**3.** err	**c.** outside of, beyond
_____	**4.** esce	**d.** equal, even
_____	**5.** eu	**e.** becoming
_____	**6.** e/ef/ex	**f.** out, out of, from, former, completely
_____	**7.** extra	**g.** to wander

SECTION VI

ANSWER	ROOT WORD	MEANING
_____	**1.** fab	**a.** before
_____	**2.** fac	**b.** to burn
_____	**3.** fer	**c.** to bring, to carry, to bear
_____	**4.** ferv	**d.** pour
_____	**5.** fid	**e.** to speak
_____	**6.** fin	**f.** end
_____	**7.** flam	**g.** break
_____	**8.** flect/flex	**h.** to bend
_____	**9.** flict	**i.** to boil, to bubble, to burn
_____	**10.** fore	**j.** to do, to make
_____	**11.** frac	**k.** bottom
_____	**12.** fund	**l.** to strike
_____	**13.** fus	**m.** faith, trust

DIRECTONS: Write the root of the <u>underlined</u> word on the line at the beginning of the sentence.

SECTION VII

> *Root Bank:* gen, grand, grat, grad, her, hetero, hom, hyper, id, inter, intra, ject, junct, jur

_____ 1. The <u>junction</u> between the two railway tracks was washed out by the typhoon.

_____ 2. Japan has a primarily <u>homogenous</u> society; most of its people are Japanese.

_____ 3. The corporate offices hope that its employees will <u>generate</u> business.

_____ 4. To <u>graduate</u> from high school in California, you have to pass the exam.

_____ 5. In wrapping gifts, most people use <u>adhesive</u> tape.

_____ 6. An <u>idiom</u> is a phrase that can be interpreted both figuratively and literally.

_____ 7. An <u>interstate</u> highway is built to connect more than one state.

_____ 8. Before giving an <u>intravenous</u> injection, a nurse needs to have thorough training.

_____ 9. The passenger was <u>ejected</u> from the car during the accident because he was not wearing a seat belt.

_____ 10. The Rose Parade floats are displayed in all their <u>grandeur</u>.

_____ 11. When you are happy with the service in a restaurant, you usually leave a <u>gratuity</u>.

_____ 12. When a witness lies under oath, he or she has committed <u>perjury</u>.

_____ 13. The United States has a <u>heterogeneous</u> society. It is made up of many different nationalities.

_____ 14. Many people believe that when children consume sugar, they become <u>hyperactive</u>.

SECTION VIII

> *Root Bank:* lect, lev, log, lus, mag, mal, man, mater, min, mit, monit, morph, mort, mut

_____   1. The police department was <u>monitoring</u> the situation in hopes that tempers would settle down.

_____   2. The <u>manufacture</u> of prescription medicines is controlled by the FDA.

_____   3. The students <u>elected</u> to have a longer lunch instead of having a break after second period.

_____   4. Environmental pollution is said to be causing the <u>mutation</u> of a certain species of frog.

_____   5. A woman often has uncanny <u>maternal</u> instincts when caring for her newborn.

_____   6. Magicians claim to be able to <u>levitate</u> their volunteers five inches from the surface of the table.

_____   7. There was an unusual <u>metamorphosis</u> of the character in Franz Kafka's novel; he believes that he becomes a dung beetle.

_____   8. As space becomes less abundant, <u>miniature</u> versions of animals and plants become more and more popular.

_____   9. To be <u>immortal</u> means to be able to live forever.

_____ 10. Her intentions were <u>malicious</u>, not thoughtful and kind.

_____ 11. The <u>dialogue</u> between the two characters in the play was hilarious.

_____ 12. In <u>illustrating</u> her point, the student displayed a graph of the statistics.

_____ 13. The news of the disaster was <u>transmitted</u> over the airwaves.

_____ 14. Using a <u>magnifying</u> glass to look at the details of a leaf was necessary.

SECTION IX

> *Root Bank:* nom, nat, nox, nym, nov, omni, pac, pan, par, para, path, pater, ped, pod, pen, pend, peri, phone, plac, port, post, pre, pro, prob, pug

_____   1. An <u>omniscient</u> narrator of a novel is all-knowing, which means he knows everything that is going on with each character.

_____   2. The widows were offered much <u>sympathy</u> and condolences upon losing their husbands in the mining disaster.

_____   3. The candidates were <u>nominated</u> in early November.

_____   4. The <u>telephone</u> is my sister's best friend.

_____   5. A <u>novice</u> is under much pressure to adhere to the demands of the program.

_____   6. Not all Californians are <u>natives</u> of the state. Many people have moved here from other places.

_____   7. His reaction to the news was very <u>placid</u>.

_____   8. My <u>paternal</u> grandfather was an important part of my life.

_____   9. Busy harbors deal with the <u>import</u> and <u>export</u> of manufactured goods.

_____ 10. To <u>pacify</u> the baby, the mother changed his diapers and gave him a bottle.

_____ 11. The <u>noxious</u> fumes were dangerous and the employees of the factory were evacuated.

_____ 12. Our fund-raising efforts were on <u>par</u> with those of the previous year.

_____ 13. The <u>podiatrist</u> was able to cure the old woman's foot problems.

_____ 14. She was awarded the Pulitzer Prize <u>posthumously</u>.

_____ 15. A <u>pediatrician</u> specializes in caring for children.

_____ 16. Charles Dickens was one of the most <u>prolific</u> writers of his time.

_____ 17. The jury decided unanimously that the murder was <u>premeditated</u>.

_____ 18. With the <u>panoramic</u> photograph, we were able to see the entire valley.

_____ **19.** Some rock stars appear to be rather <u>pugnacious</u> and their names are often in the news.

_____ **20.** The team was given a <u>penalty</u> for unsportsmanlike conduct.

_____ **21.** An <u>acronym</u> is a group of letters that abbreviate a long name; for instance, FBI is an acronym for the Federal Bureau of Investigation.

_____ **22.** The <u>probe</u> included tests of many organs to rule out disease.

_____ **23.** The students were <u>compensated</u> for their hard work by earning good grades and getting into good colleges.

_____ **24.** The frontage road was <u>parallel</u> to the highway and it was less congested and more relaxing to drive.

_____ **25.** As a punishment, our P.E. class had to run the <u>perimeter</u> of the field ten times.

DIRECTIONS: Match the root *with its meaning. Write the letter of the correct answer in the space to the left of the word.*

SECTION X

ANSWER	ROOT	MEANING
_____	1. que/quis	a. sacred
_____	2. qui	b. to look, to see
_____	3. sacr/sanct/secr	c. to stand, to be in place
_____	4. sci	d. to know
_____	5. scribe/scrip	e. above
_____	6. se	f. apart
_____	7. sec/sequ	g. below
_____	8. sens/sent	h. to seek
_____	9. sol	i. to follow
_____	10. spec	j. to feel, to be aware
_____	11. sta/sti	k. to write
_____	12. sub/sup	l. sun
_____	13. super/sur	m. quiet

SECTION XI

ANSWER	ROOT	MEANING
_____	1. tain	a. to come together, move, toward
_____	2. theo	b. god
_____	3. tract	c. truth
_____	4. trans	d. to call
_____	5. ven/vent	e. to hold
_____	6. ver	f. to see
_____	7. vers/vert	g. across
_____	8. vi	h. to wish
_____	9. vid/vis	i. life
_____	10. voc/vok	j. to drag, pull, draw
_____	11. vol	k. to turn

Words from Mythology

Take these review quizzes to insure that you have initiated the learning process for the exam. You will revisit many of these names and words stemming from mythology in your readings for the rest of your life.

DIRECTIONS: Match the name or word with its meaning. Write the letter of the correct definition in the space on the left.

SECTION XII

ANSWER	NAME OR WORD	MEANING
_____	1. Achates	a. harmonious, balanced, ordered
_____	2. Achilles' heel	b. handsome man
_____	3. Adonis	c. dedicatedly observant
_____	4. Aeolian/aeolistic	d. giving a moaning or sighing sound, like the wind
_____	5. amazon	e. referring to spiders, scorpions, mites, and ticks
_____	6. Antaean/antaean	f. one who carries a heavy burden; a bound book of maps
_____	7. Apollonian	g. a vulnerable spot
_____	8. arachnid	h. dawn; a beginning; an early period
_____	9. Argonaut	i. a large, strong, masculine woman
_____	10. Argus-eyed	j. an adventurer engaged in a quest
_____	11. atlas	k. faithful
_____	12. aurora	l. having superhuman strength

SECTION XIII

ANSWER	NAME OR WORD	MEANING
_____	1. bacchanal	a. dangerously bewitching
_____	2. berserk	b. lovestruck
_____	3. caduceus	c. symbol of the medical profession, a winged staff with serpents entwined around it
_____	4. cereal	d. an illusion or fabrication of the mind
_____	5. chaos	e. harmony and order; the orderly universe
_____	6. chimera	f. a small person or smaller-than-normal variety of plant or animal
_____	7. circean	g. a wild party; an orgy
_____	8. cornucopia	h. opposite of Apollonian, unrestrained, disorderly
_____	9. cosmos	i. commonly a breakfast food or grain product
_____	10. Cupid's arrow	j. an evil spirit; a person with great drive
_____	11. cyclopean	k. irrational; reckless
_____	12. Daedalian	l. horn of plenty; symbolic of abundance; a bountiful harvest
_____	13. demon	m. ingenious, intricate
_____	14. Dionysian	n. disorder and confusion
_____	15. dwarf	o. huge, massive

SECTION XIV

ANSWER	NAME, WORD, OR PHRASE		MEANING
_____	1. echo	a.	paradise, a place of peace and bliss
_____	2. Electra complex	b.	a diminutive person, a small, lively creature
_____	3. elf	c.	a great beauty
_____	4. Elysian Fields	d.	larger than normal being, larger than life
_____	5. erotic	e.	usually depicted as a woman, an angry violent person
_____	6. a face that could launch a thousand ships	f.	excessive attachment of a girl to her father with hostility toward her mother
_____	7. fury	g.	repetition of a sound
_____	8. giant	h.	a period of great prosperity
_____	9. golden age	i.	watch out for people with hidden motives
_____	10. beware of Greeks bearing gifts	j.	having to do with physical love, arousing desire

SECTION XV

ANSWER	NAME, WORD, OR PHRASE		MEANING
_____	1. hot as Hades	a.	a bully, a boastful person
_____	2. halcyon days	b.	a person of great courage who performs noble deeds
_____	3. harpy	c.	a shrewish or grasping person, especially a woman
_____	4. hector	d.	hard to eliminate
_____	5. Herculean/herculean	e.	foolishly daring
_____	6. hermaphrodite	f.	sweltering heat
_____	7. hero	g.	very far north, frigid
_____	8. hydra-headed	h.	extraordinary strength
_____	9. hyperborean	i.	days of perfect peace to be recalled with nostalgia
_____	10. Icarian	j.	one with the characteristics of both sexes

DIRECTIONS: Select the correct answer from the three choices. Write the answer in the space on the left.

SECTION XVI

ANSWER	WORD(S)		MEANING
_____	1. jovial	a.	disheartened
		b.	sad
		c.	merry, jolly
_____	2. labyrinth	a.	a complicated maze
		b.	a clear path
		c.	a triangle
_____	3. cover with laurels	a.	losers of major sporting events
		b.	to receive honors or recognition
		c.	what occurs after falling into shrubbery
_____	4. lethargy	a.	state of being lazy
		b.	ambitious
		c.	studious

ANSWER	WORD(S)	MEANING
_____	**5.** lunatic	**a.** the moon **b.** an intelligent and stable person **c.** a deranged person
_____	**6.** martial	**a.** marriage **b.** having to do with war or fighting **c.** having to do with shopping
_____	**7.** mentor	**a.** a teacher or counselor **b.** a deranged person **c.** a confidant
_____	**8.** mercurial	**a.** easygoing **b.** swift, changeable **c.** stable
_____	**9.** Midas touch	**a.** to fail at everything **b.** having to do with war or fighting **c.** able to be successful at anything
_____	**10.** muse	**a.** lazy **b.** an inspiration **c.** funny

SECTION XVII

ANSWER	WORD(S)	MEANING
_____	**1.** narcissistic	**a.** an orange and yellow flower **b.** a kind and generous person **c.** conceited, self-absorbed
_____	**2.** nectar	**a.** a fruit **b.** a body part **c.** something extremely delicious
_____	**3.** nemesis	**a.** an unconquerable enemy or stumbling block **b.** to regurgitate **c.** a friend and co-worker
_____	**4.** nepenthe	**a.** anything that produces euphoria **b.** a snake **c.** a medicine used for infections
_____	**5.** nestor	**a.** where birds live **b.** a wise old man **c.** a pregnant woman
_____	**6.** dressed to the nines	**a.** dressed in one's finest clothes **b.** dressed in work clothes **c.** dressed in gym clothes
_____	**7.** nymph	**a.** a beautiful young woman **b.** an ugly old hag **c.** a sea creature
_____	**8.** ocean	**a.** body of salt water that covers two-thirds of the earth; an immense expanse or quantity **b.** a small body of water **c.** a flying bird
_____	**9.** odyssey	**a.** an automobile with large wheels **b.** a long journey **c.** rest and relaxation

ANSWER	WORD(S)	MEANING
_____	**10.** Oedipus complex	**a.** a male's excessive attachment to his mother and hostility to his father **b.** a Greek city **c.** a shopping mall
_____	**11.** Olympian	**a.** godlike, majestic **b.** fearful and wimpy **c.** a city in Greenland
_____	**12.** oracle	**a.** a prisoner **b.** a person who speaks with authority and wisdom **c.** a powerful officer in the army
_____	**13.** orphean	**a.** charming and enchanting **b.** ugly and morose **c.** an orphan

SECTION XVIII

ANSWER	WORD(S)	MEANING
_____	**1.** panacea	**a.** illness **b.** cure-all **c.** pastry
_____	**2.** Pandora's box	**a.** a source for all sorts of trouble **b.** a wooden box for storing pandas **c.** a special hat
_____	**3.** panic	**a.** sudden irrational fear **b.** safe and cozy **c.** a filthy pan
_____	**4.** climb Parnassus	**a.** a mountain in the French Alps **b.** a hill in Lucerne **c.** to begin a career in the arts
_____	**5.** patience of Penelope	**a.** quick to anger **b.** endless patience **c.** anxious and out of sorts
_____	**6.** mount Pegasus	**a.** to sit on a fence **b.** to climb to the top of a mountain **c.** to soar to heights, to do inspired or creative work
_____	**7.** phaeton	**a.** a light at the end of the tunnel **b.** a dangerous emission from petroleum **c.** a light, horse-drawn carriage
_____	**8.** rise from the ashes like a phoenix	**a.** to make an unexpected comeback **b.** to smoke out dangerous criminals **c.** to fly easily in a windstorm
_____	**9.** Promethean	**a.** creative or daringly original **b.** unusually dull **c.** sleepy and unmotivated
_____	**10.** protean	**a.** the life of the party **b.** versatile, always changing **c.** boring
_____	**11.** psyche	**a.** birth **b.** death **c.** the human soul, the self

_____	**12.** pygmy	**a.** a giant of all beings
		b. a dwarf plant, animal; a small human
		c. normal and average
_____	**13.** *Rx*	**a.** a subscription to a magazine
		b. a sign of peace
		c. a symbol for prescriptions or treatment

SECTION XIX

ANSWER	WORD(S)	MEANING
_____	**1.** saturnalia	**a.** a period of unrestrained partying
		b. a time of peace and solitude
		c. a planet
_____	**2.** satyr	**a.** a lecherous man
		b. a kind and generous man
		c. an automobile with a long trunk
_____	**3.** between Scylla and Charybdis	**a.** easily decided
		b. plants of South America
		c. having to choose between two undesirable choices
_____	**4.** sibylline	**a.** a schizophrenic person
		b. prophetic; mysterious
		c. an aged and kindly woman
_____	**5.** siren	**a.** a polite form of forgiveness
		b. silence
		c. a temptress, a device that gives off a shrieking sound
_____	**6.** Sisyphean labor	**a.** a never-ending task
		b. easily accomplished
		c. before five o'clock
_____	**7.** sphinx	**a.** a king
		b. a friendly gentleman
		c. a mysterious, inscrutable person
_____	**8.** stentorian	**a.** loud; booming
		b. soft spoken politician
		c. a type of western cowboy hat
_____	**9.** stygian	**a.** happy and faithful
		b. dark and gloomy
		c. confusing
_____	**10.** syrinx	**a.** a stereo component
		b. a device used to give medicine
		c. a musical instrument/panpipe

SECTION XX

ANSWER	WORD(S)	MEANING
_____	**1.** tantalize	**a.** to give in to completely
		b. tasteful
		c. to tease, to invite but remain unattainable
_____	**2.** thersitical	**a.** soft spoken, gentle
		b. having to do with the theater
		c. loudmouth, scurrilous

_____	**3.** thunder	**a.** a soft featherlike touch
		b. a loud booming noise, sound associated with electrical storms
		c. to walk gently
_____	**4.** titan	**a.** a leader in one's field, of great ability or power
		b. a small dwarflike person
		c. one who accomplishes nothing
_____	**5.** Triton among minnows	**a.** a weak person
		b. a large fish
		c. one who stands out, a superior individual
_____	**6.** Trojan	**a.** a weakling
		b. someone with great perseverance and stamina
		c. a loud and narcissistic person
_____	**7.** Trojan horse	**a.** someone or something that subverts from within; a deceptive scheme
		b. an honorable idea
		c. a colorful wood carving from Spain
_____	**8.** troll	**a.** a handsome prince
		b. a fresh loaf of bread
		c. an ugly person
_____	**9.** typhoon	**a.** a gentle wind
		b. a powerful businessman
		c. a violent cyclonic storm

SECTION XXI

ANSWER	WORD(S)	MEANING
_____	**1.** unicorn	**a.** a mythical one-horned beast that often symbolizes virility and supreme power
		b. a one-eyed monster that is kind and gentle
		c. a small elflike beast of the woods
_____	**2.** Valhalla	**a.** where onions are grown in California
		b. a city in Hawaii
		c. a special place for persons worthy of honor
_____	**3.** Venus	**a.** a star that twinkles in the northern sky
		b. a beautiful woman
		c. a French dessert made of chocolate
_____	**4.** volcano	**a.** a vent in the earth's crust through which steam and molten rock issue forth
		b. a science experiment using clay
		c. a tide pool in the Galapagos
_____	**5.** werewolf	**a.** a lost wolf in the forest
		b. a wolf wearing sheep's clothing
		c. a man who occasionally turns into a wolf
_____	**6.** wheel of fortune	**a.** a game symbolizing loss of equity
		b. a symbol of luck or chance
		c. a large-spoked wheel on a wagon
_____	**7.** zephyr	**a.** a gentle breeze
		b. a tornado
		c. an instrument that angels play

Chapter 3

Word Analysis, Fluency, and Systematic Vocabulary Development—Part III

Another important aspect of vocabulary development that will be covered in this chapter is the knowledge of **synonyms** (if you've worked on the vocabulary foursquares in Chapter 1, you know what they are). Most words have synonyms—words that mean the same or almost the same. In your readings, you will come across words that you don't understand, but if you look at the definition in a dictionary, thesaurus, or synonym finder, chances are you will understand at least one of the words listed. Being able to understand at least one of the terms will in turn help you to understand the reading. Synonyms are extremely helpful in understanding vocabulary.

Something else that you need to understand is that some words have more than one meaning. For instance, take the word **fly.** A fly is a pesky, annoying insect with wings, (a noun). But, fly is also a verb, as in what airplanes or birds do: Let's fly to France. Fly/fly—same word, different meanings. Understanding words as they are used in the sentence is important; this is often referred to as understanding **words in context.**

Finally, we will explore even more vocabulary words that have been taken from the exams. What is important to remember about the vocabulary words is that regardless of whether they appear on the exam that you take, they are the type of word that you will encounter. The bottom line with that comment is that these words approximate the level of difficulty that you will experience on an exam. Use them as a guide for vocabulary study. There are a million and one words in the world, but the words selected for these chapters were chosen because of the level of difficulty. Now, we've got a lot to do in this chapter, so let's get going!

CHAPTER FOCUS: *Synonyms*

                        Homonyms: Words with Multiple Meanings

                        Reading Vocabulary Review V

                        Reading Vocabulary Review VI

                        Chapter Review and Quizzes

Synonyms: Words with Almost the Same Meaning

When learning new words, it is helpful to find synonyms for the words that are unfamiliar to you. Synonyms are words that can be used as substitutions and still mean the same thing or nearly the same thing. The following practice test questions will test your knowledge of the words you learned in the first chapter.

NOTE: Often you may find a synonym in the definition of a word.

Reminder: Synonyms are words that mean the same thing or almost the same thing.

Choose the word(s) that is a synonym for the word listed below.

1. **COAX**
   A ignore
   B persuade
   C hold together
   D inhabit

Your Answer:

A ☐   B ☐   C ☐   D

Choose the word(s) that is a synonym for the word listed below.

2. **BOND**
   A brute
   B convince
   C hold together
   D letter

Your Answer:

A ☐   B ☐   C ☐   D

Choose the word that is NOT a synonym for the word listed below.

3. **POPULATE**
   A inhabit
   B live
   C dwell
   D find

Your Answer:

A ☐   B ☐   C ☐   D

Choose the word that is a synonym for the word listed below.

4. **MONITOR**
   A watch
   B polluted
   C exhaust
   D manipulate

Your Answer:

A ☐   B ☐   C ☐   D

Check your Answers

For number **1** the word **COAX** means to persuade, **B.** The answer to number **2** is **C**; to **BOND** means to **hold together.** Question number **3** is tricky. Test makers like to throw in questions like this to see if you are awake. It asks for the word that is **NOT** a synonym for the listed word. The answer is **D**; **inhabit, live,** and **dwell** are all synonyms. **Find** is not. Question **4** is **A.** Nurses *monitor* their patients and probably their patience all the time. They *watch* them.

READING Vocabulary Review V

Study the list of testing words below. Become familiar with those you are unfamiliar with through the methods mentioned in the vocabulary review section of Chapter 1.

Word	Definition
seine _____	a large fishing net made to hang vertically in the water
minnows _____	any large group of very small freshwater fish used as live bait
plunge _____	to cast, throw, or jump forcefully into something
silt _____	a sedimentary material made of very fine particles between the size of sand and clay
resume _____	to begin or take up again after an interruption
startle_____	to cause to make a quick involuntary movement; to alarm
algae _____	chiefly aquatic organisms that range in size from single cell to giant kelp
tertiary_____	third in formation, place, order, or rank
alteration _____	condition resulting from a change or modification
habitats _____	an area or environment where an organism or ecological community normally lives
polls _____	a place where votes are cast and registered
suffrage _____	the right or privilege of voting
canals _____	a waterway used for travel, shipping, irrigation

Homonyms: Words with Multiple Meanings

It's happened to all of us. We are reading along very comfortably, when suddenly we approach a word that seems odd in that it is used in a way that we haven't seen it used before. Chances are it is a word that, although it is spelled the same and sounds the same, it has a different meaning. These words are called **homonyms.** There are hundreds of them. Some are easy to understand and some are very obscure. But, in both reading and *your* writing, the need to understand the way in which they are used is vital to clarifying meaning. In this section, you will find lists of homonyms. Interspersed between lists will be testlike questions that will give you practice for the exam. For those homonyms that you do not understand and that are not used in practice questions (and there are many—a book could be written on them), it is suggested that you write the definition and then use the word correctly in a sentence to help you understand them (see sample).

1. <u>ad</u>: an advertisement *In order sell my truck, I placed an ad in the newspaper.*
2. <u>add</u>: to join one thing to another as an increase *The doctor will add another medication to help cure the patient's illness.*

1) ad	add	
2) aid	aide	
3) air	err	heir
4) aisle	I'll	isle
5) all	awl	
6) away	aweigh	
7) bail	bale	
8) ball	bawl	

1. **Select the sentence with the correct usage of the word *bough*.**
   A The bough of the ship is damaged.
   B The bough on the shirt is polka dotted.
   C The bough of the tree broke last night during the storm.
   D The bough of the sail fit the sloop.

Your Answer:
A ❑   B ❑   C ❑   D ❑

9) band   banned
10) bare   bear
11) base   bass
12) beach   beech
13) beau   bow
14) been   bin
15) berth   birth
16) bloc   block
17) board   bored
18) bough   bow
19) brake   break
20) bread   bred
21) bridal   bridle
22) broach   brooch
23) cache   cash

24) capital   capitol
25) carat   carrot
26) cast   caste
27) cede   seed
28) cent   scent   sent
29) cereal   serial
30) choral   coral   corral
31) chute   shoot

32) cite   sight   site
33) clause   claws
34) coarse   course
35) colonel   kernel
36) corps   core

37) creak   creek
38) dew   do   due
39) doe   dough
40) earn   urn
41) ewe   yew   you
42) fair   fare
43) faze   phase
44) feat   feet
45) fir   fur
46) flair   flare
47) flea   flee
48) flew   flu   flue
49) flour   flower
50) foreword   forward

---

2. Select the sentence with the correct usage of the word *heir*.
  A His heir was black with some gray.
  B His heir will inherit a fortune in stocks and bonds.
  C The heir became nervous at the sounds.
  D The barber became tired of cutting heir all day.

Your Answer:

A ☐   B ☐   C ☐   D ☐

---

3. Select the sentence with the correct usage of the word *coral*.
  A The *coral* group left after their performance.
  B The horses are in their *coral*.
  C When you *coral* the animals, they will not escape.
  D *Coral* reefs off the coast of Australia are dangerous for ships.

Your Answer:

A ☐   B ☐   C ☐   D ☐

---

4. Select the sentence that does NOT use the word *fare* correctly.
  A The county *fare* is always interesting to visit in the fall.
  B The bus *fare* to Huntington Park is inexpensive.
  C From home to the market, the taxi *fare* is reasonable.
  D Airline *fares* are inexpensive these days.

Your Answer:

A ☐   B ☐   C ☐   D ☐

---

5. Select the sentence that uses the word *genes* correctly.
  A Scientists are discovering more and more about *genes*.
  B Wear your *genes* to the game tonight.
  C In China, *genes* are hard to find.
  D Oh *Genes*! Don't you have anything better to do than fish?

Your Answer:

A ☐   B ☐   C ☐   D ☐

51) foul   fowl
52) gait   gate
53) gene   jean
54) gored   gourd
55) grate   great
56) grisly   grizzly
57) groan   grown
58) hair   hare
59) hall   haul
60) halve   have
61) heal   heel
62) heard   herd

63) idle   idol
64) it's   its
65) knight   night
66) knot   not
67) lead   led
68) leak   leek

69) liar   lyre
70) links   lynx
71) loan   lone
72) locks   lox
73) main   mane
74) medal   meddle
75) mince   mints

76) moor   more
77) moose   mousse
78) morning   mourning
79) naval   navel
80) oar   or   ore
81) pair   pare   pear
82) palate   palette
83) patience   patients
84) peace   piece
85) peak   peek   pique
86) pi   pie
87) pistil   pistol
88) pleas   please

89) plum   plumb
90) pole   poll
91) poor   pore   pour
92) presence   presents
93) principal   principle
94) profit   prophet
95) rack   wrack
96) raise   rays   raze
97) rap   wrap

6. Select the sentence that does NOT use the word *mane* correctly.

A The lion's *mane* is coarse and brown.

B The *mane* idea is not clear.

C She braided the horse's *mane*.

D Most animals do not have *manes*.

Your Answer:

A ☐   B ☐   C ☐   D ☐

7. Select the sentence that uses the word *palette* correctly.

A My *palette* was burned from eating pizza last night.

B Pilgrims slept on *palettes* of straw.

C The *palette* held a ton of bricks.

D An important artist's tool is the *palette*.

Your Answer:

A ☐   B ☐   C ☐   D ☐

8. Select the sentence that does NOT use the world *presence* correctly.

A Your *presence* will be missed if you quit the team.

B It's your brithday! Open your *presence*.

C Her *presence* on the board of directors made a difference.

D His *presence* was disruptive.

Your Answer:

A ☐   B ☐   C ☐   D ☐

98) rapt	wrapped	
99) read	reed	
100) read	red	
101) reek	wreak	
102) rest	wrest	
103) retch	wretch	
104) right	write	rite
105) rye	wry	
106) sail	sale	
107) seam	seem	
108) seas	seize	sees
109) sew	so	sow
110) shear	sheer	
111) sighed	side	
112) sighs	size	
113) slay	sleigh	
114) soar	sore	
115) soared	sword	
116) stair	stare	
117) stake	steak	
118) stationary	stationery	
119) suite	sweet	
120) taught	taut	
121) tear	tier	
122) tense	tents	
123) tern	turn	
124) their	they're	there
125) threw	through	
126) throne	thrown	
127) thyme	time	
128) tide	tied	
129) to	too	two
130) toe	tow	
131) toad	towed	
132) vale	veil	
133) vain	vane	
134) vial	vile	
135) wail	whale	
136) waist	waste	
137) wait	weight	
138) way	weigh	
139) we	wee	
140) week	weak	
141) weed	we'd	
142) whine	wine	
143) wood	would	
144) yoke	yolk	
145) yore	your	

9. **Select the sentence that uses the word *wretch* correctly.**
   A Ebenezer Scrooge is a miserable *wretch*.
   B When you *wretch* out don't fall.
   C The *wretching* has to stop now!
   D When will you *wretch* Los Angeles?

Your Answer:

A ❑   B ❑   C ❑   D ❑

10. **Select the sentence that uses the word *thyme* correctly.**
    A Don't waste *thyme*!
    B She will dry the *thyme* that she grew for cooking.
    C What *thyme* do you have to go to the doctor?
    D When you go to Disneyland you can expect to have a good *thyme*.

Your Answer:

A ❑   B ❑   C ❑   D ❑

11. **Select the sentence that does NOT use the word *vile* correctly.**
    A The *vile* weather ruined our plans for the weekend.
    B The smell in the auditorium was *vile*.
    C The biology students use *viles* at least once a week.
    D Do you have to be so *vile* when you speak of your enemy?

Your Answer:

A ❑   B ❑   C ❑   D ❑

Check Your Answers

1. C
2. B
3. D
4. A*
5. A
6. B*
7. D
8. B*
9. A
10. B
11. C

> **NOTE:** The answers marked with an asterisk (*) are questions that had a distinct change in direction. All three asked that you select the sentence that was not used correctly. Reading directions are important. Hope you weren't caught sleeping!

READING Vocabulary Review VI

Study the list of testing words below. Become familiar with those you are unfamiliar with through the methods mentioned in the vocabulary review section of Chapter I.

Word	Definition
engage _____	to attract or hold the attention of
emerge _____	to come forth from
tow-headed _____	a head of white-blond hair resembling tow (flax to be spun into thread
coveralls _____	long denim jeans with attached bib
listlessly _____	lacking energy or not inclined to exert effort
nickelodeon _____	an early movie theater charging five cents admission, a player piano or a jukebox
regal _____	magnificent or splendid, befitting a monarch
lured _____	tempted or attracted with the promise of reward or pleasure
precursor _____	one that precedes another, a forerunner, a predecessor
retreat _____	a place affording peace, quiet
sultry _____	very humid and hot, torrid
soar _____	to rise suddenly above normal

Chapter Review and Quick Quizzes

In the first part of this chapter, we revisited **synonyms**. Basically, when a question on the exam asks for a word that means the same or almost the same, if you are unfamiliar with the word, you will need to use the process of elimination. Of the four answers offered, chances are you will be familiar with one or more of the words. Eliminate those that you can, and make an educated guess as to the correct answer. If you positively eliminate all but two answers, that gives you a fifty-fifty chance of getting it right. Being in possession of an extensive vocabulary is vital to success on this and other exams that you will encounter in the near future. Continually build upon your vocabulary—there are always new words to learn—words that can make a difference in your life.

The second part of the chapter focused on **homonyms**—words with multiple meanings. You were given an extensive list of homonyms. Some are easier than others, and others are more confusing and easily misused. For review purposes, take the following quizzes. You will find the answers in the appendix at the end of the book.

DIRECTIONS: *Using the word bank, fill in the blank with the word that is used correctly in the sentence.*

Word Bank: bawled, ad, bear, aisle, banned, awl, bale, aide, heir, aweigh

1. A large corporation will place an expensive _____ in the newspaper on Sunday.
2. The _____ managed to secure his boss's seat on the flight.
3. She was _____ to the estate of a famous and very successful industrialist.
4. When you walk down the _____ of a grocery store, making decisions can be difficult.
5. He used an _____ to make holes in the leather belt he was working on.
6. A sailor shouted "Anchors _____" and the ship left for the distant island on the other side of the Pacific Ocean.
7. Farmers spend many hours in the sun when they _____ hay.
8. The child _____ for his mother who had left him behind.
9. The young troublemakers were _____ from the theater.
10. I cannot _____ to watch the film because it has too much violence.

DIRECTIONS: *Using the word bank, fill in the blank with the word that is used correctly in the sentence.*

Word Bank: bored, berth, beech, block, bin, bow, bass, bred, brake, bow

11. The _____ drum was pounding loudly throughout the song.
12. The leaves of the _____ tree were falling.
13. She tied the _____ onto the package that she was wrapping.
14. The _____ was filled with grain.
15. The cruise ship was anchored at a _____ in Long Beach.
16. The store is located on the next _____ just past the corner.
17. He was _____, so he went outside to play basketball.
18. The _____ of the ship was damaged by the undetected iceberg.
19. The left _____ on my bicycle needs to be adjusted.
20. The two dogs were _____ so that their unusual traits would continue.

> **Word Bank:** brooch, bridle, carat, capital, serial, ceded, caste, coral, scent, cache

21. The horse's _____ was tangled in knots.
22. The elderly woman's golden_____ had many diamonds on it.
23. There was a _____ of weapons found hidden in the forests of Colombia.
24. You must use _____ letters for proper nouns and proper adjectives.
25. The diamond ring that she is wearing must be at least a ten-_____-size jewel.
26. India has a _____ system in place within their society.
27. The politician, realizing that he was losing, _____ the race for governor.
28. The _____of her perfume permeated the room and caused many to sneeze.
29. The _____ number on an appliance is important to take note of in case of a manufacturer recall.
30. The surfer risked his life to ride a twenty-foot wave over a _____ reef.

DIRECTIONS: Using the word bank, fill in the blank with the word that is used correctly in the sentence.

> **Word Bank:** course, urn, chute, due, pare, cite, claws, dough, squeak, kernel

31. The laundry _____ was clogged and caused a backup in the laundry room of the hospital.
32. All officers are asked to _____ anyone who does not obey the laws.
33. Cats use their _____ for protection and for climbing.
34. The Tour de France bicycle _____ is rugged and requires great endurance.
35. The farmer planted the odd-looking corn _____ in hopes that it would grow.
36. Please _____ the apples before you bake them.
37. The floors of the ancient palace _____ as a warning of someone approaching. These floors are called "nightingale floors."
38. Your library books are _____ next week.
39. The _____ was too sticky to knead so we added more flour.
40. The flowers were placed in a large copper _____ to be displayed prominently in the entryway.

> **Word Bank:** yew, flue, forward, flee, feat, phase, flour, fare, fur, flare

41. The _____ tree is an evergreen tree with red berries.
42. The subway _____ is minimal compared to the cost of owning and maintaining a car.
43. Don't worry about your two-year-old; it is just a _____ he is going through.
44. Climbing Mt. Everest is an amazing _____ for anyone to accomplish.
45. Animal Rights activists are disturbed by those who wear _____ coats.
46. The _____ burning in the street indicated that there was danger ahead.
47. The forest fire caused many residents to _____ from their homes.
48. The chimney _____ was closed, causing all of the smoke to remain in the room.
49. We added more _____ to the cookie dough.
50. If you move _____, the line will continue smoothly.

DIRECTIONS: *Using the word bank, fill in the blank with the word that is used correctly in the sentence.*

Word Bank: foul, hare, haul, grisly, gait, jeans, halve, groan, grate, gourd

51. The batter hit two _____ balls before hitting a homerun to win the game.
52. His _____ was so unusual that you could recognize him without seeing his face.
53. Her _____ had holes in the knees and were faded to light blue, but she continued to wear them.
54. The African native will use a dried _____ as an instrument.
55. The _____ covering the drainage ditch was broken and dangerous.
56. The scene after the accident was _____.
57. I heard the injured man _____ from his hospital bed.
58. The _____ hopped and ran from the wolf that was chasing him.
59. The sanitation engineers _____ trash and other castoffs daily on the job.
60. We will _____ the profits and give them to our two favorite charities.

Word Bank: idol, lead, heel, knight, herd, lyre, its, knot, leek, lynx

61. Achilles' _____ was his one vulnerable spot and eventually caused his death.
62. The _____ of elephants stormed through the jungle in search of water.
63. That rock star became the teenager's _____ .
64. Do you know what caused _____ decline?
65. She was expecting a handsome, brave _____ to ride up on his stallion and save her, but that didn't happen.
66. The sailor uses a different _____ for each task.
67. Old painted surfaces are known to contain _____, which is poisonous.
68. The French chef used a fresh _____ in cooking his delicious dish.
69. A _____ is a stringed instrument that is shaped like a "U."
70. The _____ is a member of the cat family. It has spotted fur and keen eyesight.

DIRECTIONS: *Using the word bank, fill in the blank with the word that is used correctly in the sentence.*

Word Bank: meddle, loan, ore, naval, minced, mousse, moor, lox, mane, mourning

71. Real estate agents suggest that you obtain a _____ before looking for a new home.
72. A type of smoked salmon is called _____.
73. The horse's _____ was brushed and then braided with multicolored ribbons.
74. Don't _____ in my business!
75. The clams were _____ and then added to the tomato sauce.
76. The _____ on the coast of England is at times eerie and mysterious.
77. She used a can of _____ on her hair to keep it straight.
78. There is a _____ dove who sadly cries outside my window.
79. The abandoned _____ station was to be used for an international airport.
80. Mining iron _____ is a dangerous profession.

Word Bank: poll, pistil, pare, piece, pie, patience, palette, piqued, pleas, plumb

81. If you will _____ the apples, we can make a pie.
82. The artist used a colorful _____ for his paintings.
83. Many people say that "_____ is a virtue."
84. Adding one individual _____ to another, the quilter constructs a quilt for the guild.
85. The sound of the singer's voice _____ my interest and I wandered over to the stage where he was singing.
86. Pumpkin _____ is my favorite part of the meal at Thanksgiving.
87. The _____ is the seed-producing part of the flower.
88. After hearing many _____ and much begging, the kindly aunt took her nieces to Disneyland.
89. Without a _____, a carpenter's job would be difficult and his work uneven.
90. After taking an informal _____, the students decided to take a field trip to the museum after all.

DIRECTIONS: Using the word bank, fill in the blank with the word that is used correctly in the sentence.

Word Bank: principal, profit, pore, wrap, read, rapt, presence, wracked, razed, reed

91. A clogged _____ can cause skin problems.
92. The _____ of the National Guard was appreciated by all.
93. In a few years, our school's _____ will retire.
94. Because _____ margins are down, the company's stock prices went down as well.
95. He _____ his brain trying to remember where he left his glasses.
96. The old dilapidated building was _____ and replaced by a modern structure.
97. Make certain that you _____ yourself up well before going out into the freezing cold weather.
98. To see the children so _____ in attention while listening to the story was heartwarming.
99. The _____ to my clarinet needs to be replaced.
100. She _____ the book last week and thought it was one of the best.

Word Bank: wretched, sow, wreak, sheared, wrest, seam, rite, sale, seize, wry

101. They didn't realize that the storm would _____ such havoc on the community.
102. The sword fighter managed to _____ away his opponent's weapon.
103. The witches in the play *Macbeth* are _____.
104. Growing up is considered a _____ of passage.
105. His _____ smile was noticed by the entire audience.
106. The store will have a major _____ over the holiday weekend.
107. The _____ to your pants is torn.
108. "Carpe Diem" means to _____ the day!
109. The farmers will _____ seed in the spring.
110. The sheep need to be _____ after the winter cold has gone.

DIRECTIONS: *Using the word bank, fill in the blank with the word that is used correctly in the sentence.*

Word Bank: staring, sighed, slaying, sword, soar, taut, sigh, suite, stake, stationery

---

111. The runners _____ with relief after reaching the finish line.
112. When the politician made an error in judgment during his speech the disapproving campaign manager displayed an unhappy _____.
113. It is said that the _____ of dragons was the job of the brave and fearless knights.
114. If we all had wings we could _____ like birds.
115. The knight's _____ was double-edged and very sharp.
116. Will you stop _____ at me?
117. Fasten that corner of your tent down with a _____ so that the wind will not blow it away.
118. We went to the _____ store to order the invitations to the wedding.
119. The accounting firm is located in a _____ of offices on the 27th floor.
120. The _____ wire strung across the stage enabled the circus performer to walk across it.

Word Bank: they're, tern, tide, tents, tear, towed, too, threw, throne, thyme

---

121. There was a _____ of joy streaming down her face.
122. The red-striped circus _____ are immense in size.
123. The _____ is a seabird with long pointed wings and forked tail.
124. They are running to catch the train because _____ late.
125. The pitcher _____ the ball over ninety miles an hour.
126. The prince will ascend the _____ when his father dies.
127. An herb used in cooking is called _____.
128. The rising and lowering of the _____ is caused by the attraction of the moon and the sun.
129. My sister wants to go _____.
130. The tugboats _____ the ship into port.

DIRECTIONS: *Using the word bank, fill in the blank with the word that is used correctly in the sentence.*

Word Bank: toad, weak, waste, veil, weight, yore, vial, wee, vane, wail, weighed, we'd, yolk, would, whine

---

131. The sound that a _____ makes is "ribbit, ribbit."
132. We will escape under a _____ of darkness.
133. The weather _____ shows which way the wind is blowing.
134. The _____ of blood was confused with something else and had to be redrawn.
135. The _____ of the sirens is painful to my ears.
136. We must take more care to not _____ natural resources.
137. The _____ of the world seems to be bearing down on our shoulders.
138. Trucks have to stop to be _____ on the freeways to make certain that they do not carry too much and cause damage to the road.
139. The _____ children were having a great time singing at the party.
140. I am _____ from being sick for so long.
141. If we want to complete the job before dark, _____ better hurry.
142. If only she would not _____, life would be more pleasant.
143. Your uncle _____ like you to go to the zoo with him today.
144. The egg _____ is the unhealthy part of the egg, according to health experts.
145. In days of _____, life seemed much simpler.

Reading and Vocabulary Review

DIRECTIONS: Match the word and its correct definition. Write the letter of the correct definition in the space to the left of the word. You will find the answers in the appendix in the back of the book.

SECTION V

ANSWER	WORD	DEFINITION
_____	1. seine	**a.** a sedimentary material made of very fine particles
_____	2. minnows	**b.** the condition resulting from a change or modification
_____	3. plunge	**c.** large group of very small freshwater fish
_____	4. silt	**d.** to cause to make a quick involuntary movement
_____	5. resume	**e.** a place where votes are cast and registered
_____	6. startle	**f.** chiefly aquatic organisms that range in size from single cell to giant kelp
_____	7. algae	**g.** the right or privilege of voting
_____	8. tertiary	**h.** a large fishing net made to hang vertically in the water
_____	9. alteration	**i.** an area or environment where an organism or ecological community normally lives
_____	10. habitats	**j.** a waterway used for travel, shipping, irrigation
_____	11. polls	**k.** to cast, throw, or jump forcefully into something
_____	12. suffrage	**l.** third in formation, place, order, or rank
_____	13. canals	**m.** to begin or take up again after an interruption

SECTION VI

ANSWER	WORD	DEFINITION
_____	1. engaging	**a.** white-blond hair resembling tow (flax to be spun into thread)
_____	2. emerge	**b.** lacking energy or not inclined to exert effort
_____	3. tow-headed	**c.** magnificent or splendid
_____	4. coveralls	**d.** attracting or holding the attention of
_____	5. listlessly	**e.** one that precedes another, a forerunner, a predecessor
_____	6. nickelodeon	**f.** a place affording peace, quiet
_____	7. regal	**g.** very humid and hot, torrid
_____	8. lured	**h.** to come forth from
_____	9. precursor	**i.** to rise suddenly above normal
_____	10. retreat	**j.** long denim jeans with attached bib
_____	11. sultry	**k.** an early movie theater charging five cents admission, a player piano, or a jukebox
_____	12. soar	**l.** tempted or attracted with the promise of reward or pleasure

Chapter 4

Reading Comprehension—Part I

Reading Comprehension! Why all the fuss? You've heard this before, but undoubtedly the most important thing that you learn to do in your lifetime is to **read.** How well you read can dictate the level of success and accomplishments in all areas of your life. READING IS VITAL! READING IS CRITICAL, CRUCIAL, ESSENTIAL, IMPERATIVE, URGENT, COMPULSORY, and the KEY to life! How's that for a string of synonyms? Never underestimate the power of reading. Reading can take you anywhere you want to go literally and figuratively. Read as much as possible and read a wide variety of text—from fiction to nonfiction (including newspapers, magazines, and journals): JUST READ! In this chapter, we will focus on a few tried-and-true techniques to help you understand your reading and then practice three areas of reading comprehension that will definitely be included on the exit exam and any other exam you may take in the next few years: **main idea, details,** and **inference.**

CHAPTER FOCUS: *Reading Comprehension Defined*

How to Comprehend

Main Idea

Details

Inference

Chapter Review and Quick Quizzes

Reading Comprehension—Defined

The definition of **comprehension** simply stated, is to understand; to grasp mentally. **Reading comprehension** is the understanding of the meanings of written or printed words or symbols.

Reading is a tool to help you understand an infinite number of things in life. INFINITE! Comprehending or understanding what you read can help you in driving, setting up a computer, riding a bus, following a road map, taking an exam, and even becoming a better skateboarder. Reading makes life far more interesting. But reading without understanding is not worth the time spent opening a book. Many people have difficulty focusing; they see words on a page and they may read them, but they really don't READ, meaning, they don't understand or comprehend, and it is all just words on the page. Often enough we understand certain types of reading materials, and not others. It takes practice and determination to read things you don't really care to read, but have to read for school, work, or home (warranties, instruction manuals, etc.) But in the end it is usually worth the effort—like passing the exit exam!

How to Comprehend

Like almost anything in life, you pretty much have to have a plan. For instance, your plan right now is to pass this exam so that you can get on with your life. Comprehending the short readings on the exam is going to help you with that plan. Comprehending the questions being asked is another part of the plan. We've already talked about reading the directions carefully, because the test makers like to make sure that you are awake and not sleeping through the test. Let's concentrate on the plan to understand the readings. Follow these basic steps for comprehension; a thorough explanation will follow.

Step 1: Preview the Reading. Look at the title, glance quickly at the reading, and then turn to the question section.

Step 2: Quickly read the questions to see what you need to look for in the reading. The types of questions vary; some require thorough reading, and understanding (inference and main idea), while others do not (details).

Step 3: Read the section with purpose! Knowing the questions ahead of time saves you reading time. You might want to underline sentences as you go to help you remember.

Previewing the Reading

By looking at the reading before you delve into it, you will better understand where the writer is taking you. **Previewing** the reading will help you not only on this exam, but in many types of readings that are required of you, especially science, mathematics, foreign languages, and history texts, etc. With the exit exam, you have plenty of time. It doesn't have the time restraints that SATs have. That's a good thing.

- **Look at the title.** There are many stories and poems that would not make sense if you didn't know the title. Some writers are creative that way. Sylvia Plath's poem "The Mirror" for instance, only mentions the actual subject/topic in the title. Titles are very important to many pieces of literature. Pay close attention to them.
- **Glance at the reading passage.** Scan the reading—check it out—up and down. Note the length and the number of paragraphs. If it is long, log into your thoughts that you'll need more time obviously, but again, that all depends upon the questions asked. **Note:** Normally, you would scan for unfamiliar vocabulary during the previewing, finding words that you are unfamiliar with to look up in the dictionary, but you don't have time on the exit exam, nor will you be allowed to have a dictionary. However, looking for unfamiliar vocabulary is a good thing to do with any reading, especially history, science, and math texts.

Read the Questions

After previewing the title and briefly looking at the passage itself, read the questions!

- **Read the questions first.** By reading the questions first, you will get an idea of what the test makers want you to look for in the reading passage. Don't spend a lot of time on this, but reading the questions definitely allows you to focus on the areas of the passage that are important, at least to passing the exam. The following section of this chapter will discuss in depth the types of questions asked, but if they are questions on **details**—asking for dates, measurements, etc.—you can jump right to these facts by **scanning** the reading. If they are asking for the **main idea** or asking that you **infer** something that isn't written, your reading will have to be more thorough. Chances are, you won't get out of a reading passage too easily and a thorough, but fairly quick reading will be necessary.

Purposeful Reading

After reading the questions, look at the task ahead of you as an adventure of sorts, a scavenger hunt. Reading the passage is the most challenging part when you are taking an exam like this. Some passages will be more interesting to you than others, but you need to focus on your intent, which is answering the questions correctly.

- **Scan the reading** if the questions are asking only for facts. To scan the reading, take your finger and move it quickly from left to right, looking for the detail that you need—a measurement, a figure of some sort, a date. You should be able to find the paragraph easily. But, don't do this carelessly; a passage with a lot of facts and figures thrown in could confuse you.
- **Focused reading** is needed when the questions are asking "What is the main idea of the passage?" or one of many different inference-type questions such as "What would be a good title for this story?" or "From this story you can conclude that . . ." To focus

your reading, you need to visualize the reading sentence by sentence. Do not look at the words individually, but look at them as sections or groupings. Try to draw a picture in your mind of what is being stated. See the example below.

NOTE: To visualize the sentence, draw a picture in your mind.

Charles Lindbergh flew an
airplane by himself across
the Atlantic Ocean in 1927.

- **Underlining important passages.** When you come across information that could possibly be useful for answering the questions, underline it. The information will be easier to find if you need to refer back to it to answer a question.

Step 4: Reread and answer the questions. The questions should be the easy part if you follow these steps.

Reread and Answer the Questions

Once you have followed the steps above—answering the questions should be easier than it would have been if you did not prepare yourself for reading. Reading, just like writing, is a process. Take it step by step. The more you practice, the better you become at it. Let's practice. Follow the steps above and see how it works for you.

Step 1: Preview. Look at the title and passage length.

OK—The title—It is about a woman, the passage—is not too long

---

A One-Woman Campaign

In the territory of Wyoming on September 6, 1870, for the first time anywhere in the United States, women went to the polls to cast their ballots. By 1870, the women's suffrage movement had battled unsuccessfully for thirty years on the East Coast. The big surprise to everyone was that the first victory for women's right to vote occurred in Wyoming, where there had been no public speeches, rallies, or conventions for the women's suffrage movement. Instead, there had been just one remarkable woman: Esther Morris. Her one-woman campaign is a classic example of effective politics. She managed to persuade both rival candidates in a territorial election to promise that, if elected, they would introduce a bill for women's suffrage. She knew that, as long as the winner kept his word, women's suffrage would score a victory in Wyoming. The winning candidate kept his promise to Esther Morris, which led to this historic Wyoming voting event in 1870.

Step 2: Look at the questions to the passage.

1. **According to the article, why is it surprising that Wyoming was the first state to allow women to vote?**
2. **Which sentence from the article explains specifically how Esther Morris succeeded in providing the women of Wyoming with the right to vote?**
3. **Which statement below BEST illustrates the time sequence of the events in the article?**

NOTE: Now, before you begin reading, you know to look for:
1) **something surprising;**
2) **how the one woman succeeded in getting the vote; and**
3) **you need to pay attention to the time sequence in the passage.**

Step 3: Read the passage with purpose, now that you know what you are looking for and why you are reading it.

Step 4: Answer the questions!

NOTE: Underline: When you come upon any key words such as "surprise," underline it!

---

1. **According to the article, why is it surprising that Wyoming was the first state to allow women to vote?**
   A Few people knew about formal elections.
   B There was a small population of women in the state.
   C The community showed no obvious interest in the issue.
   D The efforts on the East Coast were moving ahead quickly.

   Your Answer:

   A ❑   B ❑   C ❑   D ❑

2. **Which sentence from the article explains specifically how Esther Morris succeeded in providing the women of Wyoming with the right to vote?**
   A "The big surprise to everyone was that the first victory for women's right to vote occurred in Wyoming, where there had been no public speeches, rallies, or conventions for the women's suffrage movement."
   B "In the territory of Wyoming in September 6, 1870, for the first time anywhere in the United States, women went to the polls to cast their ballots."
   C "She managed to persuade both rival candidates in a territorial election to promise that, if elected, they would introduce a bill for women's suffrage."
   D "She knew that, as long as the winner kept his word, women's suffrage would score a victory in Wyoming."

   Your Answer:

   A ❑   B ❑   C ❑   D ❑

3. **Which statement below BEST illustrates the time sequence of the events in the article?**
   A It begins in the present and then goes back in time to explain the preceding events.
   B It begins on September 6, 1870 and then goes back in time to explain the preceding events.
   C It begins in 1865 and moves to September 6, 1870 and then goes back to 1865.
   D It all takes place on the same day—September 6, 1870.

   Your Answer:

   A ❑   B ❑   C ❑   D ❑

Analysis:

1. **C**   The article states that there were "no public speeches, rallies, or conventions for the women's suffrage movement." This is another way to say that the "community showed no obvious interest in the issue." Answer **D** is totally erroneous—the East Coast had been working for thirty years for women's suffrage. Answers **A** and **B** are both faulty—neither fact is mentioned in the article.

2.   **C**   The article states that Mrs. Morris' success was due to "effective politics," which is followed by the statement made in answer **C**. Answers **A** and **B** both state facts, but not how she succeeded. Answer **D** is close, but not the real reason she succeeded.

3.   **B**   Paying attention to the time sequence is a good habit to get into. If you had underlined dates while you were reading, **B** jumps out at you. Answers **A** and **C** are blatantly false. Answer **D** is impossible and way off course.

Reading Comprehension: Understanding the Main Idea

The **main idea** is the most important thing a writer wants you to know, the reason that the story or paragraph or article is written. If you add up the details included in the writing, they usually equal the main idea. But beware! Sometimes the main idea arrives right away, bam! in the first sentence of a paragraph, if you're lucky. There are times when the main idea is buried somewhere in the paragraph or writing, usually at the end of the passage. Then, there are times when it is not actually stated right out in the open and you have to **infer** (imply or assume) the main idea. Read the short passage below. Look for the main idea, of course, but add up the details as well.

A Chimney Swept

Chimney sweeps, you know, the ones who clean your chimneys and wear the same type of outfit that they wore over 100 years ago; the tall black hat and a scarf. In times past, throughout Europe and North America, many people were able to make a living from sweeping chimneys. It is a job that is difficult and not particularly good for your health. Although you might think that there are few, if any, chimney sweeps left in the world, you would be wrong. Because people nowadays are using their fireplaces more, the number of chimney sweeps is growing.

```
┌─────────────────────────────┐
│   Details: Details + Details │
│              =               │
│          Main Idea           │
└─────────────────────────────┘
```

- many people made a living in past as
- wear tall black hats and scarves
- more and more people using chimneys now
- job not good for your health
- the number of chimney sweeps is growing

Main Idea: Choose One from the Following

A Chimney sweeps continue to work today as in years past.
B Chimney sweeps wear tall hats and scarves.
C Chimney sweeps have an unhealthy profession.

Analysis: **The answer is A.** The other two answers, **B** and **C**, are limited in their scope, too narrow to be the **main idea.** The main idea is that chimney sweeps are still at work.

Reading Comprehension—Details

Details are the small parts of the bigger picture. These are the little things that add up to the main idea that we just reviewed. On most examinations, detail questions are probably the easiest to answer. Often the questions focus on where, what (state, size, month, year, color, and so on), when, how many, etc. Following the test-taking process we learned in the previous section, let's try it again, but this time we will focus on looking at and answering detail questions.

Step 1: Preview the title and the passage.

The Macrozamia Tree: The Oldest Living Thing

The Macrozamia trees grow in the mountains of Australia and they have been growing there for more than 10,000 years. The Macrozamia tree resembles a palm tree. Its leaves look like feathers and the trunk is very thick. On the outside of the trunk, a new ring of scales appear each year. These rings are pushed down to the bottom of the trunk as the tree grows. By counting the rings of scales on the trunk, you can usually tell the age of the tree. But, because the trees are so old, some of the rings at the bottom of the trunk have faded and it is difficult to tell the exact age.

The oldest living tree in the United States is in California. It is the redwood tree. Some of these trees are more than 4,000 years old.

The difference between the oldest plants on earth and the oldest animals is quite extensive. The oldest living animals are thought to be the giant turtles on the Galapagos Islands in the Pacific Ocean. These turtles live as long as 200 years.

Step 2: Read/review the questions.

1. Macrozamia trees grow in _____?
2. The Macrozamia tree is like a palm tree because _____.
3. The age of a Macrozamia tree is determined from _____.
4. In the United States, the oldest living thing is the _____.
5. The oldest living animals on earth _____.

Step 3: Read the passage—with a purpose. Underline key words as you read, if you would like to.

Step 4: Answer the questions!

1. **Macrozamia trees grow _____**
   A in California.
   B on an island in the Pacific.
   C in the Australian mountains.
   D in the French Alps.

Your Answer:

A ❑   B ❑   C ❑   D ❑

2. **The Macrozamia tree is like a palm tree because _____**
   A both have thick trunks.
   B both have thin trunks.
   C both trees have needles.
   D they both have coconuts growing in them.

Your Answer:

A ❑   B ❑   C ❑   D ❑

3. The age of a Macrozamia tree is determined from _____
   A counting its leaves.
   B the length of its trunk.
   C the height of its trunk.
   D the rings of scales on its trunk.

Your Answer:

A ❑   B ❑   C ❑   D ❑

4. In the United States, the oldest living thing is _____
   A a redwood tree.
   B a Macrozamia tree.
   C a turtle.
   D the Liberty Bell.

Your Answer:

A ❑   B ❑   C ❑   D ❑

5. The oldest living animals on earth _____
   E are the sheep in Scotland.
   F are the turtles in the Galapagos Islands.
   G are the trees in northern California.
   H are the whales in Baja California.

Your Answer:

A ❑   B ❑   C ❑   D ❑

Analysis: **1. The correct answer is C.** Answer **D** is way off. Answers **A** and **B** are both facts/details from the story, but not the one that is being asked, and this is when reading the questions carefully really matters. Certain details may be logged in your brain from the reading, but when you are answering the questions, be certain to read the question carefully and then read **all** of the answers before choosing the correct one. Don't let familiar facts fool you! Be careful. **2. The correct answer is A. 3. The correct answer is D. 4. The correct answer is A. 5. The correct answer is F.**

Most of the questions on exams that deal with details or facts are fairly straightforward. In answering the questions, it is a matter of accuracy. If you want to make certain that you are correct, always, *always* look back at the reading. It doesn't take that long to check. You want to be accurate and you don't want to make a careless error.

Reading Comprehension—Inferences

Are you **inferring** that I . . . ? Has anyone ever said that to you? Well, when we talk about inferring, what we mean is that you are taking information in that the writer or speaker wants you to know. You then process it around in your brain and add it to the stuff you already know. Once processed, out comes something that you are assuming to be correct. Inferences are like **deductions, conclusions, suppositions, conjectures, and presumptions** (another string of synonyms!). The tricky thing about inferences on exams is that the information they are asking for is not spelled out in so many words. You have to infer it, or draw a conclusion on your own, or make a reasonable guess. Again, you need to add up the details of the passage to come up with the proper inference.

> **Processed Details + Details**
> **+**
> **Details + Processing**
> **=**
> **Inference**

Once again we will follow the test-taking process in learning about inference questions. Inference questions require a more thorough reading of the passage because you need to process the information in your brain for awhile. Follow the steps as usual, but you will especially want to use the visualization technique discussed earlier in the chapter to make certain you understand the reading. Read the passage carefully.

Step 1: Preview the title and the passage.

Henry Noble: The Grand Imposter

Monsoon rains were pounding the tents and the generators were struggling to maintain power, but the storm mattered little to the members of the medic team. A crew member was in need of an operation. His appendix had burst and it needed to be removed immediately. The doctor quickly and knowledgeably began the operation and forty minutes later, the operation was successfully completed. With antibiotics and rest, the sailor would be fine.

But, there was something seriously wrong. The doctor doing the surgery wasn't really a doctor at all. His name was Henry Noble, a man who spent his life pretending to be something he wasn't. Noble had very little education and wasn't trained for any specific kind of work.

What Noble was particularly good at was pretending. He made up false papers about himself to fool people into hiring him. Noble tried dozens of careers. Among them, he was a professor at several colleges and a guard at a prison in Kansas. Once people discovered his fraud, he would move on to another career.

His most remarkable fraud was working as a doctor. He managed to convince the authorities of his credentials as a physician. But, what is even more remarkable, Noble performed forty-six operations during the Vietnam War, and all of them were successful.

Step 2: Read the questions to help you read with a purpose.

1. Because he _____ Noble was a fraud.
2. As a doctor, his work must have been _____.
3. Noble probably knew something about _____.
4. Catching up with Noble was challenging because _____.
5. This story is primarily about _____.

Step 3: Read with a purpose; visualize and underline.

NOTE: To visualize the sentence draw a picture in your mind.

Adrift in the middle of a storm,
the ship rolled wildly in the sea,
but the storm mattered little to the medic team . . .

Step 4: Answer the questions!

1. Because he _____ Noble was a fake.
  A was uneducated,
  B pretended to be trained for his work,
  C only looked like a doctor,
  D tried many careers,

Your Answer:
A ❑   B ❑   C ❑   D ❑

2. As a doctor, his work must have been _____
   A lengthy in training for it.
   B a career of a lifetime.
   C against the law.
   D the cause of many deaths.

Your Answer:

A ❏   B ❏   C ❏   D ❏

3. Noble was probably knowledgeable about _____
   A taking care of sick people.
   B the ways of the sea.
   C supervising a prison.
   D eating on the run.

Your Answer:

A ❏   B ❏   C ❏   D ❏

4. Catching up with Noble was challenging because _____
   A he wore the best sneakers money could buy.
   B he worked at the same job for years.
   C he attended different schools.
   D he continually changed careers.

Your Answer:

A ❏   B ❏   C ❏   D ❏

5. This story is primarily about _____
   A a man and his dog.
   B a man who was a fraud.
   C a sailor on a ship.
   D the Canadian navy.

Your Answer:

A ❏   B ❏   C ❏   D ❏

Analysis:

1. **The correct answer is B.** Remember when making **inferences,** you have to process the information, the **details** that have been given to you. Although two of the answers are correct in that they are facts from the passage, only **B** is correct because it answers the question about Noble being a fraud; he wasn't a fraud because he didn't have an education or that he tried many careers; he was a fraud because he pretended to be trained for something that he wasn't.

2. **The correct answer is C.** The key words in the question are "must have been." With these words you know that you are going to have to make a decision on your own. The only answer that stands out here as being a reasonable judgment call is **C**; the others are frauds!

3. **The correct answer is A.** Here is another question with a typical inference-type clue word—"probably." It is yet another opportunity to make a decision on your own and, as you can see, if you look at the answers carefully, only one, **A**, appears to have a measure of fulfilling that goal.

4. **The correct answer is D.**

5. **The correct answer is B.** Both questions 4 and 5 follow a similar sequence. One only needs to consider the details, which add up to the inferences of both questions.

Chapter Review and Quick Quiz

In this chapter, we discovered the importance of comprehension. In reading, as in life, there are going to be things that you will enjoy reading and things that are not going to be so pleasant for you. But, because your enjoyment is perhaps less than what you would choose, that in itself doesn't necessarily mean that it is less important. Comprehending what you read is just as important in science, math, and social studies as it is in English, even though I personally prefer the latter. Remember these comprehension techniques and practice them in your day-to-day readings. Visualizing—drawing pictures in your mind or in the margins of the book (if it is your personal copy) is extremely helpful. Underlining important facts—taking notes or outlining—all are valuable in helping you understand what you read. Use what helps you most. The answers are in the appendix.

REMINDERS:
- **Preview the reading.**
  - Look at the title
  - Glance at the reading passage
- **Read the questions first.**
  - Quickly determine what type of questions are given and what specifically you need to look for in the reading.
    - For detail questions, look for dates, numbers, measurements, and other obvious details that are easy to find and make scanning the reading possible
    - For main idea questions, read passage carefully
    - For inference questions, read passage carefully
- **Read with a purpose.**
  - Scan the reading quickly if the questions are asking for details.
  - Use visualization techniques (drawing pictures in your mind) for a focused reading if the questions are main idea or inference.
  - Underline important passages.
- **Reread the questions and then answer them.**

NOTE: Let's make certain that you understand the difference between questions that ask for details, the main idea, and inferential questions. Take the following quiz. Detailed answers are in the appendix.

---

1. **The question below is asking for what kind of information?**
   The story is mainly about _____?
   A details.
   B main idea.
   C inference.

Your Answer:

A ❑   B ❑   C ❑

2. **The question below asks for what kind of information?**
   No airplane had flown over the Atlantic Ocean before _____.
   A details
   B main idea
   C inference

Your Answer:

A ❑   B ❑   C ❑

3. **The question below asks for what type of information?**
   Paragraph 4 is mostly about _____.
   A details.
   B main idea.
   C inference.

Your Answer:

A ❑   B ❑   C ❑

4. **The question below asks for what kind of information?**
   Riders stuck on the Ferris wheel ride must have spent hours _____.
   A details
   B main idea
   C inference

Your Answer:

A ❑   B ❑   C ❑

5. **The question below asks for what kind of information?**
   Clarence Smith's idea was _____.
   A details
   B main idea
   C inference

Your Answer:

A ❑   B ❑   C ❑

Chapter 5

Reading Comprehension—Part II

In this chapter, we will look at real-life writings. **Expository** writings are writings that explain something. That's easy to remember mnemonically—**expository = explain.** You will encounter expository writings for the rest of your life. You also need to understand the technical writings that you will encounter when you buy something, when you sign a contract for a loan, or apply for a job. Types of consumer materials are: warranties, contracts, instruction manuals, and applications. Understanding them is important and occasionally, a question about one of them appears on the exam, so it is a good idea to become familiar with them. **Primary and secondary sources**—what are those, you ask? A primary source is an original publication written by the original author who originated the idea in the first place, while a secondary source is a publication that is written by another person, but quotes or uses the ideas of the primary source. Does that make sense? If it doesn't now, it will later. We will also look at the way **bibliographies** are set up, and exactly what types of information can be found in a **thesaurus,** the **Reader's Guide,** an **index,** an **atlas,** and of course the **dictionary.** The chances of an encounter with a question about any of the above items are quite high, so it is best to be prepared. We've got a lot of work to do in this chapter!

CHAPTER FOCUS: *Expository Writings*

    Consumer Materials—Structure and Function
- *Warranties*
- *Contracts*
- *Manuals*
- *Applications*

    Primary and Secondary Sources

    Bibliographic Citations

    Information Sources:
- *Thesaurus*
- *Dictionary*
- *Reader's Guide*
- *Index*
- *Atlas*

    Chapter Review and Quick Quizzes

Understanding Expository Writings

Expository writings are everywhere you read. You will find them in professional journals, editorials in the newspaper, political speeches, and in primary source material. Everywhere! Expository writings present facts, define terms, give opinions, and otherwise give examples to readers that will help them more clearly understand a specific topic. The writer makes a point or presents the **main idea** or a thesis statement and then supports it with facts or **details** in the body of the writing. The details are important in the support of the main idea. Without them, what kind of **exposition** would it be? Let's look at an example of expository writing and afterward we will review its structure and examine just why it is an expository writing.

The Seneca Falls Declaration of Sentiments
Wesleyan Chapel, Seneca Falls, New York, 1848

Drafted by Elizabeth Cady Stanton (patterned after the Declaration of Independence)

When, in the course of human events, it becomes necessary for one portion of the family of man to assume among the people of the earth a position different from that which they have hitherto occupied, but one to which the laws of nature and of nature's God entitle them, a decent respect to the opinions of mankind requires that they should declare the causes that impel them to such a course.

We hold these truths to be self-evident: that all men and women are created equal; that they are endowed by their Creator with certain inalienable rights; that among these are life, liberty, and the pursuit of happiness; that to secure these rights governments are instituted, deriving their just powers from the consent of the governed. Whenever any form of government becomes destructive of these ends, it is the right of those who suffer from it to refuse allegiance to it, and to insist upon the institution of a new government, laying its foundation on such principles, and organizing its powers in such form, as to them shall seem most likely to effect their safety and happiness. Prudence, indeed will dictate that governments long established should not be changed for light and transient causes; and accordingly all experience hath shown that mankind are more disposed to suffer, while evils are sufferable, than to right themselves by abolishing the forms to which they were accustomed. But, when a long train of abuses and usurpations pursuing invariably the same object evinces a design to reduce them under absolute despotism, it is their duty to throw off such governments, and to provide new guards for their future security. Such has been the patient sufferance of the women under this government, and such is now the necessity which constrains them to demand the equal station to which they are entitled.

The history of mankind is a history of oft repeated injuries and usurpations on the part of man toward woman, having in direct object the establishment of an absolute tyranny over her. To prove this, let facts be submitted to a candid world.

He has never permitted her to exercise her inalienable right to the elective franchise.

He has withheld from her rights which are given to the most ignorant and degraded men—both natives and foreigners.

Having deprived her of this first right of a citizen, the elective franchise, thereby leaving her without representation in the halls of legislations, he has oppressed her on all sides.

He has made her, if married, in the eye of the law, civilly dead.

He has taken from her all right in property, even to the wages she earns.

He has made her, morally, an irresponsible being, as she can commit many crimes with impunity, provided they be done in the presence of her husband. In the covenant of marriage, she is compelled to promise obedience to her husband, he becoming, to all intents and purposes, her master—the law giving him power to deprive her of her liberty, and to administer chastisement.

He has so framed the laws of divorce, as to what shall be the proper causes, and in case of separation, to whom the guardianship of the children shall be given, as to be wholly regardless of the happiness of women—the law, in all cases, going upon a false supposition of the supremacy of man, and giving all power into his hands.

After depriving her of all rights as a married woman, if single, and the owner of property, he has taxed her to support a government which recognizes her only when her property can be made profitable to it.

He has monopolized nearly all the profitable employments, and from those she is permitted to follow, she receives but a scanty remuneration. He closes against her all the avenues to wealth and distinction which he considers most honorable to himself. As a teacher of theology, medicine, or law, she is not known.

He has denied her the facilities for obtaining a thorough education, all colleges being closed against her.

He allows her in Church, as well as State, but a subordinate position, claiming Apostolic authority for her exclusion from the ministry, and, with some exceptions, from any public participation in the affairs of the Church.

He has created a false public sentiment by giving to the world a different code of morals for men and women, by which moral delinquencies which exclude women from society, are not only tolerated, but deemed of little account in man.

He has usurped the prerogative of Jehovah himself, claiming it as his right for her a sphere of action, when that belongs to her conscience and to her God.

He has endeavored, in every way that he could, to destroy her confidence in her own powers, to lessen her self-respect, and to make her willing to lead a dependent and abject life.

Now, in view of this entire disfranchisement of one-half the people of this country, their social and religious degradation—in view of the unjust laws above mentioned, and because women do feel themselves aggrieved, oppressed, and fraudulently deprived of their most sacred rights, we insist that they have immediate admission to all the rights and privileges which belong to them as citizens of the United States.

In entering upon the great work before us, we anticipate no small amount of misconception, misrepresentation, and ridicule; but we shall use every instrumentality within our power to effect our object. We shall employ agents, circulate tracts, petition the State and National legislatures, and endeavor to enlist the pulpit and the press in our behalf. We hope this Convention will be followed by a series of Conventions, embracing every part of the Country . . .

---

1. **The main idea of this expository document, which was written in 1848, is_____**
   A to declare that women are happy and content.
   B to "declare the causes that impel them" to voice their desire for equal rights.
   C to assume that men will always disrespect women.
   D to change the history of mankind the world over.

Your Answer:

A ☐   B ☐   C ☐   D ☐

---

2. **Which of the following statements is NOT one of the supportive details that Cady stated in the "Declaration of Sentiments?"**
   A He has compelled her to submit to laws, in the formation of which she had no voice.
   B He has made her, if married, in the eye of the law, civilly dead.
   C He has denied her the facilities for obtaining a thorough education, all colleges being closed against her.
   D He has made her spend hours in the scorching sun or drenching rain, planting the crops.

Your Answer:

A ☐   B ☐   C ☐   D ☐

Analysis: **The correct answer for Number 1 is B.** The answers A, C, and D are erroneous; A and C are especially off the wall. D might be negotiable had it not mentioned the "world over" because, at this point, the women's suffrage movement was a concern primarily focused in the United States. **The correct answer to Number 2 is D.** Hope you weren't falling asleep here. The question asks for the detail that is **NOT** mentioned in the "Declaration of Sentiments." **D** is the only one in that category.

Structure of Expository Writing

The "Declaration of Sentiments" is a true example of expository writing. It is also an example of a **primary source document,** which we will discuss later. As in most writings, there is an introduction, body, and conclusion. The "Sentiments," drafted for the women's suffrage movement in the mid-1800s introduces the sentiments of women and their mistreatment considering the words of the Declaration of Independence. The introduction is followed by details or facts upon facts that support the thesis. The thesis is the entire first paragraph; the second paragraph includes a hook (makes the reader want to read more), which is also called the motivator and is creative. By imitating the wording of the Declaration of Independence, Cady certainly manages to attract attention to the writing.

To support her introduction, Cady lists the many injustices that need to be addressed. These facts make up the body of her writing. Cady's conclusion, the last two paragraphs, not only summarizes the "Sentiments," but makes a bold statement as well—the clincher! "Now in view of the entire disfranchisement of one-half the people of this country . . ." That's expository writing!

> **Basic Structure of Expository Writings:**
> **Introduction with Thesis/Hook or Motivator**
> **Supporting Detail**
> **Supporting Detail**
> **Supporting Detail**
> **Conclusion/Clincher**

Structure and Function of Consumer and Workplace Documents

Warranties

These are guarantees that the manufacturer of an item purchased by the consumer will promise to repair specified defects within a specified period of time. For instance, you just bought a $500 television set. The manufacturer (RCA, Toshiba, etc.) promises to repair certain things, such as the speakers or wiring, if these is a defect and it is not accidentally or intentionally broken within a year or two or even five years depending on the cost and the manufacturer's faith in its product. Most mechanical and electronic items have warranties. The good thing about warranties is that they make you feel better that you can return the product if it is defective. Some major appliance stores offer extended warranties for, of course, expanded prices. Look at the sample of the warranty below. Answer the questions that might appear on the exit exam.

> **Warranty certificates give details of the promise from the manufacturing company.**

CERTIFICATE OF WARRANTY

To protect your purchase from manufacturer defects, ALF Manufacturing Inc. will replace or repair your television set for up to **2 years** from the date of purchase. We guarantee all parts and labor. Remember our motto, "If we can't fix it we'll replace it." We have a national repair network of over 12,000 licensed service professionals.

To speak with our repair and product support network 24 hours a day, please call 800 869-4629 and ask for Customer Service. If you prefer to communicate on-line, please go to our Internet site: www.ALFMANUFINC.org

ALF MANUFACTURING
INC.

---

1. What does ALF offer as a guarantee to their customers?
A A 24-hour customer service is available.
B If they can't repair it they will replace it.
C All parts and labor are guaranteed.
D All of the above.

Your Answer:

A ❑   B ❑   C ❑   D ❑

---

2. The company's motto is _____
A Waste not want not.
B If we can't fix it, we'll replace it.
C Bring your business to us.
D We'll replace and repair your television set for up to two years.

Your Answer:

A ❑   B ❑   C ❑   D ❑

Analysis: **The correct answer to Number 1 is D.** All of the statements are a part of the company's guarantee to their customers. **The correct answer to Number 2 is B.** Although **D** was mentioned in the warranty, it is not their motto. Answers **A** and **C** are way off and not a part of this company's credo.

Contracts

These are legal documents that you sign, for instance, when you buy something that is very expensive and you are not paying for it with cash, such as a car or a house. Contracts vary in type and legal implications and all of them have to be signed, legally. The signature binds you to the formal language of the contract, which can be really confusing at times and that is why they always tell you to "read the **small** print." Typical contracts are: employment contracts, contracts to hire an attorney, contracts to get braces on your teeth, contracts to sign when you hire a plumber or contractor, a marriage contract, contracts to purchase a vehicle, and the list goes on. Below you will find a portion of the service contract for an automobile. Look it over and then answer the questions pertaining to its terms and conditions.

A contract is a formal agreement
between people, groups, or countries
with a binding legal document setting
out terms and conditions.

PROVISIONS OF THIS VEHICLE SERVICE CONTRACT

This **CONTRACT** is between **US** and **YOU**, and is subject to all the **Terms and Conditions** contained herein.

1. **CONTRACT PERIOD**
   Coverage under this **Contract** begins on the **Contract** Purchase Date and will expire according to the time and/or mileage of the term/miles selected, whichever occurs first, as shown in the **Registration Information.**
   a. New Vehicle Plan expiration is measured in time/mileage from the **Contract** Purchase Date and zero (0) miles.
   b. Used Vehicle Plan requires a mandatory "Waiting Period" before **Coverage** takes effect. The "Waiting Period" = 30 days <u>and</u> 1,000 miles from the **Contract** Purchase Date and Odometer Mileage at **Contract** Purchase Date. 30 days <u>and</u> 1,000 miles will be added to the term of **Your Contract.**

2. **COVERAGE**
   The **Coverage** afforded **You** for **Your Vehicle** is fully described in this **Contract.** Please see section: "Schedule Of Coverages" of this **Contract.**

3. **BREAKDOWN OF COVERED PARTS**
   We will pay or reimburse **You** for reasonable costs to repair or replace any **Breakdown** of a part listed in the **Schedule of Coverages.** <u>REPLACEMENT PARTS MAY BE NEW, REMANUFACTURED, OR REPLACEMENT PARTS OF LIKE KIND AND QUALITY.</u>

4. **DEDUCTIBLE**
   In the event of a **Breakdown** covered by this **Contract, You** may be required to pay a **Deductible.** No **Deductible** payment is required with respect to Towing/Road Service, Rental, Trip Interruption, and Lost Key/Lockout, if they are provided by this **Contract.**

   If **You** have a **Deductible** as shown in the **Registration Information,** the **Deductible** amount will be applied on a repair visit basis. Should a covered **Breakdown** take more than one visit to repair, only one **Deductible** will apply for that **Breakdown.**

5. **TERRITORY**
   This **Contract** applies only to **Breakdowns** that occur and repairs made within the United States of America and Canada.

6. **LIMITS OF LIABILITY**
   a. **Per Repair Visit—Our** liability for any one (1) Repair Visit shall in no event exceed the trade-in value of **Your Vehicle** at the time of said Repair Visit, as listed in the NADA Used Car Guide.
   b. **Aggregate—**The total of all claims and benefits paid or payable while this **Contract** is in force shall not exceed the price **You** paid for **Your Vehicle** (excluding tax, title and license fees).

7. **MAINTENANCE REQUIREMENTS**
   a. You must have **Your Vehicle** checked and serviced in accordance with the manufacturer's recommendations, as outlined in the Owner's Manual. **Your** Owner's Manual lists different servicing recommendations based on **Your** individual driving habits and climate conditions. **You** are required to follow the maintenance schedule that applies to **Your** conditions. Failure to follow the manufacturer's recommendations that apply to **Your** specific conditions may result in the denial of **Coverage.** If an Owner's Manual is not provided, **You** can contact the **Administrator** and the servicing recommendations will be provided to **You.**
   b. It is required that verifiable receipts be retained for the service work. Or, if **You** perform **Your** own service, **You** must retain verifiable receipts showing purchases of all required parts and materials necessary to perform the required maintenance showing the date and mileage when the services were performed. Maintenance and/or service work receipts may be requested by the **Administrator.**

8. **TRANSFER OF YOUR VEHICLE SERVICE CONTRACT**
   a. **Your Contract** may be transferable to someone to whom **You** sell or otherwise transfer **Your Vehicle** while this **Contract** is still in force. This **Contract** cannot be transferred if the title transfer of **Your Vehicle** passes through an entity other than the subsequent buyer, or **Your Vehicle** is sold or traded to a dealership, leasing agency or entity/individual in the business of selling vehicles. This **Contract** can only be transferred once and the transfer must be initiated by the original **Contract** Holder.
   b. To transfer, the following must be submitted to the **Administrator** within 30 days of the change of ownership to a subsequent individual purchaser:
      1. A completed transfer form; with
      2. Name and Address of New owner, date of sale to new owner, current mileage; and
      3. $50.00 Transfer Fee made payable to the **Administrator.**
   c. Any remaining manufacturer's warranty must also be transferred at the same time as vehicle ownership transfer. Copies of all maintenance records showing actual oil changes and manufacturers maintenance must be given to the new owner. These maintenance records must be retained along with similar documentation for future maintenance work which the new owner has performed in accordance with the Maintenance Requirements of this **Contract.** If necessary, these documents will be verified by the **Administrator.**

9. **OUR RIGHT TO RECOVER PAYMENT**
   If **You** have a right to recover against another party for anything **We** have paid under this **Contract, Your** rights shall become **Our** rights. **You** shall do whatever is necessary to enable **Us** to enforce these rights. **We** shall recover only the excess after **You** are fully compensated for **Your** loss.

CANCELLATION OF YOUR CONTRACT

   a. You may cancel this **Contract** by contacting the **Administrator.** An odometer statement indicating the odometer reading on the date of the request will be required.
   b. **We** may cancel this **Contract** for non-payment of the **Contract** charge, or for misrepresentation in the submission of a claim. **We** may cancel this **Contract** if **Your Vehicle** is found to be modified in a manner not recommended by the manufacturer, or **Your Vehicle** is found to be used as a **Commercial** vehicle and the applicable surcharge has not been marked in the **Registration Information** and payment has not been received for this surcharge.
   c. If this **Contract** is cancelled within the first sixty (60) days and no claims have been filed, **we** will refund the entire **Contract** charge paid. If this **Contract** is

cancelled after the first sixty (60) days or a claim has been filed, **We** will refund an amount of the **Contract** charge according to the pro-rata method reflecting the greater of the days in force or the miles driven based on the term/miles selected and the date **Coverage** begins, less a twenty five ($25.00) dollar administrative fee. In the event of cancellation, the lienholder, if any, will be named on a cancellation refund check as their interest may appear.

Your Signature   Date:

_____   _____

---

1. **Provision #5 "Territory" refers to** _____
   A the areas (Canada and the United States) where the contract will cover repairs for breakdowns
   B the Oregon Territory explored by Lewis and Clark
   C the territory where the car is forbidden to break down
   D all of the above

Your Answer:

A ❑   B ❑   C ❑   D ❑

---

2. **Under the "Contract Period," how long does the buyer of a used vehicle have to wait before the coverage takes effect?**
   A 2 years and 60,000 miles
   B 60 days
   C 30 days and 1,000 miles
   D contract purchase date and 0 miles

Your Answer:

A ❑   B ❑   C ❑   D ❑

Analysis: Reading the provisions of a vehicle service contract is not particularly exciting reading, but it is important reading. The best advice is to read carefully. Take your time, especially when you are doing this in the real world. But for now, answering a few questions to check understanding is your goal and the goal of the exam makers. The correct answers to the questions are: **1 A** and **2 C**. To find both answers, it takes careful reading to make certain you are not confused by the details.

Manuals

These are offered, for instance, to the consumer or to the employee for many reasons. To the consumer, manuals are used for instructions on how to put something together such as a barbecue, a bike, or a computer, or to instruct in art, plumbing, or yoga. Employee manuals give specific instructions as to job descriptions. They tell you just exactly what you are supposed to be doing at your job. Whatever the type of manual, it will be informative and instructional. Some are well written and easy to follow, while others are extremely difficult and full of **jargon,** which is language that is used in one specific field (teacher jargon, doctor jargon, skater jargon, journalist jargon, electrician jargon, and so on) and the people in that field understand it better than people outside the field. Below is a sample of an instruction manual. It is attempting to teach someone to throw a Frisbee forehand. Although many manuals have illustrations, this one doesn't. Many instructions are difficult to follow without a visual to help. Read on.

Teaching Beginners How to Throw Forehand

GRIP: Your grip is like this: the middle finger is straight and flat against the inside rim of the disk. The outside rim of the disk makes contact with the web between thumb and index finger. Beginners may need to keep the index and middle fingers separated to gain more control of the disk. The part of the middle finger must still be against the rim of the disk.

STANCE: Assume a stance with the balls of the feet a shoulder width apart. Initially, it appears easier to learn to throw side on and/or with the elbow close to the hip. This may be a crutch later when you have to look upfield and extend around a marker.

The thrower must have the disk cocked, ready to impart spin before throwing. It can either start wound as far back as it can go or wind just before the throw.

SWING: The main trick is to keep the outer tip of the disk down. For the more advanced beginner, the following points may help. The motion of the disk while in the hand should not be so much as an arclike swing, but a whiplash with increasing speed, motion toward the target starts from the shoulder, to the elbow, then wrist, and finally the fingers. Stepping forward and the nonpivot foot may help. The pivot should be on the opposite side as the throwing hand.

RELEASE: Until now, there has been little spin in the disk. The whiplash effect of the swing should culminate in a "snap" imparting maximum spin plane. [i.e, if the spin axis is not perpendicular to the flight plate, the disk launch should lie within this plane]. The time of release is when it all must come together. The last motions imparted to the disk are the ones it takes with it to combat the wind and gravity. Yet, this instant happens so quickly and beginners have so many things to concentrate on that it's hard to tell what went on.

FOLLOW-THROUGH: Any action by the thrower after letting go of the disk cannot influence the flight of the disk. Nevertheless, some specific follow-through tips are suggested in the next section as an aid to correct specific problems in a throw.

---

1. Instruction manuals are provided for instructional use in the
   _____ and for the _____
   A workplace; consumer.
   B baby; toddler.
   C giant; ant.
   D car; passenger.

Your Answer:

A ❑   B ❑   C ❑   D ❑

---

2. In the instructional manual above, the directions for throwing would be more easily understood if _____
   A the instructions were in a foreign language.
   B the instructions were double-spaced.
   C the instructions were illustrated.
   D they were in red ink and not black.

Your Answer:

A ❑   B ❑   C ❑   D ❑

Analysis: **The correct answer to Question 1 is A.** The other answers in this set are wrong. The only logical answer is **A. The correct answer to Question 2 is C.** Reading the answer choices carefully is the key. The answer to this question is inferred in the introductory paragraph to the section. However, most of the answers can be eliminated with a thorough and careful reading.

Applications

There is a time in everyone's life that requires the completion of an application. Applications are completed for employment, driver's licenses, renting or leasing apartments, qualifying for auto or home loans, and so on. Below is a typical application for employment. Become familiar with the information that is asked on these forms. Be prepared to answer a few questions regarding this information.

APPLICATION FOR EMPLOYMENT
Print or type all information.

Section 1: Personal

Date of Application: Phone: (   )

Name: Social Security Number:

Address:

Are you over eighteen years of age?   YES   NO

Person to contact in an emergency:

Address: Phone: (   )

Section 2: Availability

Total Hours Available Per Week:	Hours Available:	M	T	W	T	F	S	S

Date Available for Employment:

What transportation will you use to get to work?

Section 3: Education

Circle the highest grade completed   1   5   6   7   8   grade/middle   9   10   11   12   high school
   1   2   3   4   college/technical   1   2   3   4   post graduate

If education in progress, give name and address of school:

Section 4: Work Experience (List previous employers, starting with the most recent, whether part or full time)

Employer	Address	From	To	Position	Salary

Are you able to perform all the essential functions of the job
for which you are applying with or without accommodations?   (Circle One)   YES   NO

If no, what accommodations will you need:

If hired, do you agree to abide by the safety rules of the company?   (Circle One)   YES   NO

Applicant's Signature: Date:

---

1. What information belongs in Section 2?
   A The applicant's name and address.
   B The signature of the applicant.
   C The hours that the applicant is available to work.
   D The emergency information of the applicant.

Your Answer:

A ❑   **B** ❑   **C** ❑   **D** ❑

---

2. In what section will you circle the highest grade that you completed in school?
   A Section 1
   B Section 2
   C Section 3
   D Section 4

Your Answer:

A ❑   **B** ❑   **C** ❑   **D** ❑

---

3. What is meant by "accommodations" in the last section of the application?
   A That you will need to sleep in a hotel room every night.
   B The use of a wheelchair, hearing device, or other aid to help in fulfilling job duties.
   C That the office be the executive suite on the 37th floor of the building.
   D The use of six secretaries.

Your Answer:

A ❑   **B** ❑   **C** ❑   **D** ❑

Analysis: **The answer to Question 1 is C.** The layout of the application form makes it easy to find information quickly; that's the good thing about test questions like this. Occasionally though, the test makers may attempt to fool you with the wording of either the questions or the answers. Just read them carefully. **The answer to Question 2 is C.** Again, the information is easy to find with this format. You don't have to plow through a lot of words to get to the information you need. **The answer to Question 3 is B.** According to the federal government, all employers must accommodate those with disabilities providing they are capable of performing the essential functions of the job. This question in the application asks the job applicant whether there is a need for the accommodations (wheelchair, hearing aid, Braille, etc.)

Primary and Secondary Sources

Primary sources are exactly that—sources upon which subsequent interpretations or studies are based. Without primary sources, there would be no **secondary sources.** One begets the other. The "Declaration of Sentiments" that was included earlier in the chapter is a sample of a primary source document. The Declaration of Independence is also an example of a primary document. **Secondary sources,** on the other hand, are works that interpret or analyze an historical event or phenomenon. These documents usually contain bibliographies or a works cited page that documents the use of primary sources and other secondary sources.

Primary Source Documents

- diaries
- journals
- speeches
- interviews
- letters, memos
- manuscripts
- memoirs
- autobiographies
- government records
- organization records
- published materials (books, magazine and journal articles, newspaper articles) written at the time of a particular event
- photographs
- audio recordings
- video recordings, films, documentaries
- public opinion polls (taken at time of event)
- research data (anthropological field notes, scientific data, etc.)
- artifacts (physical objects, buildings tools, furniture, clothing, original artworks, etc.)

NOTE: Primary Source documents enable the researcher to get as close as possible to what actually happened during an historical event or time period.

Secondary Source Documents

- textbooks
- encyclopedias
- biographies
- critiques and reviews of art/literature
- dictionaries
- books and articles that review or interpret research works

1. **Which one of the following is NOT an example of a primary source document?**
   A memoirs
   B autobiographies
   C biography
   D government documents

Your Answer:

A ☐   B ☐   C ☐   D ☐

2. **Which one of the following is an example of a secondary source document?**
   A biographies
   B memoirs
   C original art
   D interviews

Your Answer:

A ☐   B ☐   C ☐   D ☐

Analysis: **The answer to Question 1 is C.** Understanding the difference between the two types of sources is the key to knowing the answers to these questions. If you didn't know what types of documents belong to which source, these questions would be difficult. Just remember, that a biography is a **secondary source document** because it is not written by the person it is about; it is written from research and no doubt many **primary source documents.** The **answer to Question 2 is A.**

Bibliographic or Works Cited Citations

When you write a research paper in one of your classes, chances are that your instructor will ask for a bibliography or a works cited page. This is the page that is needed for you to give credit to the sources whose information you borrowed for your paper (which by the way is a secondary-type source). Giving credit to the person whose work you are borrowing is mandatory. Plagiarism is what it is called if you don't, and that's a legal battle that you would want to avoid at all costs. It is much easier to credit your source. An individual **citation** contains only enough information to enable the reader to look up the source if they so desire. There are different ways to document different types of sources (such as periodicals/magazines, web sites, encyclopedias, etc.), as well as different types of research papers for different classes. Some subjects require that you document according to the rules of the American Psychological Association or APA. But, because this book focuses on English, we will become familiar with the Modern Language Association (MLA) format. What will be asked on the test are specific questions about the setup of a **bibliographic** or **works cited** entry. Look at the following entry carefully. Note the position of each of the components; author, title, city of publication, publisher, and year of publication. Please be aware that punctuation in the entry is very important.

> Orwell, George. <u>Animal Farm.</u> New York: Harcourt Brace Jovanovich, Inc., 1946.

> **NOTE: Bibliographic Entries**
> **Author (last name, first name). Title of book (<u>underlined</u>). City of Publication: Publisher, Year of publication.**

> **NOTE: The second line of the entry must be indented**

1. **Which of the following bibliographic entries is incorrect?**
   A Finley, M.I. <u>The World of Odysseus</u>. New York: Penguin Books, 1956.
   B Tolkien, J.R.R. <u>The Hobbit</u>. New York: Ballantine Publishing Group, 1937.
   C McCourt, Frank. <u>Angela's Ashes: A Memoir.</u> New York: Simon and Schuster, 1996.
   D Houston, Jeanne Wakatsuki, and James Houston. <u>Farewell to Manzanar</u>. 1973.

Your Answer:
A ☐   B ☐   C ☐   D ☐

Analysis: **The correct answer to Number 1 is D.** The question is asking which entry is **incorrect**. Remember: punctuation is important. Period, colon, and comma placement is the key to answering this question correctly, plus the fact that the incorrect answer left out the city of publication and the publisher. Both should be placed before the date of publication with the proper punctuation.

Informational Sources

You can usually count on a test question that asks you what you will find in various informational sources. A thesaurus, *Reader's Guide to Periodical Literature*, an index, an atlas, and the dictionary are the key sources to the questions. Although your school librarian has no doubt explained these to you many times before, it is helpful to review the functions of these informational sources. Study the entries and then answer the preview questions that follow.

Thesaurus

When you know the definition of a word, but you need a word that has the same or similar meaning, you go to a thesaurus or a synonym finder. Thesauruses are set up alphabetically like a dictionary or they are indexed (see sample below). If you have an indexed version, look up the word in the back of the book and then go to the number that it refers to.

Sample of Indexed Thesaurus

> **NOTE: First look up the referenced number.**

Hypochondria 437
sickness 889

437. HYPOCHONDRIA
See also 889. Sickness

1. imagined ill-health, valetudinarianism, anxiety, neurosis, psychoneurosis.
2. depression, melancholy, *Psychiatry*. melancholia, hypochondriasis, despondency, doldrums, dejection, low spirits, megrims, the blues, *Archaic*. hyp.

Dictionary

In addition to helping you define or understand the meaning of a word, a dictionary is also helpful with spelling, syllabication (splitting up the word properly), pronunciation, parts of speech (noun, pronoun, verb, adjective, etc.), etymology (the history of the word and any root or derivatives), as well as capitalization.

Example of a dictionary entry

> **ex•tro•vert (ek**-strö-vurt) *n.* a person
> more interested in the people and things
> around him than in his own thoughts
> and feelings, a lively sociable person.
> **extrovert** *adj. extroverted.* **ex•tro•**
> **version** (ek-strö-**vur**-zhŏn) *n.*

- **ex•tro•vert** = syllabication; this separates the word for you in case you ever need to write part of the word on one line and part of the word on another line
- **(ek**-strö-vurt) = pronunciation—phonetically demonstrates how to say the word
- *n.* = part of speech this word happens to be a noun
- "a person more interested in the people and things around him than in his own thoughts and feelings, a lively sociable person." ⎬ the definition or word meaning
- **extrovert** *adj. extroverted.* **ex•tro•ver•sion** (ek-strö-**vur**-zhŏn) *n.* ⎬ additional forms of the word

Reader's Guide to Periodical Literature. *The Reader's Guide to Periodical Literature* is a book found in the library and is one of the most used magazine reference tools used. The

Reader's Guide is easily identified by its green cover. If you are looking for information on a current topic in a magazine, this is the source to tap. The guide is indexed alphabetically according to subject and author. Before you go to a lot of work in using this guide, make certain your library has the magazines that it refers you to before you go searching the shelves and wasting time. An entry (see below) in this book will provide you with the following information: the topic, page numbers, volume, name of magazine, name of author, subtopic, date, cross-references, title of article, subject entry, and author entry.

SAMPLE NAME ENTRY

AUTHOR ENTRY
This article is *by* Robert J. Dole.

DOLE, ROBERT J., 1923-

The establishment clause, *Policy Review* no 15 p36-7 Ja7 '96

about

All about Dole. R. Lowry, *National Review* v48 p79+

SUBJECT ENTRY
This article is *about* Robert J. Dole.

SAMPLE SUBJECT ENTRY

FISHING

See also
Bass
Bass Fishing
Fish keepers
Fly Fishing

SEE REFERENCE
The subject heading for articles on this topic is *Fly Fishing*.

SEE ALSO REFERENCE
This reference leads you to related or more specific subject headings.

FLY CASTING *see* Fly fishing

TITLE ENHANCEMENT
This had been added by the indexer to clarify the meaning of the title. Square brackets are used to indicate these editorial interpretations.

SUBJECT HEADING
This article is about Fly fishing.

AUTHOR
The author of this article is Lou Tabory.

ARTICLE TITLE

FLY FISHING

ILLUSTRATIONS
This article is illustrated and includes a map.

MAGAZINE CITATION
This article appears in *Outdoor Life*.

Working the edge [salt water fly fishing] L. Tabory. il map *Outdoor Life* v197 p56-58+ Ap '96

DATE OF MAGAZINE
The issue is dated April 1996.

VOLUME NUMBER
The volume of this issue is 197.

PAGING
This article can be found on pages 56 through 58 (continued on later pages of the same issue).

Index and Other Parts of a Book.

- Beginning in the beginning, the **title** page is normally the first page in the book with print on it. The title of the book, the author's name, the publisher's name, and the place of publication are all located on this page.
- The **copyright** page is located usually on the reverse side of the title page. It provides information about the date or dates the book was published. It also has the Library of Congress information (the number that almost all published books are given) or an International Standard Book Number [ISBN], which uniquely identifies the book.
- Often there is a **preface** or a **forward, introduction,** or an **acknowledgment,** where you will discover some background information to the book, who may have been involved in writing it, and why it was written.

- The **table of contents** lists the divisions of the book into units, chapters, or topics.
- The **body** of the book is the main course—the meat and potatoes.
- An **appendix,** near the end of the book is necessary when additional information is needed to explain something within the book itself. Maps, charts, tables, diagrams, letters, or other documents will be found here.
- A **glossary** provides definitions of words or terms that may be unfamiliar to the reader. It is like a mini-dictionary.
- The **index** is one of the most valuable parts of a book. It is an alphabetical listing of all the important topics included in the book. Although it is a distant cousin to the table of contents, the index is far more detailed and it tells which page in the book you will find the topic or specific information that you need.
- And, last but not least, a **bibliography**, which we've spoken of earlier in the chapter. The bibliography is where the author credits any primary or secondary sources from which he or she may have borrowed information. It also suggests further readings.

Atlas.   An **atlas**—where would we be without one? This is a book of maps. Open this book and you will see more than you realize. Cities, states, countries, continents, rivers, mountains, major lakes and bodies of water, deserts, rain forests, and peninsulas among the many hundreds of other geographical data. Maps contain valuable sources of information. Different types of map offer different types of information:

- **Physical maps** show elevation, natural landscapes (mountains, deserts, etc.), elevations (see example below), mineral resources, vegetation, land use, and ecoregions, among others.

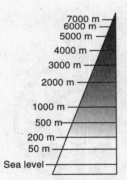

The diagram at left is an approximate key to elevation colors on the relief maps. Red characters are used for land features (mountains, islands, plains, etc.) and blue characters are used for lakes, rivers, oceans, and other water features.

As with the political maps, the relief maps in the World Atlas use the Equidistant Cylindrical projection, which is characterized by severe distortion of area, shape, and distance, particularly near the poles.

- **Political maps** show population density, transportation density, time zones, and of course political information.

Type Styles

ALBANIA	Independent country
ANTARCTICA	Antarctica
GUADELOUPE (FRANCE)	Dependency, overseas territory, etc.
MINNESOTA	Internal division (state, province, etc.)
CHECHNYA	Region with separatist movement(s)
KASHMIR	Disputed territory
Kingston Paris	National capital(s)

POLITICAL MAPS

Cities with less than 200,000 inhabitants are not shown unless they are either a national capital or the center of a large urban area.

Cities

Orlando	Population under 200,000
Zurich	Population 200,000 - 499,999
Lubumbashi	Population 500,000 - 999,000
Jilin	Population 1,000,000 -1,999,000
Melbourne	Population over 2,000,000

Urban areas

■	Population 1,000,000 - 2,999,999
▲	Population 3,000,000 - 4,999,999
●	Population over 5,000,000

Colors

Disputed territory

Antarctic ice shelf

- **Climate and weather maps** show precipitation (rainfall), snow cover, and temperatures.

Precip	Temp	Probability anomaly as shown on map	Probability of occurrence for each class			Most likely category
			A	N	B	
		40%-50%	73.3%-83.3%	23.3%-13.3%	3.3%	"Above"
		30%-40%	63.3%-73.3%	33.3%-23.3%	3.3%	"Above"
		20%-30%	53.3%-63.3%	33.3%	13.3%-3.3%	"Above"
		10%-20%	43.3%-53.3%	33.3%	18.3%-28.3%	"Above"
		5%-10%	38.3%-43.3%	33.3%	28.3%-23.3%	"Above"
		0%-5%	33.3%-38.3%	33.3%	28.3%-33.3%	"Above"
		0%-5%	30.8%-33.3%	33.3%	30.8%-33.3%	"Near Normal"
		5%-10%	28.3%-30.8%	33.3%	28.3%-30.8%	"Near Normal"
		0%-5%	28.3%-33.3%	33.3%	33.3%-38.3%	"Below"
		5%-10%	23.3%-28.3%	33.3%	38.3%-43.3%	"Below"
		10%-20%	28.3%-18.3%	33.3%	43.3%-53.3%	"Below"
		20%-30%	13.3%-3.3%	33.3%	53.3%-63.3%	"Below"
		30%-40%	3.3%	33.3%-23.3%	63.3%-73.3%	"Below"
		40%-50%	3.3%	23.3%-13.3%	73.3%-83.3%	"Below"
		0%	33.3%	33.3%	33.3%	"Climatology"

Also located on most maps are:

- The **compass rose**, which directs you north, south, east, and west on the map. Usually, north is at the top of the map, south at the bottom, east is right, and west is left. The compass rose has been included on maps since the 1300s. It originally was an indicator of the direction of the winds (N, NE, E, SE, S, SW, W, and NW).

- The **legend or key** is in a little box that shows what certain colors or symbols mean. Note the example of the political map legend on the previous page; it illustrates what specific colors and symbols are intended for cities of various sizes.

- The **scale** provides the user with an idea of how large or small an area is. For instance, a one-inch scale could represent 1,000 miles or it could represent 10 miles, depending upon the map. Note the scale on the examples below.

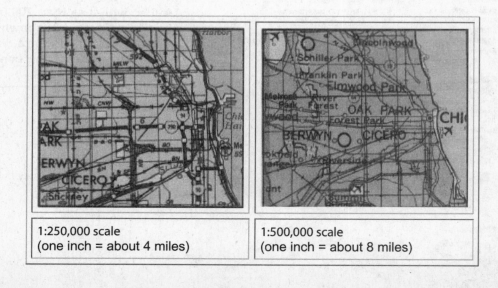

1:250,000 scale
(one inch = about 4 miles)

1:500,000 scale
(one inch = about 8 miles)

• **Longitudinal and latitudinal lines** indicate exactly where in the world the area you are looking for is located. Longitudinal lines are the lines you see running up and down from the North Pole to the South Pole all the way around the globe. Latitudinal lines are the lines that run around the globe and are parallel with the equator. This table gives the latitude and longitude of various major cities in California. The first column gives the latitude in degrees and minutes. The second column gives the longitude in degrees and minutes.

CALIFORNIA	Latitude	Longitude
Bakersfield AP	35° 25' N	119° 3' W
Barstow AP	34° 51' N	116° 47' W
Burbank AP	34° 12' N	118° 21' W
Chico	39° 48' N	121° 51' W
Covina	34° 5' N	117° 52' W
Crescent City AP	41° 46' N	124° 12' W
Downey	33° 56' N	118° 8' W
El Cajon	32° 49' N	116° 58' W
El Cerrito AP (S)	32° 49' N	115° 40' W
Escondido	33° 7' N	117° 5' W
Eureka/Arcata AP	40° 59' N	124° 6' W
Fresno AP (S)	36° 46' N	119° 43' W
Laguna Beach	33° 33' N	117° 47' W
Livermore	37° 42' N	121° 57' W
Long Beach AP	33° 49' N	118° 9' W
Los Angeles AP (S)	33° 56' N	118° 24' W
Los Angeles CO (S)	34° 3' N	118° 14' W
Modesto	37° 39' N	121° 0' W
Monterey	36° 36' N	121° 54' W
Napa	38° 13' N	122° 17' W
Needles AP	34° 36' N	114° 37' W
Oakland AP	37° 49' N	122° 19' W
Oceanside	33° 14' N	117° 25' W
Ontario	34° 3' N	117° 36' W
Oxnard	34° 12' N	119° 11' W
Palmdale AP	34° 38' N	118° 6' W
Palm Springs	33° 49' N	116° 32' W
Pasadena	34° 9' N	118° 9' W
Petaluma	38° 14' N	122° 38' W
Pomona Co	34° 3' N	117° 45' W
Redding AP	40° 31' N	122° 18' W
Redlands	34° 3' N	117° 11' W
Richmond	37° 56' N	122° 21' W
Riverside-	33° 54' N	117° 15' W
Sacramento AP	38° 31' N	121° 30' W
Salinas AP	36° 40' N	121° 36' W
San Diego AP	32° 44' N	117° 10' W
San Fernando	34° 17' N	118° 28' W
San Francisco AP	37° 37' N	122° 23' W
San Francisco Co	37° 46' N	122° 26' W
San Jose AP	37° 22' N	121° 56' W
San Louis Obispo	35° 20' N	120° 43' W
Santa Ana AP	33° 45' N	117° 52' W
Santa Barbara MAP	34° 26' N	119° 50' W
Santa Cruz	36° 59' N	122° 1' W
Santa Maria AP (S)	34° 54' N	120° 27' W
Santa Monica CIC	34° 1' N	118° 29' W
Santa Paula	34° 21' N	119° 5' W
Santa Rosa	38° 31' N	122° 49' W
Stockton AP	37° 54' N	121° 15' W
Ukiah	39° 9' N	123° 12' W
Visalia	36° 20' N	119° 18' W
Yreka	41° 43' N	122° 38' W
Yuba City	39° 8' N	121° 36' W

Chapter Review and Quick Quiz

A lot going on in this chapter! We reviewed information about **expository** writings, **consumer materials, primary and secondary sources, bibliographic citations,** and **informational sources.** Let's make certain you understand each of them. Take the following quick quiz for a review. The answers are listed in the appendix in the back of the book.

1. **Which of the following is not an example of expository writing?**
   A newspapers
   B political speeches
   C novels
   D editorials

Your Answer:

A ❑   B ❑   C ❑   D ❑

2. **Which of the following is an example of a primary source document?**
   A a comic book
   B the Declaration of Independence
   C a novel
   D an appliance warranty

Your Answer:

A ❑   B ❑   C ❑   D ❑

3. **Warranty certificates are** _____
   A not functional.
   B used to decorate a product box.
   C sold separately at all times.
   D guarantees of the manufacturer for an item purchased.

Your Answer:

A ❑   B ❑   C ❑   D ❑

4. **True or False. A contract is a formal agreement between people, groups, or countries with a binding legal document setting out terms and conditions.**
   A True
   B False

Your Answer:

A ❑   B ❑

5. **Manuals are used for** _____
   A job descriptions.
   B instructions for various appliances.
   C care and maintenance of an automobile.
   D all of the above.

Your Answer:

A ❑   B ❑   C ❑   D ❑

6. **In general, applications will always ask for** _____
   A your name, address, and telephone number.
   B whether or not you like to wear jeans.
   C the color of your hair.
   D your shoe size.

Your Answer:

A ❑   B ❑   C ❑   D ❑

7. **Which of the following is NOT an example of a secondary source document?**
   A textbooks
   B encyclopedias
   C dictionaries
   D poems

Your Answer:

A ❑   B ❑.   C ❑   D ❑

8. **A bibliographic citation or works cited citation for a book asks for the** _____
   A author, title, city of publication, publisher, and year of publication.
   B author, title, city in which the author resides.
   C author, title, publisher and the author's year of birth.
   D author, title, city of publication, publisher, and today's date.

Your Answer:

A ❑   B ❑   C ❑   D ❑

9. **A thesaurus is used to locate words that** _____
   A can be divided into three syllables.
   B mean the same or almost the same.
   C are biographical.
   D have six suffixes.

Your Answer:

A ❑   B ❑   C ❑   D ❑

10. **True or False. A dictionary definition includes syllabication.**
   A True
   B False

Your Answer:

A ❑   B ❑

11. **The title page is** _____ **and names the title, author, and publisher.**
   A at the end of the book
   B the first page with printing on it
   C used as an index
   D the same as a table of contents

Your Answer:

A ❑   B ❑   C ❑   D ❑

12. **True or False. The table of contents lists the divisions of the book into units, chapters, or topics.**
   A True
   B False

Your Answer:

A ❑   B ❑

13. **The glossary of the book** _____
   A provides a biography of the author.
   B instructs the reader on good reading habits.
   C provides a glossy coating to the pages of the book.
   D provides definitions of words or terms that may be unfamiliar to the reader.

Your Answer:

A ❑   B ❑   C ❑   D ❑

14. **The index is** _____
   A in the front of the book and lists the chapters.
   B scattered throughout the book to prevent boredom.
   C an alphabetical listing of important topics included in the book.
   D a random list of names, places, and dates.

Your Answer:

A ❑   B ❑   C ❑   D ❑

15. **The compass rose was originally included on the map to show the direction of** _____
   A the winds.
   B large fish swimming.
   C the South Pole.
   D the French countryside.

Your Answer:

A ❑   B ❑   C ❑   D ❑

Chapter 6

Literary Response and Analysis—Part I

In this chapter, we will review literary **genres.** Genres are the broad categories under which all literature is type-cast or categorized—for instance; fiction, nonfiction, poetry, and drama are all genres of literature. However, within these genres are **subgenres,** which are mini-categories within the large category. Example: within the fiction category its subgenre includes: historical fiction, fantasy, science fiction, mystery, romance, etc. Once we have a clear understanding of genre, we will look at questions on the exam that will ask you to respond to a specific genre.

CHAPTER FOCUS: ***Understanding Genres***
                                                   Fiction—The Novel

- ***Historical Novels***
- ***Science Fiction***
- ***Fantasy Novels***
- ***Mystery or Detective Stories***
- ***Romance Novels***
- ***Bildungsroman***
- ***Picaresque Novels***
- ***Epistolary Novels***
- ***Stream of Consciousness Novels***

Nonfiction

- ***Speeches***
- ***Diaries and Memoirs***
- ***Autobiographies***
- ***Biographies***
- ***Magazine, Newspaper, Journal Articles, and Editorials***
- ***Essays***

Poetry

- ***Ballads***
- ***Blank Verse***
- ***Concrete Poetry***
- ***Didactic Poems***
- ***Dramatic Monologues***
- ***Elegies***
- ***Epic Poems***
- ***Free Verse***
- ***Limericks***
- ***Narrative Poems***
- ***Sonnets***

Drama

Chapter Review and Quick Quiz

Understanding Genres

Fiction—The Novel

The first **genre** that we are going to look at is **fiction** (writings that are invented and not true) or more specifically, the **novel.** This genre is by far the most common in all of literature. You read several novels each year in your English class. The novel is a long narrative (a writing that tells a story) that deals with characters, settings, and incidents upon which the story is built or developed. The author invents the characters and situations with the intent of entertaining the reader. There are many different types of novels, which are the **subgenres.** Let's take a look at them.

Historical Novels.   Usually set in times of great conflict or social change, historical novels attempt to recreate a historically important series of events or depict specific personae, or people vital to that event. Although the foundation of the historical novel is based upon actual events, as are the details of dress, manners, and other aspects of daily life, the author fictionalizes the story in many other ways by adding and subtracting details to move the story along. Examples of historical novels are: Sir Walter Scott's *Rob Roy* and *Ivanhoe*, Victor Hugo's *Les Miserables*, Leo Tolstoy's *War and Peace*, and Margaret Mitchell's *Gone with the Wind*.

1. **Which of the following novels would be categorized as an example of historical fiction?**
   A *The Pearl* by John Steinbeck
   B *War and Peace* by Leo Tolstoy
   C *Fahrenheit 451* by Ray Bradbury
   D *The Color Purple* by Alice Walker

Your Answer:

A ❑   B ❑   C ❑   D ❑

Analysis: **The correct answer is B.** *War and Peace* by Leo Tolstoy is a historical novel based on the events surrounding the invasion of Russia by Napoleon of France. There are over five hundred characters as well as a variety of themes and action that makes *War and Peace* a monumental work. *The Pearl* and *The Color Purple* are novels that depict characters who deal with major conflict. *Fahrenheit 451* is a science fiction novel written by Ray Bradbury. It is set in the future and deals primarily with censorship and the burning of books.

Science Fiction.   This subgenre is set usually in the future or in an imaginary world. The themes, settings, plots, and characters are based on some scientific or technological speculation or theorization. Jules Verne's *Around the World in Eighty Days* and *20,000 Leagues Under the Sea*, H. G. Wells' *The War of the Worlds* and *The Time Machine*, Ray Bradbury's *Fahrenheit 451* and *The Illustrated Man*, and Arthur C. Clarke's *2001: A Space Odyssey* are examples of the subgenre of science fiction.

2. **Which of the following novels would be included in the subgenre of science fiction?**
   A *Romeo and Juliet* by William Shakespeare
   B *Wuthering Heights* by Emily Brontë
   C *A Farewell to Arms* by Ernest Hemingway
   D *The War of the Worlds* by H. G. Wells

Your Answer:

A ❑   B ❑   C ❑   D ❑

Analysis: *Romeo and Juliet* is a play about "two star-crossed lovers," which was written by Shakespeare. *Wuthering Heights* is a novel of a family torn apart by the adoption of a homeless waif and the subsequent years of revenge and hate. *A Farewell to Arms* is the love story of a nurse and a wartime ambulance driver. **A, B,** and **C** are incorrect. **The correct answer is D.** *The War of the Worlds* is about an alien invasion. It caused quite a controversy when it was read on the radio; people believed that the invasion was actually happening.

Fantasy Novels.   These are written for either pure enjoyment or as serious or satirical (writing that blends humor and wit with criticism on human affairs or institutions, most often politics). Fantasy novels are set in an imaginary, unreal, or utopian (an ideal) world and usually involve fantastic or unbelievable characters. Examples of fantasy novels include: *Gulliver's Travels* by Jonathan

Swift (a utopian and a political satire), *Alice's Adventures in Wonderland* by Lewis Carroll, J. R. R. Tolkien's *The Lord of the Rings*, and the *Harry Potter* novels by J. K. Rowling.

3. **Which of the following novels would be considered a part of the subgenre of fantasy?**
   A *The Lord of the Rings* by J. R. R. Tolkien
   B *The Old Gringo* by Carlos Fuentes
   C *Don Quixote* by Miguel de Cervantes
   D *Moby Dick* by Herman Melville

Your Answer:

A ☐ **B** ☐ **C** ☐ **D** ☐

Analysis: **The correct answer is A.** The *Lord of the Rings* is a trilogy of novels set in the world of Middle Earth. J. R. R. Tolkien is widely admired for his fantasies that are based on small people he calls Hobbits. Answers **B, C,** and **D** are novels, but definitely not fantasy, although the whale in *Moby Dick* could possibly be considered fantastic in a sense.

Mystery or Detective Stories. This is a subgenre in which a mystery or crime is solved by a detective. The reader is presented with the clues at the same time that the detective uncovers them. Usually, in a detective story, the emphasis is on the plot. However, many authors develop very strong main characters (or protagonists) as well as plot.

4. **Read the following passage and then select the literary subgenre to which it belongs.**

   At three o'clock precisely I was at Baker Street, but Holmes had not yet returned. The land-lady informed me that he had left the house shortly after eight o'clock in the morning. I sat down beside the fire, however, with the intention of awaiting him, however long he might be. I was already deeply interested in his inquiry, for, though it was surrounded by none of the grim and strange features which were associated with the two crimes which I have already recorded, still, the nature of the case and the exalted station of his client gave it a character of its own. Indeed, apart from the nature of the investigation which my friend had on hand, there was something in his masterly grasp of a situation, and his keen, incisive reasoning, which made it a pleasure for me to study his system of work, and to follow the quick, subtle methods by which he disentangled the most inextricable mysteries. So accustomed was I to his invariable success that the very possibility of his failing had ceased to enter into my head.

   A Fantasy
   B Historical fiction
   C Detective
   D Picaresque

Your Answer:

A ☐ **B** ☐ **C** ☐ **D** ☐

Analysis: From reading the passage, the words "crime" and "case" are mentioned and the tone of the writing seems mysterious. Answers **A, B,** and **D** can be ruled out easily by paying close attention to the wording of the passage carefully. **The correct answer is C.**

Romance Novels. These depend upon the very fertile imagination of the author rather than on real-life events. The settings, characters, and action are often depicted in a series of episodes that involve adventure in exotic settings, gallant love, heroic deeds, and mysterious events. In the Middle Ages, **chivalric** (the brave knight on the white horse type) **romances** such as *Sir Gawain and the Green Knight* dealt with damsels in distress as well as the knight's many encounters with monsters and giants. Today, we think of the romance novel as the **popular romance** typified by the Harlequin Romances.

5. Read the passage below and determine which subgenre of literature it belongs to.

Mara had never expected to see the man again. She wasn't sure she wanted to see him now.

But there he stood, dominating the doorway of Books and Such. Mara owned the bookstore just off the picturesque main square in Freeburg, a small, close-knit town in southern Maryland.

There he stood, Mick Swanson, the man who, a year ago, had pretended to love her and then had broken off their brief but intense relationship as if it meant nothing.

His neatly trimmed, sandy hair and the tailored overcoat stretching across his broad shoulders gave Mick the air of a man in charge. But there was wariness in those blue eyes that touched Mara more than she wanted to admit.

A Fantasy
B Science Fiction
C Historical
D Romance

Your Answer:

A ☐   **B** ☐   **C** ☐   **D** ☐

Analysis: **The correct answer is D.** After reading the passage, one can easily determine the answer with all of the references to "love." The tone of the writing is mushy—gooey, and certainly could not be identified with fantasy, science fiction, or historical fiction. This is definitely a romance novel.

Bildungsroman.   This is a type of novel that follows the development of a character or hero's education or life from youth to experience. The term actually translated from German means "development novel." It was originally coined to describe Wolfgang von Goethe's novel *Wilhelm Meister's Apprenticeship*. Other examples of the bildungsroman are *David Copperfield* by Charles Dickens, Charlotte Brontë's *Jane Eyre*, Hermann Hesse's *Demian*, Saul Bellow's *The Adventures of Augie March*, and Doris Lessing's *Children of Violence*.

6. The subgenre of fiction that follows the education of a hero from youth to experience is called _____
A bildungsroman.
B fantasy.
C romance.
D science fiction.

Your Answer:

A ☐   **B** ☐   **C** ☐   **D** ☐

Analysis: **The correct answer is A.**

Picaresque Novels.   These are novels whose main character lives by his or her wits and becomes involved in one predicament after another. It usually takes the form of a series of journeys in which the main character's many adventures involve people from all walks of life. The picaresque tales originated in Spain and the most famous of all is the novel by Miguel de Cervantes, *Don Quixote*. Mark Twain's *Huckleberry Finn*, Henry Fielding's *Tom Jones*, and Daniel Defoe's *Moll Flanders* are all examples of the picaresque novel.

7. A picaresque novel is one whose main character becomes involved in one predicament after another. Which of the following does NOT represent a picaresque novel?
A *Don Quixote* by Miguel de Cervantes
B *The Grapes of Wrath* by John Steinbeck
C *Moll Flanders* by Daniel Defoe
D *Tom Jones* by Henry Fielding

Your Answer:

A ❑   B ❑   C ❑   D ❑

Analysis: Make certain you read the questions carefully. This is one of those that could fool you. It asks for the answer that does *not* represent a picaresque novel. **The correct answer is B.** *The Grapes of Wrath* is about a desperate family that moves from Oklahoma to California in search of work during the depression. Choices **A, C,** and **D** are all examples of picaresque novels.

Epistolary Novels.   These are written through correspondence or letter-writing between characters. It was a form of novel writing that was made popular in the eighteenth century. Examples of the epistolary novel are: Samuel Richardson's *Pamela and Clarissa Harlowe*, but more recently are Alice Walker's *The Color Purple* and John Barth's *Letters*.

8. **An epistolary novel is one that is written through _____ between one or more characters.**
   A oral conversations
   B written correspondence
   C first-person fiction
   D third-person fiction

Your Answer:

A ❑   B ❑   C ❑   D ❑

Analysis: The correct answer is B. The epistolary novel is correspondence between one or more characters. Answers **A, C,** and **D** are wrong. First-person fiction uses "I" as the narration, while third-person fiction uses "he," "she," or "it" in narrating the story.

The Stream of Consciousness Novel.   This is one that might appear to be a bit unusual at first. It is a type of psychological novel in which the story emerges through the inner workings of one (or more) of the main characters. On the page, the stream of consciousness novel appears to be made of fragmented sentences, unusual capitalization and punctuation and spacing. The author's use of dashes and other typographical oddities are intended to present the character's thoughts as disjointed and illogical, which they usually are. Examples of this type of novel are: James Joyce's *Ulysses*, Virginia Woolf's *Mrs. Dalloway* and *To the Lighthouse*, as well as William Faulkner's *As I Lay Dying*.

9. **Read the following passage and identify the subgenre to which it belongs.**

   STATELY, PLUMP BUCK MULLIGAN CAME FROM THE STAIRHEAD, bearing a bowl of lather on which a mirror and a razor lay crossed. A yellow dressing gown, ungirdled, was sustained gently behind him by the mild morning air. He held the bowl aloft and intoned:

   — Introibo ad altare Dei.

   Halted, he peered down the dark winding stairs and called up coarsely:

   — Come up, Kinch. Come up, you fearful jesuit.

   Solemnly he came forward and mounted the round gunrest. He faced about and blessed gravely thrice the tower, the surrounding country and the awaking mountains. Then, catching sight of Stephen Dedalus, he bent towards him and made rapid crosses in the air, gurgling in his throat and shaking his head. Stephen Dedalus, displeased and sleepy, leaned his arms on the top of the staircase and looked coldly at the shaking gurgling face that blessed him, equine in its length, and at the light untonsured hair, grained and hued like pale oak.

   Buck Mulligan peeped an instant under the mirror and then covered the bowl smartly.

— Back to barracks, he said sternly.

He added in a preacher's tone:

— For this, O dearly beloved, is the genuine Christine: body and soul and blood and ouns. Slow music, please. Shut your eyes, gents. One moment. A little trouble about those white corpuscles. Silence, all.

A Science Fiction
B Fantasy
C Epistolary
D Stream of Consciousness

Your Answer:

A ☐   **B** ☐   **C** ☐   **D** ☐

Analysis: The correct answer is D. After a brief review of the passage things just don't appear normal do they? Stream of consciousness novels are a bit odd when compared to the "normal" writing of a typical novel. Answers **A** and **B** are obviously incorrect. And, if you didn't know that an epistolary novel was one that is written in the form of letters, you might be confused. But, **D is the correct answer.**

Nonfiction

As you know, nonfiction is a generalized term for writing that is based on truth. It is real and not imagined like that of novels. Although nonfiction is considered a literary genre, or the main category, it is important to become familiar with the types of nonfiction that are among its many subgenres. Biographies, autobiographies, speeches, diaries, memoirs, essays, editorials, journal articles, and magazine and newspaper articles are all examples of nonfiction.

Speeches.   These are given by all sorts of people for all sorts of reasons. Most often we listen to speeches being given by a speaker, however, in school, especially in history or English classes; we read and study them to help us understand what exactly was going on during a specific period of time. Most often speeches are given to either inform the listener or to persuade the listener. It would be impossible to go into detail about the number and subjects of speeches given around the world, but the following list of quotes are from speeches that are well known and often referred to not only on examinations, but in daily life as well.

From: Abraham Lincoln's Gettysburg Address given on November 19, 1863: "Four score and seven years ago our fathers brought forth, on this continent, a new nation, conceived in Liberty, and dedicated to the proposition that all men are created equal."

From: Martin Luther King, Jr.'s "I Have a Dream" speech given at the Lincoln Memorial in Washington D.C. in 1963 during the March on Washington: "I have a dream that my four little children will one day live in a nation where they will not be judged by the color of their skin but by the content of their character."

From: President Franklin D. Roosevelt's inaugural address in 1933: "The only thing we have to fear is fear itself."

From: U.S. Supreme Court Justice William O. Douglas's speech on the court: "The court is really the keeper of the conscience, and the conscience is the Constitution."

From: President John F. Kennedy's inaugural address: "Ask not what your country can do for you, ask what you can do for your country."

From: The lunar surface, 240,000 miles from Earth on July 20, 1969, Neil Armstrong said to the world as he took that first historic step: "That's one small step for man, one giant leap for mankind."

10. "We have nothing to fear, but fear itself," is a statement made famous by _____, who was speaking at his inauguration in 1933.
  A Abraham Lincoln
  B Frank Sinatra
  C John F. Kennedy
  D Franklin D. Roosevelt

Your Answer:

A ❑   B ❑   C ❑   D ❑

Analysis: The question is very specific in what it is asking, but you need to know a little about American history. First of all, Answer **B** is there and completely wrong because Frank Sinatra was a singer and was never inaugurated as president. Abraham Lincoln and John F. Kennedy (**A** and **C**) were presidents, but their inaugurations are at completely different times than the one stated in the question. So, by process of elimination, **the correct answer is D.**

Diaries and Memoirs.   These are similar in that they are written to remember incidents in our lives; diaries, however, are usually written by people to record events and thoughts on a regular basis. Undoubtedly, one of the most famous of all diaries is *Anne Frank: A Diary of a Young Girl*. Of course, there are hundreds of other notable diaries published; many of them are the writings of politicians and often the writings of well-known authors or poets such as: Jonathan Swift, Ralph Waldo Emerson, Theodore Roosevelt, and Charles Lindbergh. Diaries are often published after the author dies—posthumously. Memoirs, on the other hand, are usually written to record a single period of the author's life that will often coincide with an historical event. Homer Hickam's *Rocket Boys: A Memoir* (a.k.a.: *October Sky*), Ji-li Jiang's *Red Scarf Girl: A Memoir of the Cultural Revolution*, and Frank McCourt's *Angela's Ashes: A Memoir*, are examples of memoirs.

11. True or False. Memoirs are usually written to record a specific period of the author's life.
  A True
  B False

Your Answer:

A ❑   B ❑

Analysis: A is the correct answer.

Autobiographies.   These are written as an account of all or a part of a person's life. In most cases, the writing is in the form of narration or telling the story of important life events, but often, the author manages to weave into the writing introspective thoughts as well as imagination. Autobiographical writings offer glimpses into the author's world through his or her own eyes. We are able to more clearly experience the author's personality, attitudes, and thoughts we probably would not experience otherwise. Examples of autobiographies are: *Up from Slavery* by Booker T. Washington, *Autobiography* by Benjamin Franklin, *The Education of Henry Adams* by, of course, Henry Adams, *I Know Why the Caged Bird Sings* by Maya Angelou, *Confessions* by Jean-Jacques Rousseau, *True Relation of My Birth, Breeding and Life* by Margaret Cavendish, and the *Confessions* of St. Augustine.

12. True or False. Autobiographies are NOT written by the authors about themselves.
  A True
  B False

Your Answer:

A ❑   B ❑

Analysis: **The correct answer is False, B.** Autobiographies are written by the authors about themselves.

Biographies. These are written by someone about someone else. As opposed to autobiographies, which are written by someone about themselves. Biographies, usually fact-based writings, ideally (because some of them are unauthorized) are accurate accounts of the person's character, personality, and career. Biographies have been written about people in all walks of life including: artists, actors, inventors, explorers, mathematicians, doctors, businessmen and -women, scientists, anthropologists, saints, composers, musicians, and politicians, to name but a few—and everyone from Archimedes to Max Zorn is included in this large subgenre of literary works.

13. Nonfictional literary works that are written specifically about a real person are called
_____

  A fantasies.
  B diaries.
  C biographies.
  D science fiction.

Your Answer:

A ❑   **B** ❑   **C** ❑   **D** ❑

Analysis: **The correct answer is C.** Both **A** and **D** are fictional (not real) and diaries (**B**) are writings by people who record their thoughts and impressions of life or events that are happening around them.

Included in this last category of nonfiction are **magazine articles, newspaper articles, journal articles, editorials,** and **essays.**

Magazine Articles. These need little explaining; they are what they are, depending primarily on the type of magazine. There are newsmagazines, fashion magazines, women's magazines, men's magazines, children's magazines, and motorcycle, sewing, automobile, running, and skiing magazines—magazines for almost all interests and hobbies. The articles are obviously written to help sell the magazine, which means they must be interesting to the reader. The structure of the article again depends upon the magazine type. Most often though, the beginning of the articles usually have a **hook,** as you would use bait on a hook to attract a fish's attention, or something that will attract the reader's attention and invite or encourage him or her to read further. A hook might be a question or a quote or some other strong statement, interesting fact, or an anecdote (brief story) that catches the reader's attention like this quote:

> "I personally believe that each and every one of us was put here for a purpose, and that's to build and not to destroy. And if by chance some day you're not feeling well, you should remember some silly little thing that I've said or done, and it brings back a smile to your face or a chuckle to your heart, then my purpose as the clown has been fulfilled." (Red Skelton)

or this fact:

Sharks are carnivorous. There are over 250 species of the torpedo-shaped fish with strong jaws and bony teeth and at least 10 species are known to attack humans.

These are hooks—something that will interest the reader. The remainder of the article builds upon and around the hook.

14. **A magazine article often begins with a device that attracts the reader's attention and encourages him or her to read more of the article. This device is called a _____**

    A sinker.

    B worm.

    C hook.

    D pole.

Your Answer:

A ❑   **B** ❑   **C** ❑   **D** ❑

Analysis: **The correct answer is C.** Although the remaining answers are related to the topic of fishing, which is what a hook does—fishes for readers, **A, B,** and **D** are incorrect.

Newspaper Articles. These provide the reader with information that is usually tied to current events or things that are happening at the moment or within a recent period of time. When you read a newspaper article, notice the organization of the article. The manner in which this information is given to the reader is very important. In the newspaper business, they call it the **inverted pyramid.** In the inverted pyramid, you will find the **lead,** which is the really long sentence (or first paragraph) that begins the article and usually includes the "5 Ws and an H" (who, what, where, when, why, and how). The rest of the information that is included is listed according to its importance to the article and that is how the remainder of the pyramid is set up: important information at the top, least important at the bottom. An example of a lead might be:

> "An earthquake measuring 4.3 on the Richter scale, but causing no major damage, was reported by Cal Tech to have been centered in the Big Bear area northeast of Los Angeles and jolted Southern Californian's from their sleep last night at 11:30 P.M. as far away as Oceanside."

Another type of article published in the newspaper is not tied to current events (most of the time), but written for human interest. These articles are called **feature stories** or **features.** Features can be written about any one of a million subjects. Sometimes, they are tied into a current event. For example, if the current event is about the discovery of a new planet or comet, the feature article might be about a powerful telescope or the history of astronomy. Newspaper articles are intended to provide facts about current events or about human interest stories. Whether the article is about international, national, state, or local, political, sports, tragic, or otherwise, the newspaper article keeps the reader informed.

15. **The first line of a news story is called a _____**

    A lead.

    B editorial.

    C feature.

    D tragedy.

Your Answer:

A ❑   **B** ❑   **C** ❑   **D** ❑

Analysis: **The correct answer is A. D** is easy to eliminate; **B** and **C** are both parts of a newspaper, but **A** is the only one that is a specific part of an article and the obvious correct answer.

Editorials. In keeping with the newspaper/magazine subgenre, editorials are writings that are included in most newspapers and in many magazines. These writings express the opinions of the editors of either the newspaper or the magazine. The editorial may be about an event in the news or an important topic of some sort. For instance, a Supreme Court ruling on censorship of the Internet might prompt an editor to write an opinion piece on the subject. In most cases, these opinions reflect the nature of the paper or magazine: some newspapers are conservative, some are liberal, and some are middle-of-the-road, meaning they don't take a strong stance either way. In many newspapers, the editorial section (which is usually two pages of writings) includes **letters to the editor**

and **op-ed** pieces. Letters to the editor are short writings submitted by readers with varying opinions on a certain topic. Op-ed writings, which are usually on the page opposite the editorials, and usually include opinions that are opposite those of the editor, are intended to provide the reader with a broader view of an issue. A well-informed reader is one who has read or understands both sides of the issue and is capable of making an informed or intelligent judgment on it. Knowing both sides of an issue is extremely important for all citizens.

16. **Editorials express the opinion of the newspaper or magazine and are written by the _____**
    A printer.
    B staff writer.
    C editor.
    D chief executive officer.

Your Answer:

A ❑   B ❑   C ❑   D ❑

Analysis: **The correct answer is C.** The editorial staff is responsible for writing the editorials of the newspaper. Answers **A, B,** and **D** are all members of the newspaper organization, but none are responsible for the opinion pieces.

Journal Articles.   These are articles written by the author for a specific audience, usually a profession or career. For instance, doctors, educators, attorneys, accountants, scientists, and computer engineers who write about their professions, usually submit these writings to a journal that interests people in their field. The articles are used to inform, to keep people in the profession aware of new methods, techniques, equipment, or studies that could affect what they do professionally on a daily basis. Of course, these articles contain **jargon** that is unique to the profession. For instance, doctors use words that most likely only they would understand. Asking a doctor to read a journal article written for a structural engineer would be as challenging for the doctor as it would be for the structural engineer to understand a medical journal. However, journal articles are vital in keeping up with the latest information possible in a specific profession.

17. **Professional journals are written for a specific audience. The language that is used in the journal is unique to the audience being targeted. This language is called _____**
    A slang.
    B dialect.
    C academic language.
    D jargon.

Your Answer:

A ❑   B ❑   C ❑   D ❑

Analysis: **The correct answer is D. C** might confuse you because some journals use academic language, but not all journals are academic; therefore, **C** is incorrect. Answers **A** and **B** are both wrong because slang is language used informally with friends, and dialects are the words and pronunciations used in a specific area of the country.

Essays.   There are many of these around, and they have been around since at least the sixteenth century. Essays are written for many reasons and believe it or not, people who are not in school write essays! Some are published in journals and magazines or in literature anthologies. Here are a few of the essays that you will most likely be asked to write: **expository** (explains something), **narrative** (tells about something), **comparison/contrast** (explains the similarities and differences between two things), **persuasive** (meant to encourage the reader to your opinion), and **autobiographical** (about yourself), among others. The styles in which these essays are written vary as well. Some essays are **formal** and others are **informal**. Formal essays are serious and logically organized, similar to those you write in your English class or your history class. However, informal essays are usually humorous or whimsical and <u>less</u> formal in their structure. Informal essays are intended for entertainment and less conclusive than formal essays. Yes, essays are everywhere. We will discuss essay writing later in the book because you are going to write two of them for the exit exam.

18. **Essays are written in two basic styles:** _____ **and** _____

    A messy and neat.
    B formal and informal.
    C confusing and clear.
    D cohesive and noncohesive.

Your Answer:

A ❏   **B** ❏   **C** ❏   **D** ❏

Analysis: **The correct answer is B.** Answer **A** is the odd answer out—the one that is most obviously wrong. Answers **C** and **D**, while certainly they could apply to an essay as being either clear or confusing, or structurally cohesive or not, they don't appropriately apply to the manner in which the essay is written in a more authoritarian sense.

Poetry

As the English poet William Wordsworth wrote, poetry is "the spontaneous overflow of powerful feelings . . . recollected in tranquility." Or, as the American poet Marianne Moore states, poetry consists of "imaginary gardens with real toads in them." However you want to describe or define it, poetry is intense, imaginative, and rich in meaning. Written differently on the page than prose (paragraph writing), poets choose their words very carefully. The words are chosen not only for meaning, but for sound and rhythm as well. Poets are able to express meaning through a number of **literary devices;** it has been said that poetry is painting with words. And, if you look closely at poetry, you will find the poet's use of words inspiring. We are going to take a look at various types of poems and address the literary devices used in them.

Ballads.   The ballad is a form of narrative poetry (tells a story). It often tells a story of tragedy, for instance, a doomed love affair, family feuds, historical events, battles, shipwrecks, or murders, as well as the stories of outlaws and rebels like Robin Hood or Jesse James, or admired heroes like John Henry and Casey Jones. Ballads have a distinct rhyme scheme. This is the way the lines are written and which words rhyme at the end. For instance, the ballad rhyme scheme is *abcb*. This means that the first three lines, which are lines *a*, *b*, and *c*, do not rhyme with each other. But, the fourth line rhymes with line *b*, which is the second line. Look at the example of the ballad rhyme scheme below:

From: Ballad of Birmingham by Dudley Randall
(On the bombing of a church in Birmingham, Alabama, 1963)

"Mother dear, may I go downtown	(a)
Instead of out to play,	(b)
And march the streets of Birmingham	(c)
In a Freedom March today?"	(b)

Notice how the ending words on lines 1, 2, and 3 do not rhyme? But, notice how the ending words on lines 2 and 4 *do* rhyme—(play rhymes with today). That's the ballad rhyme scheme! Ballads have been written for centuries and are often sung. A slightly more recent example is a song written by Paul Simon in 1966. In this poem, Simon adapts a poem that was written by Edwin Arlington Robinson titled "Richard Cory." Look at the first four lines of the song, which is another example of the ballad rhyme scheme.

They say that Richard Cory owns
One half of this old town,
With elliptical connections
To spread his wealth around.

19. A ballad is a narrative poem that is often written about a tragedy, a disaster, a hero, or a rebel. The rhyme scheme of the ballad is _____

   A *abab.*
   B *abcabc.*
   C *abac.*
   D *abcb.*

Your Answer:

A ❑   **B** ❑   **C** ❑   **D** ❑

Analysis: **D** **is the correct answer.**

Blank Verse. This is unrhymed **iambic pentameter.** And what is iambic pentameter? Well, iambic pentameter is a line of poetry that has words that are unstressed and stressed (or 5 metrical feet). What does that mean? Basically, a line of blank verse has 10 syllables. These 10 syllables are broken up into groups of 2 syllables, which means there are 5 groups and these are called metrical feet. The first syllable of the 10 is unstressed, meaning that it is softer in sound. The second syllable is stressed, which means it sounds louder than the first syllable. Since we are talking about feet, think of it as walking. If you were to walk toe-to-heel, which is opposite of your normal heel-toe walk, putting your toe down first is softer (like walking on tiptoes) than if you did it the other way. Toe-to-heel = unstressed—stressed. In other words, every other syllable in a line of blank verse, which is written in unrhymed iambic pentameter, is either unstressed (soft) or stressed (loud). Look at the example from Christopher Marlowe's play Dr. Faustus:

> Was this the face that launched a thousand ships
> And burned the topless towers of Ilium?

> **Now once again, but this time with *syllabication*:**
> ˘ = unstressed syllable
> ´ = stressed syllable

    Wăs/ thís/ thĕ/ faće/ thăt/ launched/ ă/ thóu/ sănd/ shíps
     1   2   3   4   5   6   7   8   9   10

Blank verse has been used for centuries. William Shakespeare in particular, used blank verse extensively throughout his plays. Below is a sample of blank verse.

From "Mending Wall": By Robert Frost

Something there is that doesn't love a wall.
That sends the frozen-ground-swell under it,
And spills the upper boulders in the sun;
And makes gaps even two can pass abreast.
The work of hunters is another thing:
I have come after them and made repair
Where they have left not one stone on a stone,
But they would have the rabbit out of hiding,
To please the yelping dogs. The gaps I mean,
No one has seen them made or heard them made,
But at spring mending-time we find them there.

20. **True or False. Blank verse is unrhymed iambic pentameter and contains five metrical feet or a total of ten syllables.**
    A True
    B False

Your Answer:

A ❑   B ❑

Analysis: **The correct answer is A.** Blank verse is unrhymed iambic pentameter.

Concrete Poetry. It is easier to refer to this type of poem as a shape poem, because the poem is written about and usually in the shape of its subject. For instance, think about a feather; if you were to write a poem about a feather, you would probably mention its airy lightness of being, among other things, and then you would write the poem on the paper, in the actual shape of a feather. See the example below, a poem in the box!

Have you ever wondered about a box with its lines so simple, so straight and unassuming? Its life is defined by containment—at times cooperative and at others rebellious—screaming at its fullness bursting with discontent. Ah yes, the life of a box, fulfilling, empty, or somewhere in between. Plain brown cardboard, intricately carved wooden teak or mahogany inlaid with mother of pearl or the haughtiness of gold disguising its undemanding ranks. The box, have you ever considered?

21. **Concrete poetry is a poetry that** _____
    A is written in the shape or form of something.
    B is written with words that are backwards.
    C is sonnetlike in its structure.
    D has a rhyme scheme of *abab*.

Your Answer:

A ❑   B ❑   C ❑   D ❑

Analysis: **B** is a nonsense answer. **C** and **D** have nothing to do with being concrete, or taking a shape that is what concrete poetry does. **The correct answer is A.**

Didactic Poems. These are poems that teach morals, the good life, or instruct in specific areas of knowledge. This type of poem was favored by the classical Latin poets and eighteenth-century English poets. Below is an example of a didactic poem written by Ovid, a Roman poet who lived from 43 B.C.–17 A.D.

Ovid's

METAMORPHOSES

BOOK XV

Translated by Mr. **Dryden,** *and Others.*

The **PYTHAGOREAN**

PHILOSOPHY.

By Mr. **DRYDEN**

A king is sought to guide the growing State,
One able to support the Publick Weight,
And fill the Throne where *Romulus* had fate.
Renown, which oft bespeaks the Publick
Voice,

Had recommended *Numa* to their Choice:
A peacefull, pious Prince; who not content
To know the *Sabine* Rites, his Study bent
To cultivate his Mind; to learn the Laws
Of Nature, and explore their hidden Cause.
Urg'd by this Care, his Country he forsook,
And to Crotona thence his Journey took.
Arriv'd, he first enquir'd the Founder's Name
Of this new Colony; and whence he came.
Then thus a Senior of the Place replies,
(Well read, and curious of Antiquities)

22. True or False. Didactic poetry is considered instructional or teaching poetry.
   A True
   B False

Your Answer:

A ❑   **B** ❑

Analysis: The correct answer is A.

Dramatic Monologue.   These are poems that allow a single character to speak out about a dramatic situation and the entire episode is overheard by a silent listener. The poet Robert Browning who wrote "My Last Duchess" is famous for his poetry using this technique. The dramatic monologue below was written by Johann Wolfgang Goethe, a German poet, playwright, and novelist.

May Day Celebration (MAILIED)
by Johann Wolfgang Goethe

Translation by John Sigerson

How grandly nature
Shines upon me!
How glistens the sun!
How laughs the mead!

From countless branches
The blossoms thrust,
A thousand voices
From underbrush,

And joy ecstatic
Fills everyone.
O sun! O earth!
O risk! O fun!

O love, oh, lovely,
So golden fair
Like morning cloudlets
On that hill there!

You prosper grandly
The dew-fresh fields
With breath of flowers;
The whole Earth yields!

O maiden, maiden,
How I love thee!
Your eye's a-sparkle—
How you love me!

Just as the lark loves
Singing and sky,
And morning-blooms thrive
On heav'n-mists high—

So do I love you,
Joy, courage, art
Who give me the youth,
With throbbing heart,

To fashion new songs,
New dances free.
Be ever happy,
As you love me!

23. True or False. Poetry that is considered dramatic monologue has more than three speakers or narrators in the poem.

  A True
  B False

Your Answer:

A ❑   B ❑

Analysis: **The correct answer is B, false.** A monologue is one person speaking. Mono— means one. Dramatic monologue poetry is one-person narration.

Elegies.   Originally, an elegy in classical times, which refers to ancient Greece, was a poem written in elegiac meter, which is rhyming iambic pentameter, and we all know what that is, right? Well, an elegy is a sad or mournful poem whose mood and tone are both sad and mournful and is written for someone who has died. The following poem is an example of an elegy.

from Adonais (1821) By Percy Bysshe Shelley

  I

  I weep for Adonais—he is dead! Oh weep for Adonais! though our tears
  Thaw not the frost which binds so dear a head!
  And thou, sad Hour, selected from all years
  To mourn our loss, rouse thy obscure compeers,
  And teach them thine own sorrow, say: "With me
  Died Adonais; till the future dares
  Forget the past, his fate and fame shall be
  An echo and a light unto eternity!"

  II

  Where wert thou, mighty Mother, when he lay,
  When thy Son lay, pierc'd by the shaft which flies
  In darkness? where was lorn Urania
  When Adonais died? With veiled eyes,
  'Mid listening Echoes, in her Paradise
  She sate, while one, with soft enamour'd breath,
  Rekindled all the fading melodies,
  With which, like flowers that mock the corse beneath,
  He had adorn'd and hid the coming bulk of Death.

24. An elegy is a poem written in a tone that is _____

  A odd and sarcastic.
  B happy and full of life.
  C sad and mournful.
  D friendly and light.

Your Answer:

A ❑   B ❑   C ❑   D ❑

Analysis: **The correct answer is C.** Answer A is way off, and answers **B** and **D** are total opposites of the true definition of an elegy.

Epic Poems.   These are very long narrative poems that tell a story of a remote time and place and have characters who are larger than life. The story of the epic poem begins in the middle of the action or, as it is properly referred to, *in media res*. The epic poem uses many literary devices or conventions throughout its length such as catalogs (long lists), formal speeches, and epic similes (longer or extended), among others. Its style is considered elevated, meaning formal or dignified. There are two types of epics; the folk epic and the literary epic. Folk epics are thought to have been passed along by oral tradition (or told aloud like storytelling), and their original authors are uncertain or unknown. The *Iliad*, the *Odyssey*, *Beowulf*, *Song of Roland*, the *Poem of Cid*, and *Mahabharata* are considered folk epics and come from various cultures—Greek to East Indian. Literary epics, on the other hand, are poems that are written and meant to be read like John Milton's *"Paradise Lost"* and Dante's *"Divine Comedy."* Below is a preview of John Milton's *Paradise Lost*.

"Invocation" to Book I of *Paradise Lost*: By John Milton

Of man's first disobedience, and the fruit
Of that forbidden tree whose mortal taste
Brought death into the world, and all our woe,
With loss of Eden, till one greater Man
Restore us and regain the blissful seat,
Sing, Heavenly Muse, that, on the secret top
Of Oreb, or of Sinai, didst inspire
That shepherd who first taught the chosen seed
In the beginning how the Heavens and Earth
Rose out of Chaos: or, if Sion hill
Delight thee more, and Siloa's brook that flowed
Fast by the oracle of God, I thence
Invoke thy aid to my adventurous song,
That with no middle flight intends to soar
Above th' Aonian mount, while it pursues
Things unattempted yet in prose or rhyme

25. Epic poems incorporate _____

  A minimal literary conventions.
  B many literary conventions.
  C French in at least one part.
  D short and abrupt conventions.

Your Answer:

A ❑   **B** ❑   **C** ❑   **D** ❑

Analysis: The correct answer is B. Epic poems are known for incorporating many literary conventions. Answer A is the opposite and the other two answers make little sense at all.

Free Verse

Literally, this is a poem that is free of meter, rhyme, and other formalities of traditional verse. American poet Walt Whitman, French poets Charles Baudelaire and Paul Verlaine, and English poet Gerard Manley Hopkins were the frontrunners of this style of poetry in the nineteenth century. Most twentieth- and twenty-first-century poetry is free verse, although a few poets choose to revisit some of the older forms. Free verse allows the poet more freedom to play with words and sounds without the restrictions of iambic pentameter or rhyme schemes.

Calvary Crossing a Ford by Walt Whitman

A line in long array, where they wind betwixt green islands;
They take a serpentine course—their arms flash in the sun—hark to the musical clank;
Behold the silvery river—in it the splashing horses, loitering, stop to drink;
Behold the brown-faced men—each group, each person, a picture—the negligent rest
   on the saddles;
Some emerge on the opposite bank—others are just entering the ford—while,
Scarlet, and blue, and snowy white,
The guidon flags flutter gaily in the wind.

26. True or False. Free verse poetry is restrictive and follows very precise rhythms and meter.
  A True
  B False

Your Answer:

A ❏   B ❏

Analysis: **The correct answer is B, false.** As the name implies, free verse is exactly that. There are no restrictions to the poems; poets are free to express themselves without following rigid formats of more formal types of poetry.

Limericks.   A limerick is a nonsense poem that has a specific pattern. It has five lines and the rhyme scheme is *aabba* (which we learned about earlier). Lines one, two, and five are longer and rhyme and lines three and four are shorter and rhyme. These poems were popular in the nineteenth century. The following example of a limerick is by Edward Lear.

> There was an Old Man with a beard,
> Who said, "It is just as I feared!
> Two Owls and a Hen,
> Four Larks and a Wren,
> Have all built their nests in my beard!"

27. A limerick poem is a _____ poem.
  A nonsense
  B serious
  C concrete
  D lengthy

Your Answer:

A ❏   B ❏   C ❏   D ❏

Analysis: **The correct answer is A.** The limerick is silly and fun and full of nonsense. Answer **B** is the opposite; answers **C** and **D** are completely erroneous.

Narrative Poems.   Narrative poems simply tell a story. If you look at the ballad and the epic poem explanations above, you will see two examples of narrative poems. Narrative poems have a beginning, a middle, and an end. Geoffrey Chaucer's *Canterbury Tales* is another example of a narrative poem. This is a series of tales about a variety of people who make a pilgrimage to a shrine in Canterbury, England. Each has their own tale to tell and all come from a wide spectrum of classes and occupations, which makes for an interesting read.

28. True or False. Narrative poems tell a story and have a beginning, middle, and end.
  A True
  B False

Your Answer:

A ❏   B ❏

Analysis: **The correct answer is A, true.** Narrative poems tell a story and have a beginning, middle, and end.

Sonnets.   Sonnets, sonnets—fourteen-lines of iambic pentameter (unstressed, stressed, toe, heel) originating in the thirteenth century by an Italian poet named Petrarch. The form arrived in England via Thomas Wyatt and it was then modified and made famous by William Shakespeare. So, we have the Italian sonnet and the Shakespearean sonnet. In English, the Shakespearean sonnet is easier to construct than the Italian sonnet because we have less rhyming ability in our language than do the Italians. Their rhyme schemes are different. Let's take a look at the rhyme schemes and then look at a sonnet written by Shakespeare.

The Italian or Petrarch sonnet rhyme scheme: **abba, abba, cde, cde**
The Shakespearean sonnet rhyme scheme: **abab, cdcd, efef, gg**

18

Shall I compare thee to a summer's day?
Thou art more lovely and more temperate:
Rough winds do shake the darling buds of May,
And summer's lease hath all too short a date;
Sometime too hot the eye of heaven shines,
And often is his gold complexion dimmed;
And every fair from fair sometime declines,
By chance or nature's changing course untrimmed:
But they eternal summer shall not fade,
Nor lose possession of that fair thou ow'st,
Nor shall death brag thou wand'rest in his shade,
When in eternal lines to time thou grow'st.
    So long as men can breathe or eyes can see,
    So long live this, and this gives life to thee.

29. Sonnets have _____ lines.

  A twelve
  B eighteen
  C six
  D fourteen

Your Answer:

A ❑   **B** ❑   **C** ❑   **D** ❑

Analysis: **The correct answer is D.** The sonnet has fourteen lines—no more, no less.

Drama

This is our final category in the genre section. Dramas have been around for ages. They originated in ancient times with the Greeks who used drama for various religious ceremonies. The evolution of drama continued on into medieval times and the Renaissance, and up to the present. Drama is a literary work that is written using dialogue between characters that was performed on stage in front of an audience. There are all different types of plays: tragedy, comedy, history, farce, absurd, morality, one-act, and on and on. A play is distinct in the way that it is written, as it includes (usually) stage directions, scene settings, and the dramatis personae or characters named for each act. It is not typical reading that you are used to in fiction or nonfiction; it is more interrupted by the details that an author writing a novel would include in a paragraph; instead, a playwright usually adds settings, expressions, and so on as stage directions. There are thousands of playwrights, but the one you will be reminded of over and over again is William Shakespeare. To the English language, he is probably the best known and respected of them all.

30. Drama is written with _____

  A spunk.
  B confusion.
  C character dialogue.
  D darkness.

Your Answer:

A ❑   **B** ❑   **C** ❑   **D** ❑

Analysis: **The correct answer is C.** Answers **A, B,** and **D** are incorrect.

Chapter Review and Quick Quiz

Another chapter with a lot to say! We've covered everything from speeches to drama. Let's see how you remember what you've learned. The answers are in the appendix.

DIRECTIONS: Match the letter of the correct definition of the literary term, put it in the space to the left.

ANSWER   **LITERARY TERM**   **DEFINITION**

_____   1. historical fiction   **a.** work that depends on the fertile imagination of the author, romantically farfetched in nature

_____   2. science fiction   **b.** narrative poem telling the story of a tragedy

_____   3. fantasy   **c.** a broad category in which all literature is placed or typecast

_____   4. mystery   **d.** verbalization of specific topic for audience

_____   5. romance   **e.** work in which a single character speaks out in the poem

_____   6. bildungsroman   **f.** written records of specific events in one's life

_____   7. picaresque   **g.** work written by someone about someone else

_____   8. epistolary   **h.** work that recreates historically important events

_____   9. stream of consciousness   **i.** two types: formal and informal

_____   10. speeches   **j.** a story written in dialogue

_____   11. diaries   **k.** a sad and mournful poem about death

_____   12. autobiography   **l.** work set in a futuristic or imaginary world

_____   13. biography   **m.** a 14-line poem, either Italian or Shakespearean

_____   14. news articles   **n.** writings by people about themselves

_____   15. editorials   **o.** describing a story written through letter writing

_____   16. essays   **p.** work in which random thoughts of characters are revealed

_____   17. ballad   **q.** a mystery or crime solved by a detective

_____   18. blank verse   **r.** writings that teach morals or about the good life

_____   19. concrete   **s.** a category of writings that are not true

_____   20. didactic   **t.** a poem that tells a story

_____   21. dramatic monologue   **u.** work in which the main character becomes involved in one predicament after another

_____   22. elegy   **v.** long narrative poem with heroes of epic proportions

_____   23. free verse   **w.** a category of writings that are factual, true

_____   24. limerick   **x.** written opinions by an editor of a newspaper

_____   25. narrative   **y.** a five-line nonsense poem

_____   26. sonnet   **z.** work set in an imaginary or unreal utopian world

_____   27. drama   **aa.** writings that usually contain the 5 Ws and H in the lead

_____   28. fiction   **bb.** a poem free of rhyme and meter

_____   29. nonfiction   **cc.** unrhymed iambic pentameter

_____   30. genre   **dd.** work that follows a main character from innocence to experience.

Chapter 7

Literary Response and Analysis—Part II

In this chapter, we will be looking at what happens within a **narrative** text that is basically anything in the way of writing—short to long—that tells a story, whether it is factual or not. In the last chapter, we looked at a variety of narratives from ballads, histories, epics, biographies, and all the others we reviewed, but here we will dig a little deeper and examine what goes on within a narrative.

CHAPTER FOCUS: *Understanding Narrative Texts*
- *Dialogues*
- *Monologues*
- *Soliloquies*
- *Asides*
- *Character Foils*
- *Character Traits (Characterization)*
- *Themes*
- *Plot and Conflict*
- *Foreshadowing*
- *Flashbacks*
- *Imagery*
- *Symbols and Symbolism*
- *Allegories*
- *Irony*
- *Narrator/Point of View*
- *Mood*

Chapter Review and Quick Quiz

Understanding Narrative Texts

Dialogues

A **dialogue** is conversation between two or more people or characters in a narrative text. Dialogue provides clues not only about the characters themselves, but about the plot as well. Reading dialogue is like eavesdropping in on someone's conversation, and from the information you receive as a reader in overhearing this conversation, you can either predict what might happen next, or discover what has happened before. Dialogue is written in plays, short stories, scripts, novels, and narrative poems. Dialogues written for scripts are straightforward; they don't bother with stage directions for the most part because that's the director's job. On the other hand, plays are written with fairly specific stage directions because the playwright has something specific in mind when he/she wrote the play.

1. **Read the two brief dialogues below. Determine which dialogue has been written for a script, and which has been written for a play.**

#1 Band Camp California

Fred: Hey Lucy, the reed to my clarinet is broken, do you have a spare?
Lucy: If I had one I wouldn't give it to you.

Fred: Thanks Lucy, it's great to see you again too.
Lucy: Have you totally lost it or have you been playing your clarinet too long?
Fred: Look Lucy, what happened last summer, was last summer. Can we just move on and start over? I admit what we did was a little crazy, but this year is different . . . I've matured you'll see.

#2 The Secret of Life

Characters: Franny, a homemaker
　　　　　　Lewis, her retired neighbor

Setting: The scene opens in Franny's small, dimly lit and cluttered kitchen. It has one windowed door, which is stage right. There is an old, grungy-looking table covered with a wrinkled plastic tablecloth. There are two chairs at either end of the table and Franny is sitting at one. Wearing an old housecoat with her hair tied in a bandana on her head, Franny seems to be pondering something and stares off across the room when she hears a knock at the door. Seeing that it is her neighbor Lewis, she motions for him to come into the kitchen. Lewis, an elderly man and quite handy to have around is wearing dirty overalls and a stained white T-shirt underneath. He enters the kitchen.

Lewis: (*Loudly, as he is hard of hearing*) Top o' the mornin' to ya' Franny!
Franny: (*Meekly*) Good morning Lew, how are you? Won't you sit and have a cup of coffee with me? (*Franny motions for him to sit as she stands to get the coffee from the stove.*)
Lewis: I'd love to take you up on that. (*Lewis sits down in the chair at the table.*) What you been up to Fran? I know I ain't no psychologist, but I can see somthins' bothrin' ya.' You seem mighty quiet this mornin'.
Franny: Well, Lewis. (*She pauses as she pours the coffee, serves it to him and then sits across the table.*) I don't rightly know how to explain just what I'm feeling, but something's come over me and I think my life has suddenly turned for the . . . well, I'm not real sure.

    A #1 is written for a play and #2 for a script.
    B #1 is written for a novel and #2 for a script.
    C #1 is written for a script and #2 for a poem.
    D #1 is written for a script and #2 for a play.

Your Answer:

A ❑　　**B** ❑　　**C** ❑　　**D** ❑

Analysis: **The correct answer is D.** The dialogue of #1 was written as a script; note the simplicity and no stage directions, while #2 is specific about characters and stage directions, which is typical for a play. The other answers are either all or partially wrong; two of them, **B** and **C**, throw in answers that are really off base from the original question.

Monologues

When a character in a play (or in a narrative) is on stage alone, he or she begins to speak that is a monologue. It is usually a long speech and it usually reveals something important either about the action or about the thoughts of the character. The monologue is closely related to the **soliloquy**, which you will learn about next. There are two types of monologues. The **interior monologue**, which demonstrates the characters inner thoughts, is similar to the **stream of consciousness** that we learned in the last chapter. You can hear the character thinking out loud. The **dramatic monologue** is found when the character is overheard speaking to a silent listener. It reveals not only the speaker, but a dramatic situation as well.

2. **The monologue is a long speech given by a character who is _____ on stage. It usually reveals something important either about the action or about the thoughts of the character.**
   A alone
   B eating dinner
   C crying and sobbing
   D dressing

Your Answer:

A ☐   B ☐   C ☐   D ☐

Analysis: **The correct answer is A.** A person in the middle of a monologue is alone and speaking on stage. Answers **B** and **C** are rather obscure and answer **D** is just wrong.

Soliloquies

A **soliloquy,** like an interior monologue, is when a character in a play on stage alone begins to think aloud. It is used to tell the audience what the character is thinking and what his motives or plans are. It is also used to provide information about earlier events that have occurred elsewhere or simply to provide additional background information. Below you will find an example of one of the most famous of all soliloquies. This is Hamlet (à la Shakespeare) thinking aloud.

Act III, Scene 1

Hamlet

To be, or not to be; that is the question;
Whether 'tis noble in the mind to suffer
The slings and arrows of outrageous fortune,
Or to take arms against a sea of troubles,
And, by opposing, end them. To die, to sleep—
No more—and by a sleep to say we end
The heartache and the thousand natural shocks
That flesh is heir to—'tis a consummation
Devoutly to be wished. To die, to sleep.—
To sleep, perchance to dream. Ay, there's the rub,
For in that sleep of death what dreams may come
When we have shuffled off this mortal coil
Must give us pause. There's the respect
That makes calamity of so long life,
For who would bear the whips and scorns of time,
Th' oppressor's wrong, the proud man's contumely,
The pangs of disprized love, the law's delay,
The insolence of office, and the spurns
That patient merit of th' unworthy takes,
When he himself might his quietus make
With bare bodkin? Who would these fardels bear,
To grunt and sweat under a weary life,
But that the dread of something after death,
The undiscovered country from whose bourn
No traveler returns, puzzles, the will,
And makes us rather bear those ills we have
Than fly to others that we know not of?
Thus conscience does make cowards of us all,
And thus the native hue of resolution
Is sicklied o'er with the pale cast of thought,
And enterprises of great pitch and moment
With this regard their currents turn awry,
And lose the name of action.

3. **A soliloquy is very similar to** _____
   A a character in a play.
   B the climax of a novel.
   C an interior monologue.
   D an exterior monologue.

Your Answer:

A ❑   B ❑   C ❑   D ❑

Analysis: **The correct answer is C.** The soliloquy is very similar to the interior monologue; in fact, they could be considered synonyms. Answers **A** and **B** are nonsense and Answer **D** is there to confuse you—exterior? Interior!

Asides

Interesting name isn't it? But, an **aside** is when an actor on stage turns to the audience or someone standing nearby, and tells it something <u>allegedly</u> without being heard by the other actors. Asides are used for comic effect or for melodramatic effect and they reveal (like the monologue and soliloquy) inner thoughts or feelings of the character or a personal evaluation or interpretation of what is going on in the scene at the time.

4. **True or False. An aside is an actor speaking to a group of actors on stage about an ongoing conflict.**
   A True
   B False

Your Answer:

A ❑   B ❑

Analysis: **The correct answer is B, false.** An aside is when an actor on stage turns to the audience and makes a comment, either comic or dramatic.

Character Foils

This is another interesting name and an interesting concept. **Character foils** are contrast characters or nearly the complete opposites of another character. What comes to mind right away are the Danny DiVito and Arnold Schwarzenegger characters in a film of the recent past (*Twins*). In drama however, the character foil who, for instance, may not be extremely bright, provides the opposite (or foil) for the intelligent or wise character. The foil's lack of intelligence makes the wise person look even more intelligent.

5. **The character foil is a near opposite of another character. The foil makes the other character appear** _____ **in whatever personality trait the character foil is weakest.**
   A stronger
   B weaker
   C ill at ease
   D wild

Your Answer:

A ❑   B ❑   C ❑   D ❑

Analysis: **The correct answer is A.** The character foil, as an opposite, allows the other character to appear stronger in whatever personality strength the character foil is lacking. Answers **B** and **C** could possibly confuse you if you didn't know what a foil was, but answer **D** is the throwaway answer—the first to eliminate.

Character Traits (or Characterization)

Characters come in all shapes, sizes, colors, and types. The technique that an author uses to develop the characters is called characterization. A character in any narrative could be a main character (or the **protagonist**), or as a main character he or she/it could be an **antagonist** (someone who works against or who is in opposition of the protagonist). Characters can also be considered **minor characters.** Minor characters add a little bit of flavoring, but they are less important than the main character(s). Before we get into specific traits, you need to know that characters can be **static** or **dynamic:** static characters (remember the root system!) *stay* the same; they hardly change at all. On the other hand, dynamic characters are the opposite of static characters. Dynamic characters *change* from the beginning of the story or narrative, until the end. That's a lot of information in a little bit of time; let's quickly review.

NOTE: Remember the root system—
<u>pro</u> means for or in favor of
<u>ant</u> or <u>anti</u> means against (hence, protagonist and antagonist!)
<u>Sta</u> means stationary or stays the same = static
<u>dyn</u> means energetic or dynamic

- Main character = protagonist = the most important player or character in the story or narrative
- Main character = antagonist = in opposition to the protagonist, the bad guy <u>most</u> of the time
- Minor character = adds flavoring and spice but is less important
- Dynamic character = changes from beginning to end of the story
- Static character = remains the same or the changes are hardly noticeable

Now that *that* is clear, let's continue with the way authors develop their characters or characterization. Authors provide the reader with a broad spectrum of details about their characters: physical appearance, personality, speech, actions, thoughts and feelings, behavior, and interactions with other characters. Throughout a lifetime of reading, you will meet characters who assume all sorts of traits. Look at the list below and these are just a few:

OUTGOING	AGGRESSIVE	ANTISOCIAL	CHIVALRIC	ENTHUSIASTIC
FORCEFUL	NEAT	CHARISMATIC	MESSY	APATHETIC
ORGANIZED	SENSITIVE	CHARMING	UNKEMPT	BOHEMIAN
IMPULSIVE	PERSUASIVE	CAREFUL	ATHLETIC	STONG
HONEST	CONVENTIONAL	CONVINCING	IGNORANT	WEAK
CALM	ALERT	ANNOYING	EVIL	PERSISTANT
QUIET	LETHARGIC	RISK-TAKING	MEAN	PLEASANT
SLY	MANIPULATIVE	GENTLEMANLY	VULGAR	GUARDED
UNDERSTANDING	PERCEPTIVE	LADYLIKE	KIND	COMPETITIVE
DETERMINED	BOLD	SINFUL	CARING	DEXTEROUS
TALKATIVE	INTELLIGENT	IMMORAL	GENEROUS	ENERGETIC
DEMANDING	SOCIABLE	SAINTLY	STERN	

6. An antagonist is an important character in a narrative, but this character's role is _____

    A to make the minor characters look bad.
    B to make the protagonist laugh and sing.
    C to take the place of the character foil.
    D to be in opposition of the protagonist.

Your Answer:

A ❑   **B** ❑   **C** ❑   **D** ❑

Analysis: **The correct answer is D.** The antagonist's job is to be in opposition of the protagonist—almost complete opposites. Answers **A** and **B** are easily eliminated. There is a chance that **C** might confuse you if you were uncertain about the protagonist.

Themes

The author's message or the main idea of a work is the **theme.** Although the theme is not expressed overtly or specifically stated, it is represented through various images, characters, events, or actions. In reading a novel or any other narrative, discovering the theme can be more like detective work. At times it is very subtle and difficult to figure out, but at other times it's right there in front of you. Below is a list of themes.

LONELINESS	FAMILY	VIOLENCE
COURAGE	FREEDOM	TRUTH
AMBITION	PATIENCE	REGRET
GREED	LOYALTY	SUCCESS
JEALOUSY	HATE	TRUST
HAPPINESS	HOPE	NATURE
RACISM	INDEPENDENCE	GROWING UP
FRIENDSHIP	LOVE	PEACE
FAITH	JUSTICE	SELF-IMPROVEMENT

7. **Read the poem below and select the correct theme of the poem.**

Those Winter Sundays By Robert Hayden

Sundays too my father got up early
and put his clothes on in the blueblack cold,
then with cracked hands that ached
from labor in the weekday weather made
banked fires blaze. No one ever thanked him.

I'd wake and hear the cold splintering, breaking.
When the rooms were warm, he'd call,
and slowly I would rise and dress,
fearing the chronic angers of that house,

Speaking indifferently to him,
who had driven out the cold
and polished my good shoes as well.
What did I know, what did I know
of love's austere and lonely offices?

A regret
B peace
C war
D success

Your Answer:

A ❑   B ❑   C ❑   D ❑

Analysis: **The correct answer is A.** Reading the poem carefully, the narrator is remembering his father's simple kindnesses: getting up early on his one day off to make the fire, polishing his shoes. The narrator also expresses his regret: in speaking to him indifferently, never thanking him. Regret appears to be the theme of the poem. Answers **B, C,** and **D** don't really fit in.

Plots

These are the actual events or happenings that take place in a narrative. The author chooses the events and arranges them, usually in a time sequence, but occasionally authors toss in a

flashback (you'll learn about that soon) or **stream of consciousness** that causes the plot to become not so logically arranged. However, there is a logical arrangement of the plot, a gradual up, reach the top, and then a gradual down, or any version close to that (remember—as mentioned earlier, some authors jump into conflict a little earlier than others so the gradual part may not be so gradual).

- **Exposition—or the opening.** This is the beginning of the plot. The author introduces the characters and setting and provides the reader with background information. Sometimes authors take quite awhile to do this (three or four chapters) and you must be patient in reading. Other times they jump right into the action, taking less time with the introductions.
- **Rising action—or complication.** This is where the author begins to describe the conflict or the problem that the characters are about to face. The situation has caused tension to rise at this point of the story.
- **Climax**—the turning point in the story. This is where the problem is at its peak literally and the characters begin charting their descent, how are they going to solve the problem?
- **Falling Action**—where the author explains how the solution is going to occur.
- **Resolution or Denouement—the ending.** The story is brought to conclusion here; it may or may not be the way you would like it to be. Endings are a personal thing; some people like them happy; some people like them tragic or sad.

Now, what you also must understand is that this rise in action is most likely some kind of **conflict.** Conflict also is expressed by the author in many different ways depending on the nature of the narrative. Let's look.

- **External Conflict**
  - Person against nature (storms, beasts, etc.)
  - Person against person (main character against another character)
  - Person against society (character has difficulty with laws, beliefs)
  - Person against fate (a problem out of the character's control)
- **Internal Conflict**
  - Man against himself (making a difficult decision, inner turmoil)

8. The denouement of the plot is the same as the _____
   A climax.
   B rising action.
   C resolution.
   D introduction.

Your Answer:

A ❑   B ❑   C ❑   D ❑

Analysis: **The correct answer is C.** The resolution and the denouement are the same thing. Answer **D** would be easy to eliminate, but **A** and **B** might give you problems if you didn't know exactly what denouement was.

Foreshadowing

This is a technique that authors use to create suspense and to prepare the reader for what is about to happen in their writing. **Foreshadowing** is the hint or clue given earlier in the book that suggests later events without completely giving the plot away. Foreshadowing can be very subtle, meaning there are times in your reading when you might read on and not realize that it was foreshadowing until the event actually happened. S. E. Hinton foreshadows future events through the character Johnny in her book *The Outsiders*, when the protagonist, Ponyboy, tells Johnny to be careful with his cigarettes at the abandoned church where they were hiding and later, the church catches on fire. Johnny and Ponyboy rescue several young children, but Johnny is badly injured and burned and later . . . well, you'll have to read the book to find out what happened. That's foreshadowing.

9. **Foreshadowing** _____
   A is the hints and clues about what might occur later in the book.
   B is a television show about shadow puppets.
   C is the introduction of the characters.
   D is the rising action of the story.

Your Answer:

A ☐   **B** ☐   **C** ☐   **D** ☐

Analysis: The correct answer is A. Foreshadowing is the hints and clues about what might occur later in the book. Answers **C** and **D** are related to the plot, while Answer **B** is one of those throwaway answers.

Flashbacks

These are techniques that allow the author to go back in time through the characters and to present scenes or incidents that happened before the opening of the narrative. Remember when we discussed plots and the rising action and climax and the fact that some authors jump right into the action and then catch the reader up later through flashbacks? Well, now you know. The author may choose to have the reader understand through character dialogue when one character tells another character about the past, or the author may choose to have a character dream about it or simply just remember.

10. **A flashback is** _____
   A telling a story from the end to the beginning.
   B scenes presented that took place before the action or conflict.
   C a summer lightning storm.
   D hinting or previewing what might happen later in the story.

Your Answer:

A ☐   **B** ☐   **C** ☐   **D** ☐

Analysis: The correct answer is B. Flashback tells the readers what happened before all of the action takes place. Answers **A** and **D** might be a little confusing if you are unsure of the answer, but Answer **C** is completely wrong.

Imagery

Imagery is words that are used by an author to create an image in the reader's mind. Usually, the words used, appeal to the five senses in some way—visual, auditory (hearing), kinesthetic (touch), olfactory (smell), and taste. In writing, especially fiction and poetry, authors need to get the images across to the reader in order for the reader to visualize what they are attempting to impress upon the reader in their writing. Not having the benefit of a screen that can actually show you the elegant woman's long fur-lined red coat without telling you (like film or television), authors need to be able to get you, the reader, to see that image in your mind. Authors literally paint word pictures in their works. Without imagery, reading fiction and poetry would be far less exciting.

11. **Read the following two stanzas of a poem and select which of the five senses it most affects.**

From; I Wandered Lonely as a Cloud
by William Wordsworth

I wandered lonely as a cloud
That floats on high o'er vales and hills,
When all at once I saw a crowd,
A host, of golden daffodils;
Beside the lake, beneath the trees,
Fluttering and dancing in the breeze.

> Continuous as the stars that shine
> And twinkle on the milky way,
> They stretched in never-ending line
> Along the margin of a bay:
> Ten thousand saw I at a glance,
> Tossing their heads in sprightly dance.

A touch
B hearing
C smelling
D vision

Your Answer:

A ❑   B ❑   C ❑   D ❑

Analysis: The correct answer is D. Wordsworth provides the reader with strong visual imagery in this segment of his poem. "Lonely as a cloud," A host of golden daffodils," "beside the lake," and "beneath the trees" are a few examples of the visual imagery that you could actually paint if you had to.

Symbols and Symbolism

A **symbol** implies a connection between things. A symbol is something that is concrete (something you can touch) that stands for something that is abstract (a feeling, an idea, or an emotion). For instance, a dove implies a connection to peace, a heart is a symbol that implies love, white is a symbol that implies purity or goodness, and the American flag as a symbol implies for Americans freedom and democracy. There are symbols almost everywhere you look. When you read, you will often find symbols that the author has strategically placed to deepen the meaning of the text; this is called symbolism. The symbols themselves can be objects and actions, and even the characters themselves become symbols—standing for good or evil, for instance. Regardless of the symbol and whether it is abstract or literal, symbolism adds another dimension to writing.

12. **True or False. Symbolism is an abstract object that stands for something that is concrete.**
    A True
    B False

Your Answer:

A ❑   B ❑

Analysis: The correct answer is B, false. Read the question carefully. The terms abstract and concrete are reversed.

Allegories

Definitely a more challenging concept to understand, an **allegory** is the use of characters, events, or even the settings of a narrative to represent something abstract such as an idea, emotion, or feeling. The reader in this case is treated to a second or underlying meaning in addition to the surface meaning of the narrative. For instance, an underlying meaning might be social, satirical, political, or religious. Many times the author presents the characters as abstractions come to life: a character could represent greed, hope, charity, and envy, for example. George Orwell's novel *Animal Farm* is an allegory. In this book, Orwell uses animals who take over a farm as an allegory that represents communism and its repressive control over the citizens of the former Soviet Union.

13. **An allegory uses characters, events, or settings to represent something <u>abstract</u>. In this sentence <u>abstract</u> means _____**
   A a style of painting.
   B something bizarre or ludicrous.
   C a person, place, or thing.
   D something nonconcrete; an idea, emotion, or feeling.

Your Answer:

A ❑   B ❑   C ❑   D ❑

Analysis: The correct answer is D. An allegory uses characters, events, or setting to represent something that is abstract. Abstract is something you cannot really touch, an idea, an emotion, or a feeling. Answer **B** is way off, Answer **A** is actually true, but not in the sense that it is being used here, and answer **C** lists things that are concrete—things you can actually touch.

Irony

Irony is using a phrase or a word to mean the exact opposite of its normal or the expected meaning. In other words, it is a contrast between what it *really* is and what it *appears* to be. There are three types of irony used in writing:

- **Dramatic irony:** The reader (or audience) sees a character's faults or mistakes; the character himself does not. In Shakespeare's play *Romeo and Juliet*, the dramatic irony occurs when Romeo, believing that Juliet is dead, kills himself; meanwhile, the readers know that she is merely in a coma from which she will be awakening soon.
- **Verbal irony:** The author states one thing, but means another, for instance when someone says to you "Thanks a lot," but saying it in a mean or sarcastic way. That person is stating one thing, but meaning another.
- **Irony of situation:** A situation that demonstrates a large difference between the reason for a particular action and the result. In Daniel Keyes' short story, "Flowers for Algernon," Charlie Gordon, the main character, who has a very low IQ, hears of an experimental brain operation that will allow him to become intelligent. It has worked for a mouse named Algernon, so he believes that it will work for him as well. Charlie has the surgery and is given a good-luck disk by another character named Gimpy that has "Sta-Brite" (stay bright?) written on it. Sta-Brite is the name of a metal polish. Anyway, the irony of this situation is that Charlie's intelligence does improve, but it subsequently begins to degenerate into a condition far worse than it was originally, so, ironically, Charlie was unable to "Sta-Brite."

14. **The three types of irony are _____, _____, _____**
   A allegory, situational, and abstract.
   B verbal, dramatic, and irony of situation.
   C verbal, abstract, and occasional.
   D irony, allegory, and concrete.

Your Answer:

A ❑   B ❑   C ❑   D ❑

Analysis: The correct answer is B. The three types of irony are verbal, dramatic, and irony of situation. The other three answers include several literary terms that might confuse you if you did not know the background to irony.

Narrator or Point of View

All works of literature must have a narrator, or someone who tells the story. Depending upon which narrator the author uses determines how much information the reader will be given. There are two major points of view: *first-person* and *third-person*. The first-person narrator stands within the story and describes it from an "I" perspective, which means that when you read a story and you see the word "I," you'll know it is a first-person narrator. This narrator reveals only his or her own feelings and thoughts. However the third-person narrator is an outsider looking in and there are three third-person narrator types. The first is third-person *omniscient*. As an outsider, this person knows *everything* about the characters and about what is going on in their minds, emotions, and their actions. This narrator is referred to as *all-knowing*. The second type of third-person narrator is the *third-person limited*. This narrator enters the mind of only one character and presents the details from that person's perspective only. This type of narrator is limited in what can be presented. The final type of third-person is called *third-person objective*. This narrator offers the readers only facts—only the facts. There are no thoughts, feelings, or emotions presented by this narrator. He or she takes an objective point of view. Let's review again.

- **First person:** Using "I" this narrator has a limited perspective in that he or she only sees the situation from his or her perspective. This person sees the story from the inside.
- **Third-person omniscient:** The all-knowing narrator. As an outsider, this person can enter the characters' minds and relate their thoughts, feelings, and actions.
- **Third-person limited:** As a narrator, this person enters the mind of only one character and sees everything from that character's perspective, hence the limited perspective.
- **Third-person objective:** This narrator states only the facts. He or she does not bother with emotions, feelings, or thoughts—just the facts.

15. **Which of the following narrators is referred to as the "all-knowing" narrator.**
    A first person
    B third person omniscient
    C third person limited
    D third person objective

Your Answer:

A ❑   B ❑   C ❑   D ❑

Analysis: **The correct answer is B.** The all-knowing narrator is the third-person omniscient. Answers **A, C,** and **D** are incorrect.

Mood

This is a rather *emotional* concept. Just as doing something or not doing something depends upon the mood you are in at the time, the same goes for the author when he or she is writing the story—not his or her mood personally, but the mood in the story. When an author chooses the setting, words, details, objects, and images in a piece of literature, he or she is creating a mood for the work. The mood of a literary work may be happy, sad, lonely, dark, somber, jubilant, empty, isolated, etc. The author chooses the appropriate details to match the mood he or she is attempting to portray in the work. The difficult part of mood is weaving it in throughout the characters, and all that goes on in the course of a story or narrative. It is complex.

16. **The mood in a narrative sets up an _____ aspect of the story.**
    A introduction
    B psychotic
    C emotional
    D resolution

Your Answer:

A ❑   B ❑   C ❑   D ❑

Analysis: **The correct answer is C.** Answer **B** is exaggerated and answers **A** and **D** deal with plot and are wrong.

Chapter Review and Quick Quiz

If you stop to really think about it, the amount of work and the number of decisions that need to be made regarding characters, plots, mood, theme, and all the other things that go into writing a novel that were discussed in this chapter must certainly leave an author exhausted. But, that's another reason why reading is so much fun—someone else agonized over all the details, and we get to sit back and enjoy their efforts. To check your learning, take this quick quiz. The answers are in the appendix in the back of the book.

DIRECTIONS: Write the letter of the correct definition in the space to the left of the word it defines.

ANSWER	WORD(S)		DEFINITIONS
_____	1. dialogue	a.	speech in which a character alone on stage begins thinking aloud
_____	2. interior monologue	b.	most important character in a story
_____	3. dramatic monologue	c.	words that create images that appeal to the five senses
_____	4. soliloquy	d.	a character who does not change during a story
_____	5. asides	e.	something concrete that stands for something abstract
_____	6. character foils	f.	speech that reveals characters thoughts
_____	7. dynamic character	g.	the series of actual events in a narrative
_____	8. static character	h.	the use of characters, settings, events to represent something abstract
_____	9. protagonist	i.	revisiting past events through a character
_____	10. antagonist	j.	hints or clues given about future events in a story
_____	11. theme	k.	a character in opposition of the protagonist
_____	12. plot	l.	speech in which a character is overheard speaking to a silent listener
_____	13. foreshadowing	m.	the emotional aspect of the writing
_____	14. flashback	n.	contrasting or near opposites of another character
_____	15. imagery	o.	characters that change somehow through the story
_____	16. symbolism	p.	the voice of the person telling the story
_____	17. allegory	q.	conversation between two or more characters
_____	18. irony	r.	remarks by a character to the audience without being heard by other characters
_____	19. narrator	s.	a message or main idea of a narrative
_____	20. mood	t.	the use of a word or phrase to mean the exact opposite of what is being said

Section II

Writing

Chapter 8

Written and Oral Language Conventions—Part I

That's a fancy title for **grammar.** Grammar is what we are going to be reviewing in this chapter. The English language is filled with rules about everything, but what is confusing is that there is always an exception to the rule, which makes our language challenging in some ways. But, the more you understand about these little things, the better your writing and speaking will become. We will look specifically at clauses, phrases, and punctuation, but wait, there is a method to this madness! By looking at the little things such as phrases and clauses that make up the bigger things called sentences and paragraphs, we are building upon the basics of writing, which is the final step in this review for the exit exam.

CHAPTER FOCUS:　　*Clauses*
- *Independent or Main*
- *Subordinate or Dependent (Parts I and II)*
- *Adjective/Adverbial/Noun Clauses*

Phrases
- *Prepositional Phrases*
  - *Adjective*
  - *Adverb*
- *Verbal Phrases*
  - *Participial Review*
  - *Participial Phrases*
  - *Gerund Review*
  - *Gerund Phrases*
  - *Infinitive Review*
  - *Infinitive Phrases*
- *Appositives*
  - *Appositive Review*
  - *Appositive Phrases*

Punctuation
- *End Marks—a brief word*
- *Apostrophes*
- *Colons*
- *Semicolons*
- *Commas*
- *Hyphens*

Chapter Review and Quick Quizzes

Clauses

A **clause** is a group of words that has a **subject** and a **predicate** (the verb part) and is used as part of a sentence. All clauses contain a subject and a verb, but not all clauses express complete thoughts. That is why we are going to look at the two kinds of clauses: **independent** (is also know as a **main clause,** but we will use the word independent to make it less confusing), and **subordinate clauses** (also called **dependent clauses,** but we will use subordinate clause to be less confusing).

Independent Clause

Think of the word independent; it means not having to depend upon anyone or anything. That's what an independent clause is: a complete thought, and it can stand by itself as a sentence. In other words, it doesn't need any help; it can be a simple sentence. In looking at the samples below, notice that these independent clauses have a subject and a verb and that they express a complete thought. Note: the subject is boxed, and the verb is highlighted in each clause.

- Charles Dickens wrote many books.
- Ben stopped the car.
- The moon is full.
- Meredith ate the apple.
- Dominic sold the painting.

1. **Select the independent clause from the following list.**
   A when he drives slowly
   B which tell the entire story
   C he was a captain
   D because I told her

Your Answer:

A ❑   **B** ❑   **C** ❑   **D** ❑

Analysis: **The correct answer is C.** The only clause that can stand independently is this one; the others are subordinate clauses and cannot stand alone as a sentence.

Subordinate Clauses—Part I

Subordinate means of lesser importance and perhaps that is a good way to remember the meaning of this clause. Subordinate clauses are underqualified—they do not express a complete thought and cannot stand alone. Although subordinate clauses do have a subject and a verb, they are still dependent upon an independent clause to make them a complete sentence. Review the samples below.

Notice that these clauses begin with words such as: *that, where, which, since,* and *what.* When you see or hear a clause that begins with one of these, you know that it has to have at least one more clause to make it a sentence and one of those clauses must be an independent clause (because the subordinate clause is dependent). The subject of the clause is boxed and the verb is highlighted.

- that I prefer
- where he put the phone
- which she just bought
- since you've been away
- what they saw

2. **Which of the following clauses is NOT a subordinate clause?**
   A when the movie is over
   B she works in an office
   C because I told you
   D what a senator does

Your Answer:

A ❑   **B** ❑   **C** ❑   **D** ❑

Analysis: **The correct answer is B.** All of the clauses except for **B** are subordinate. They cannot stand alone as a sentence. She works in an office is an independent clause.

Subordinate Clauses—Part II

There are three additional (bonus) clauses in the subordinate category. Let's take a look at them. There is an **adjective clause** (modifies or describes a noun or a pronoun), an **adverb clause** (modifies or describes a verb), and a **noun clause** (person, place, or thing). Don't let the actual definitions (below) frighten or confuse you; if you keep this organized in your mind, all of this clause talk shouldn't bother you. You know that an **adjective** describes or (the fancy word) "modifies" a *noun* (person, place, or thing) or a *pronoun* (he, she, it, they, we, etc.) right? The red boat sailed on the blue water. Red is an adjective describing/modifying boat and blue is an adjective describing/modifying water. Well, apply this same idea to the adjective clause; it is going to modify a noun (person, place, or thing) or a pronoun (he, she, it, they, we, etc.). When you review these bonus subordinate clauses, just keep your mind organized and connect and apply what you already know about parts of speech (nouns, verbs, pronouns, adjectives, prepositions, and conjunctions) to the clauses and you will be fine.

Adjective Clause

An adjective clause is a subordinate clause that modifies a noun or a pronoun, just as a normal adjective (smart, small, blue, or inquisitive) modifies a noun or a pronoun in an everyday sentence. These clauses are usually introduced with a **relative pronoun: that, which, who, whom, whose.** A relative pronoun *relates* the adjective clause to the word it modifies.

Relative Pronouns That Introduce Adjective Clauses:

that, which, who, whom, whose

Example: Botero is the artist *who paints and sculpts very large rounded people.*

> **NOTE: The adjective clause *"who paints and sculpts very large rounded people,"* begins with the relative pronoun *who and it modifies the noun artist.***

Adverb Clause

This is a subordinate clause that modifies a verb, an adjective, or an adverb. Adverb clauses are introduced by a subordinating conjunction, which is a word that connects the adverb clause to the word or words that the clause modifies. The subordinating conjunctions were listed earlier, but review is always good:

Subordinating Conjunctions That Introduce Adverb Clauses:

after, although, as, as if, as long as, as soon as, as though, because, before, how, if, in order that, since, so that, than, though, unless, until, when, whenever, where, wherever, whether, while

Example: *Though the sun refuses to shine*, we will continue to plan our trip to the beach.

> **NOTE: The subordinating conjunction "though" begins the adverb clause "Though the sun refuses to shine" which modifies the verb "plan."**

Noun Clause

A noun clause is a subordinate clause that is used as a noun. It is common for the list of words below to be introduced as a noun clause:

Words That Commonly Introduce Noun Clauses:

who, whom, what, whoever, whomever, whatever, which, whichever, that

Example: *That Sammy is very angry* is obvious.

> **NOTE: The noun clause "that Sammy is very angry" is used as the subject in this sentence.**

3. The three types of subordinating clauses are _____, _____, and _____.
   A adverb, preposition, verb.
   B adverb, subject, predicate.
   C noun, adjective, adverb.
   D noun, adjective, verb.

Your Answer:

A ❑   B ❑   C ❑   D ❑

Analysis: **The correct answer is C.** This is one of those questions that could really throw you off if you didn't know exactly what the answer was. The three subordinating clauses are noun, adverb, and adjective. Answer **D** might confuse you if you were wavering back and forth about the answer, but Answers **A** and **B** are more easily eliminated.

Phrases

A **phrase** is a group of words that are related in some manner, but they do not have a *verb and its subject*. There are several categories of phrases. We will be reviewing the following: **prepositional phrases** with adjective and adverb phrases. **Verbal phrases** with participial, gerund, and infinitive phrases, and finally, **appositive phrases.**

Prepositional Phrases

Before we get into describing what prepositional phrases are, you need to make certain that you remember what a preposition is. A *preposition* is a word that deals with the relationship of a *noun* or a *pronoun* to another word in the sentence. Look below at the list of prepositions. Review them. Study them. Log them into a permanent part of your brain! Knowing these words for what they are will help you in many ways, not just for parts of speech and grammar, but in the writing that we will be working on in a chapter or two.

PREPOSITIONS—THOSE WITH MORE THAN ONE WORD ARE COMPOUND PREPOSITIONS

aboard	before	from	out
about	behind	in	over
above	below	in addition to	past
according to	beneath	in front of	since
across	beside	inside	through
after	besides	in spite of	throughout
against	between	instead of	to
along	beyond	into	toward
along with	but (except)	like	under
amid	by	near	underneath
among	concerning	next to	until
around	down	of	up
aside from	during	off	upon
as of	except	on	with
at			within
because of	for	on account of	without

Those are prepositions. Now for prepositional phrases. These are easy as long as you know prepositions. A prepositional phrase is a group of words that begin with a *preposition* and end with a *noun* or a *pronoun*. Review the examples below. The preposition is boxed and the noun or pronoun is highlighted.

> Reminder: All prepositional phrases begin with a preposition and end with a noun or pronoun

- because of the flu
- on the stove
- through the window
- out of the zoo
- within a month

4. **Which of the following is NOT a prepositional phrase?**
   A into the night
   B under the clouds
   C off the wall
   D system is down

Your Answer:

A ❏   B ❏   C ❏   D ❏

Analysis: **The correct answer is D.** Just making sure you are paying attention, the question asks which one is *not* the prepositional phrase. The first three phrases all have *prepositions*—into, under, and off. Look at Answer **D.** Down is a preposition right? It's on our list. Well, you need to remember that prepositions are always followed by a *noun* or a *pronoun*. Down is a preposition, but not here. In this question it is used as an adverb.

Adjective Phrases

Simply stated, an adjective phrase is a prepositional phrase used as an *adjective*. Reminder: An adjective is a word that describes or modifies the noun or pronoun and the one-word adjective usually precedes or goes before the noun or pronoun like this: The yellow light means caution. "Yellow" is an *adjective* describing or modifying "light." Similarly, with an adjective phrase the noun precedes the prepositional phrase, making it an adjective phrase. The prepositional phrase hasn't changed; it still has the preposition at the beginning, and the noun or pronoun at the end. Let's take a look at the adjective phrases below; The nouns are boxed and the **adjective phrases are highlighted.**

- The light in the intersection is out of order.
- The package on the shelf is Betsy's.
- Catalina is an island off the coast of California.
- The basket inside the garage is empty.
- The dog with the black spots seems happy.

Adverb Phrases

An adverb phrase, much like an *adverb*, is used to tell *when, where, how, how much,* or *how far,* but in the form of a prepositional phrase. Remember: an *adverb* modifies a *verb,* an a*djective,* or *another adverb.* Let's look at the samples below. The adverb phrases are highlighted and the function of the phrase is in parentheses.

- The rain fell over the meadow. (where)
- My friends and I drove throughout the city looking for a CD. (where)
- Peter will finish reading the book by Thursday. (when)
- I will call you early in the morning. (when)
- The clerk answered with a smile. (how)

5. **Adjective phrases modify _____ or pronouns and adverb phrases modify _____, adjectives, or another adverb.**
   A verbs, adjectives
   B nouns, conjunctions
   C nouns, verbs
   D interjections and conjunctions

Your Answer:

A ☐   B ☐   C ☐   D ☐

Analysis: The correct answer is C. Knowing exactly what adverbs and adjectives modify is beneficial for this question. Although Answer **D** can be eliminated quite easily, **A** and **B** might cause a little confusion at first glance.

Verbal Phrases

The **participial, gerund,** and **infinitive phrases** are known as verbal phrases. Before delving into their backgrounds, we need to review the definitions of the three verbals standing alone before we get into the phrase part of the review.

Participle Review and Participial Phrases

- **Participle Review:** a verb that can be used as an adjective
  - **Present** participles end in *-ing.* Example:
    The article was encouraging. Notice that the word encouraging in its true form is a *verb,* but it is used as an *adjective* in this sentence because it describes or modifies the *noun* article.
  - **Past** participles end in *-d* or *-ed.* Example: The student searched the abandoned hall for her backpack. Again, the verb form abandoned is used as an *adjective* in the past tense and modifies the noun hall, making it a past participle.
  - Participial phrases: Used as an adjective, the participial phrase is comprised of a participle, its modifiers, and its complements. Review the examples below. The **participial phrase is boxed** and the noun it modifies is highlighted.

    Examples: Flapping its wings, the bird took flight.
    Living in California, Eric learned to appreciate the ocean.
    Laughing at my joke, Lisa fell from the chair.

6. **In the following sentence locate the participial phrase: "Destined for fame, my cousin practiced singing every day."**
   A practiced singing every day
   B my cousin practiced
   C singing every day
   D Destined for fame

Your Answer:

A ❑   B ❑   C ❑   D ❑

Analysis: **The correct answer is D.** "Destined for fame" is the participial phrase and it modifies the *noun* "cousin." Answers **A**, **B**, and **C** are incorrect. Taking this a step further, is the word "Destined" past or present participle? (Past) Remember past participles end in *-d* or *-ed*, and present participles end with an *-ing*.

Gerund Review and Gerund Phrase

- **Gerund Review:** A form of *verb* that ends in an *-ing* but is used as a *noun*. *Not* to be confused with the present participle (above), which also ends in an *-ing* but it is used as an *adjective*. That's the major difference. Example: Cooking is an art form for some people. The word cooking—the gerund of this sentence would under normal circumstances be a verb; however, it is used as a *noun*. Gerunds are common but we don't often attach a title to them or think to ourselves "Oh, that's a gerund!" Skating, painting, exercising are commonly used as gerunds.
- **Gerund Phrase:** A gerund phrase includes of course, the gerund and its complement and modifiers. They all act together as a *noun*. Review the following gerund phrases. The gerund phrases are boxed. Remember, gerund phrases act as *nouns*, which mean they might be the *subject* of the sentence, the *direct object*, the *object of the preposition*, etc.

   Examples: Approaching the freeway onramp may require caution.
   The song spoke of the gentle blossoming of friendship.
   By speaking to the audience, the politician was able to relay his message.

7. **Identify the gerund phrase in the following sentence: "Sweeping the floor was one of his many duties."**
   A Sweeping the floor
   B was one of
   C his many duties
   D the floor was

Your Answer:

A ❑   B ❑   C ❑   D ❑

Analysis: **The correct answer is A.** A gerund phrase contains a gerund, which is a *verb* form that ends in *-ing* and is used as a *noun*. Answers **B**, **C**, and **D** are incorrect.

Infinitive Review and Infinitive Phrase

- **Infinitive Review:** Another *verb* form that can be used as a *noun*, an *adjective* **or** an *adverb*. This form usually begins with "to." Review the following examples.
  - Infinitives as *nouns*: To build the bridge took two years. His ambition is to become a musician. Ann likes to ski but not to skate.
  - Infinitives as *adjectives*: The best time to visit California is anytime. If you want information about cameras and photography, that is the magazine to read.
  - Infinitives as *adverbs*: The cyclists were eager to ride in the race. The players stopped at halftime to rest.
- **Infinitive Phrases:** An infinitive phrase consists of an infinitive and its modifiers and complements. Again, infinitive phrases can be used as *nouns*, *adjectives*, and *adverbs*. The infinitive phrases are boxed.

- Infinitive Phrases as *nouns*: To run fast takes a lot of training. To succeed in business takes patience and determination. They wanted to travel around the world beginning in September.
- Infinitive Phrases as *adjectives*: He is the cyclist to watch in this stage of the Tour de France. He wanted to join the club. They like apples and oranges to eat on the plane.
- Infinitive Phrases as *adverbs*: The students became quiet to hear the teacher. They are delighted to visit the elderly. The artist was proud to display his sculptures.

8. **Identify the infinitive phrase in the following sentence: "After surgery, the football player will complete many leg exercises to strengthen his knee."**
   A After surgery
   B to strengthen his knee
   C the football player
   D will complete many leg exercises

Your Answer:

A ☐   B ☐   C ☐   D ☐

Analysis: **The correct answer is B.** The infinitive phrase is "to strengthen his knee." It is used as an adverb in the sentence. Answers **A, C,** and **D** are wrong.

Appositives

Appositive Review and Appositive Phrases

- **Appositives** are *nouns* or *pronouns* that follow another *noun* or pronoun in order to either explain it or to identify it. **Example:** astronaut, John Glenn, was one of America's early space travelers. The word "astronaut" is the appositive and "John Glenn" is the noun(s) that identifies it. **Example:** Lewis and Clark, leaders of an expedition west, are well known in American history. "Lewis and Clark" are the nouns and "leaders of an expedition west" explain.
- **Appositive Phrases** are a phrases made up of an appositive and its modifiers. The appositive is boxed, and the appositive phrase is highlighted.

   Examples: The respected and admired French diplomat, Jean Paul Gautier, is visiting Sacramento.
   The next train to San Diego, the Coaster, boards in fifteen minutes.
   Yo Yo Ma, a well-known and talented cellist, will have a recital next week.

9. **Identify the appositive in the following sentence: "The writer, Sandra Cisneros, is creative and talented."**
   A creative and talented
   B the writer Sandra Cisneros
   C Cisneros is
   D writer

Your Answer:

A ☐   B ☐   C ☐   D ☐

Analysis: **The correct answer is B.** An appositive is a *noun* or a *pronoun* placed beside another noun or pronoun to identify or explain it. In this case the noun "writer" is placed next to the proper noun "Sandra Cisneros" and is therefore the appositive.

Punctuation

Punctuation is the practice of using marks such as periods, exclamation points, commas, hyphens, and question marks, to separate sentences and to make their meanings clear. Can you imagine if there were no punctuation marks or a sentence without the spaces that separate the words? youwouldntknowwhereathoughtbeganorendedeverythingwouldblendtogetherandunderstanding-wouldbeextremelychallenging. Whether you are writing by hand (as you will be doing on your exam essays) or typing on a computer, punctuation, from a tiny little period to a Capital letter, or space between words is mandatory and obviously very necessary.

End Marks—a Brief Word about Them!

Although we all know to use end marks at the ends of our sentences, a few of us forget from time to time. When you get to the writing portion of the CAHSEE, you cannot afford to forget. As a reminder about end marks, please review the following:

- Use a **period** at the end of a statement.

  Example: Autumn is my favorite time of year**.**

- Use a **question mark** at the end of a question.

  Example: How many pencils do you have**?**

- Use an **exclamation point** at the end of an exclamation.

  Example: Look at that view**!**

- Use a **period** or an **exclamation point** at the end of a request or a command.

  Example: Please pass the milk**.** (a request)
  Give me the milk**!** (a command)

- Use a **period** after most abbreviations.

  Example: Mr., Mrs., Ms., Dr., Jr., St., Rd., Blvd., Corp., Inc., A.M., P.M., B.C., A.D., B.A., B.S., Ph.D., W.E.B. DuBois,

  Example: Government agencies and other widely used abbreviations are written without periods: FBI, PTA, NAACP, PBS, CNN, VHS, HUD, and YMCA, etc. Words that are abbreviated (such as television = TV) are not written with periods.

Apostrophes

These are used for the possessive case of nouns (and some pronouns), to indicate a contraction, and to form some plurals. Let's look at the use of apostrophes in each case.

- **Use of apostrophes in possessive case:**
  - **Possessive case of singular noun** shows ownership or relationship. To form the possessive case of a singular noun, add an apostrophe and then an "s."
    (singular noun + ' + s = possessive singular noun)
    - the cat's tail
    - Joe's drum set
    - Kyle's guitar
    - one dollar's worth
    - a moment's notice
  - **Possessive case of plural noun ending in "s."** When a plural noun already ends in an "s," add only an apostrophe. This is also true with proper nouns that end with an "s"; add only an apostrophe.
    (plural noun with "s" ending + ' = possessive case of plural noun)
    - the cats' tails
    - Los Angeles' population
    - doctors' opinion
    - ten dollars' worth
    - the students' lockers
  - **Possessive case of plural nouns not ending in "s."** For plural nouns that do not end in "s" add an apostrophe and then an "s."
    (plural noun-no "s" + ' + s = possessive plural noun)
    - men's suits
    - children's toys

- women's clothing
- geese's noise
- mice's tracks
  ○ **Possessive personal pronouns** do not use an apostrophe with possessive personal pronouns.
    - yours, ours, theirs, hers, its, his, mine
  ○ **Possessive case of indefinite pronouns.** With some indefinite pronouns, add an apostrophe and an "s" to form the possessive case.
    - Everyone's, everyone's, no one's, somebody's, someone's, anyone's, another's, etc.
- **Use of apostrophes in contractions.** An apostrophe is a shortened form of a word, figure, or a group of words. The apostrophe in the contraction shows where the letter that was left out would be if it were still there. Contractions are shortcuts. Review the following list of contractions. Note that an apostrophe is added where a letter is removed.

COMMON CONTRACTIONS

I am = I'm	2003 = '03
has not = hasn't	let us = let's
she would = she'd	of the clock = o'clock
they had = they'd	where is = where's
cannot = can't	we are = we're
were not = weren't	he is = he's
should not = shouldn't	you will = you'll
there has = there's	is not = isn't
there is = there's	are not = aren't
who is = who's	does not = doesn't
who has = who's	they are = they're
they are = they're	will not = won't

- **Use of apostrophes for plurals.** To form the plurals of letters, numerals, and signs, and for words referred to as words. Review the examples below.
  ○ They hope to get all A's and B's on their report cards.
  ○ When you write your essay, do not use ampersands (&'s).
  ○ You use too many and's in your essay.

10. In the following sentence, choose the correct form of the word that is underlined.
"The Senate members approved Senator Kennedys plan for reorganization."
A Kennedy's
B Kennedys'
C Kennedys's
D correct as is

Your Answer:

A ❏   B ❏   C ❏   D ❏

Analysis: **The correct answer is A.** This form shows ownership; it's Senator Kennedy's plan. Therefore, there is an apostrophe and then an "s." Answer **B** is plural possessive case; Answer **C** is erroneous, as is **D.**

Colons

These are used for the following reasons. Please review them.
- After the salutation of a business letter.
  ○ Dear Governor Davis:
  ○ Dear Mayor Hahn:
  ○ Dear Mr. Miyayami:

- Between the parts of a number indicating time.
    - 9:17
    - 12:30
    - 17:48
- To emphasize a word, phrase, clause, or a sentence that explains or adds impact to the main clause.
    - She has worked here longer than anyone in the district: thirty-two years.
    - There are two things you must remember: drink plenty of water, and get plenty of sleep.
- To introduce a list.
    - We have many things in common: sports, academics, friends, and music.
    - Working for this organization requires: loyalty and long hours.
- To distinguish between a title and a subtitle, volume and page, chapter and verse in literature.
    - *English for Everyone: A Handbook of Grammar, Mechanics, and Usage*
    - *Encyclopedia Britannica* X: 135
    - Garden of Truth 23: 1–6
- To formally introduce a sentence, a question, or a quotation.
    - William Shakespeare wrote: "O, it is excellent to have a giant's strength; but it is tyrannous to use it like a giant."

Semicolons

These are related to the colon in a sense; the semicolon is used in a variety of ways. Let's take a look.

- Use to join two or more independent clauses (clauses that could stand alone as a sentence) that are not connected with a coordinating conjunction (and, but, nor, for, or, yet, so).
    - She didn't cause any trouble; she made us laugh and cry at the same time.
    - The dog waited before he pounced; he jumped straight up in the air.
- Use between independent clauses that are joined by a conjunctive adverb (accordingly, besides, consequently, furthermore, however, indeed, instead, meanwhile, moreover, nevertheless, otherwise, therefore) or a transitional expression (as a result, in addition, for example, in spite of, for instance, that is, in conclusion, in fact).
    - Our trip to Japan was all that we expected it to be; nevertheless, it will be an experience we shall never forget.
    - The fog continues to block the sun most mornings in June; as a result, the beaches are not too crowded.
- Use to separate independent clauses that are long or contain commas.
    - To the members of the club, meetings and special functions were just a part of the regular routine; but before each and everyone of them, there was always time for socializing.

11. **In the following sentence, select the word that should be followed by a colon to separate the two clauses:**

    "The first aid kit contained the following items bandages, antiseptic pads, flares, aspirin, gauze, tweezers, a knife, rain poncho."
    A kit:
    B contained:
    C bandages:
    D items:

Your Answer:

A ❑   **B** ❑   **C** ❑   **D** ❑

Analysis: **The correct answer is D.** Use a colon before a list of items, especially after the expression "the following items." Answers **A, B,** and **C** are definitely wrong.

Commas

These are one of the most used and abused of punctuation marks. As you can see, below is a list of some of the more common usage rules.

- Use between two independent clauses that are joined by *coordinating conjunctions* (but, or, nor, for, yet, and, so).
  - I would like to visit with her, but my life is very hectic right now.
  - Both of the kids went shopping for clothes, so they weren't here when the package arrived.
- Use to separate individual words, phrases, or clauses in a series (a series contains at least three items).
  - At the grocery store I bought eggs, bread, and milk.
  - When I baby-sat last night the children ate dinner, took a bath, and read books.
- Use to separate adjectives that equally modify the same noun.
  - The time passes quickly during the long, hot days of summer.
  - Time passes slowly during the short, cold days of winter.
- To enclose an explanatory word or phrase.
  - Ray Charles, a blind and very talented musician and singer, is touring Europe right now.
  - The two pilots, flying over Fresno, ejected safely and landed in a field.
- Use after *yes*, *no*, or other mild exclamations such as *well*, or *why* at the beginning of a sentence.
  - Yes, I would like to go to the river next weekend.
  - Well, I believe there is a better answer to the question.
- Use to set off words used in direct address.
  - Dominic, it is your turn to wash the dishes.
  - Please, Meredith, call me when you get home.

12. **In the following sentences, which one is NOT punctuated with commas correctly.**
    A Please, take me to see your counselor.
    B When you go to the store would you pick up some lettuce, tomatoes, and onions?
    C Behind the stage door the actors embrace each other in celebration of their opening night.
    D Over a period of time, the French have become known for their excellent cooking skills.

Your Answer:

A ❑   **B** ❑   **C** ❑   **D** ❑

Analysis: **The correct answer is C.** There should be a comma after door. The other sentences are punctuated properly.

Hyphens

These are used to either join two words together or to divide one word into two parts. Let's review the examples below.

- Use a hyphen to divide a word that is too long and won't fit at the end of the line—but remember these rules: divide a word only between syllables (check the dictionary if you are unsure) and do not divide one-syllable words. Also, divide an already hyphenated word at the hyphen and do not separate a word so that one letter remains alone or orphaned.
  - Yesterday, there were so many complicated things that had to be completed before our vacation that I was exhausted by bedtime.
  - On our way to work today we were stopped in traffic, when my brother-in-law cruised by on his motorcycle.

- Use with compound names, places, and numbers from twenty-one to ninety-nine and for fractions that are used as adjectives.
  - Daniel Day-Lewis is a talented dramatic actor.
  - Stratford-upon-Avon is the borough where Shakespeare was born.
  - There are twenty-three students in my English class.
  - I will need one-half cup of milk for the dessert.
- Used to make a compound word.
  - great-great-grandfather
  - brother-in-law
  - sixteen-year-old
- To join a capital letter to a noun or participle.
  - T-shirt
  - U-turn
  - S-shaped
- When two or more words have a common element that is omitted in all but the very last term.
  - There are two-, three-, and four-foot lengths of rope ready to use.
  - The sunglasses were available in blue-, amber-, gray-, and brown-tinted lenses.
- To form new words beginning with the *prefixes self*, *ex*, *all*, *great*, and *half*, and with the *suffix elect*, as well as joining any *prefix* to a *proper noun*.
  - half-eaten
  - half-baked
  - senator-elect
  - post-Depression
  - ex-governor
  - mid-July
- To indicate the life span of a person or the score of a contest or vote.
  - The Dodgers beat the Yankees 6-0.
  - William O. Smithson lived from 1764-1828.

13. In the following, which sentence is hyphenated correctly.
   A After you turn sixty-five, you will be able to retire from work.
   B Can you name the thirty ninth state?
   C Kareem Abdul Jabbar is a respected basketball player.
   D At the zoo today, we saw many animals and our favorites we-re the giraffes.

Your Answer:

A ❑   B ❑   C ❑   D ❑

Analysis: The correct answer is **A.** Numbers between twenty-one and ninety-nine are hyphenated. Answer **B** needs a hyphen between thirty and nine. In Answer **C,** Abdul-Jabbar should be hyphenated, and in Answer **D,** the one-syllable word *were* should not be hyphenated at all.

Chapter Review and Quick Quizzes

After all of this clause, phrase, and punctuation talk, you are probably anxious to test your memory. Let's see what you remember about the chapter. Take the following quizzes and check your answers in the appendix.

DIRECTIONS: Using the word bank below, complete the sentences by filling in the blanks with the word that best completes the sentence. Some words are used more than once, but they are listed the number of times that they are used in the paragraph.

> *Word Bank:* adjective, adverb, noun, two, subordinate, subordinate, independent, verb, subject, predicate, subject, clause, independent

SECTION I—CLAUSES

A _____ (1) is a group of words that have a _____ (2) and a _____ (3). All clauses contain a _____ (4) and a _____ (5), but not all clauses express a complete thought. There are _____ (6) kinds of clauses: _____ (7) and _____ (8) clauses. _____ (9) clauses express a complete thought, but _____ (10) clauses do not. An _____ (11) clause modifies a noun or a pronoun. An _____ (12) clause modifies a verb, an adjective, or another adverb. A _____ (13) clause is used as a noun.

DIRECTIONS: Using the word bank below, complete the sentences by filling in the blanks with the word that best completes the sentence. Some words are used more than once, but they are listed the number of times that they are used in the paragraph.

> *Word Bank:* appositive, nouns, –ing, adjective, infinitive, gerunds, phrase, verbal, adverb, phrase, noun, pronoun, adjective, preposition, infinitive, gerund, verbal participial, verb, subject, prepositional

SECTION II—PHRASES

A _____ (1) is a group of words that are related, but they do not have a _____ (2) and a _____ (3). There are _____ (4) phrases, adjective, and adverb phrases. There are _____ (5), _____ (6), _____, (7) and _____ (8) phrases as well as appositive phrases. A _____ (9) phrase begins with a preposition and ends with a _____ (10) or a _____ (11). An _____ (12) phrase is a prepositional _____ (13) used as an _____ (14). An _____ (15) phrase is used to tell when, where, how, how much, or how far. _____ (16) phrases include participial, gerund, and infinitive phrases. Participial phrases are used as an _____ (17). This phrase usually begins with a word that has an _____ (18) ending. Gerund phrases act as _____ (19). Gerunds are verb forms that end in an -ing, but are used as nouns. _____ (20) phrases begin with the word "to" and are used as a noun, adjective, or an adverb. _____ (21) phrases are noun or pronoun phrases that follow another noun or pronoun.

SECTION III—PUNCTUATION

DIRECTIONS: In the following paragraph there are many punctuation and capitalization errors. Underline the errors and then check the corrected version of the paragraph in the Appendix.

the word machiavellian has become synonymous (a synonym) for political immorality niccolo machiavelli, who lived form 1469–1527 wrote a book titled *the prince* which is remembered for its insistence that while his subjects are bound by conventional or the normal moral obligations, a ruler may use any means necessary to maintain power and it doesn't matter how unscrupulous. therefore machiavellian has come to mean cynical political scheming which is characterized by deceit and bad faith Evidently, niccolo was a thin-lipped man who was very hyperactive and sarcastic isn't it amazing how the memory of one man with theory of political morality can be so appropriate to modern times

Chapter 9

Written and Oral Language Conventions—Part II

It is mind-boggling to think about the amount of work that goes into speaking, reading, and writing English. The rules and their exceptions alone fill books. But, it is all a part of the learning process. This chapter is no different. We have a fair amount to cover in the area of grammar, a continuation of the previous chapter, so we'd better get busy. This is where we are going.

CHAPTER FOCUS: *Capitalization*

           Sentence Construction
- *Fragments*
- *Declarative, Imperative, Exclamatory, Interrogative*
- *Subject—Simple, Complete, Compound*
- *Predicate—Simple, Complete, Compound Verbs*

           Subject/Verb Agreement

           Double Negative

           Comparison of Modifiers
- *Positive Form*
- *Comparative Form*
- *Superlative Form*

           Chapter Review and Quick Quizzes

Capitalization

The list of capitalization rules is extensive. Much of it comes naturally to you, but reviewing all of the rules is valuable for test taking.

Capitalize . . .

- The first word in every sentence.
  - **My** shoes need to be repaired.
  - **Last** night we went to a concert.
- The pronoun **I**.
- The first word in a full-sentence quotation.
  - Piri Thomas said that, "**Every** child is born a poet and every poet is a child."
- All proper nouns and proper adjectives.
  - **Mrs. Jones, Doctor Smith, Ludvig van Beethoven**
  - **Great Wall of China, Sacramento Kings, Colorado River**
  - **Spanish** dancing, **Thai** food, **Japanese, Morse** code
  - **Korean** barbeque, **Dutch** chocolate, **Nigerian** masks, **Victorian** dress
- Words that name a particular section of the country; these are proper nouns. But, do not capitalize if the sentence merely indicates direction: Birds fly south in the winter.
  - Many birds spend their winters in the **South.**
  - The **North** was industrialized in the late 1800s.
- Names of planets, stars, and other heavenly bodies.
  - **Pluto, Earth, Mars,** the **Milky Way,**
- Races, nationalities, languages, and religions.
  - **Asian, African-American, Latino, Hispanic**

- - French, Spanish, Japanese, Canadian, Armenian
  - German, Danish, English, Chinese, Portuguese
  - Hindu, Buddhism, Catholic, Protestant, Muslim
- All words in a title except for articles (*a, an, the*), short conjunctions (*and, but, for, nor, or, so, yet*), and short prepositions (*at, for, from, with*).
  - *Romeo and Juliet, Of Mice and Men, To Whom the Bell Tolls*
  - *A Beautiful Mind, Shadowlands,*
  - *Los Angeles Times, Chicago Tribune, Time Magazine*
  - *The Nine Muses: A Mythological Path to Creativity*
  - *"Flying to the Sun: The Story of Icarus"*
- Names of organizations, an association, businesses, government bodies, and a team and its members.
  - Reading is FUNdamental, Democratic Party, Palos Verdes Peninsula Snowboarding Club, the Civil Rights Movement, the Department of Health, Education, and Welfare
- Abbreviation of titles and organizations.
  - M.D., Ph.D., B.A., FBI, NAACP, B.C., A.D.
- Brand names of business products.
  - IBM, Honda, Dodge, Hewlett-Packard, Sony, Farmer John, Wheaties
- Letters used to indicate a form or shape.
  - U-turn, V-neck, S-shaped
- Mother, father, uncle, and senator when they are being used as part of their title or when they are used in place of proper nouns.
  - My Uncle Jeff has a great personality.
  - Did you know that Senator Boxer is from California?
  - I told you that Mom would be upset.
- Nouns or pronouns that refer to a supreme being or deities, holy days, sacred writings, or religious followers.
  - God, Allah, the Koran, the Talmud, the Lord, Book of Psalms
- Names of historical events, and periods, special events, and calendar items.
  - The Renaissance, the Depression, the Middle Ages, the Dust Bowl, the Battle of Bunker Hill, Spanish-American War, Cinco de Mayo, Valentine's Day, the Olympic Games, Oscars
- Names of trains, ships, airplanes, and spacecraft.
  - The *Titanic*, the *Queen Mary, Mayflower*, Amtrak, Orient Express, Carnival Cruises, *Spirit of St. Louis, Apollo 11*
- Names of buildings and other structures.
  - Eiffel Tower, the Empire State Building, Tokyo Tower, the Sears Building
- Names of monuments and awards.
  - Washington Monument, Lincoln Memorial, Vietnam Memorial, the Pulitzer Prize, the Nobel Prize, the Newbury Award
- Cities, towns, and villages.
  - Torrance, Long Beach, Del Mar, Julian, Palm Springs, Fremont
- Streets, roads, highways.
  - Artesia Boulevard, the 405 Freeway, Interstate 5, Gaffey Street
- Landforms, continents, bodies of water, public areas.
  - The Cascade Mountains, Death Valley, Sahara Desert, the Alps, Asia, Africa, Antarctica, Mt. Etna, Glacier National Park, Sherwood Forest
- Titles, the title of a person when it comes before the name, the title used alone or following a person's name only when you want to emphasize the position.
  - The Secretary of Defense was speaking at the convention.
- Do **not** capitalize the names of school subjects except languages and course names followed by a number.
  - English, Latin, French, Japanese, German, Spanish, Algebra 101, Biology 120
- The words *freshman, sophomore, junior,* and *senior* only when they are part of a title.
  - The Senior Banquet, Frosh-Soph. Basketball, the Junior Prom.

- Holidays, months, and days of the week.
  - Thanksgiving, Memorial Day, June, July, August, Monday, Tuesday

1. Select the sentence that does NOT have correct capitalization.
A During the long road trip to Tucson, we visited the Grand Canyon.
B The american revolution freed us from england's rule.
C The Declaration of Independence is the heartbeat of our nation.
D Creating the Statue of Liberty must have been an enormous task.

Your Answer:

A ☐   B ☐   C ☐   D ☐

Analysis: **The correct answer is B.** American Revolution and England should be capitalized. Answers **A, C,** and **D** are correctly written.

Sentence Construction

A sentence is a group of words that expresses a complete thought. It begins with a capital letter, and ends with an end mark of some sort (period, question mark, or exclamation point), depending upon the type of sentence. When you have a group of words that look somewhat like a sentence, but reading it carefully you notice that it really doesn't have a complete thought or, rather, something is missing, it is called a fragment, and these are what you want to avoid in writing sentences. Fragments may have a verb, or subject, or some other important part of the sentence missing to make it that way, and it is our job to make certain we understand the difference. But, before we get into the parts of a sentence and their functions, let's look at the types of sentences there are and how to tell a good sentence from a bad one.

Declarative Sentences

These make a statement. They tell something and are probably the most common type of sentences. They are always ended with a period. Review the following two examples: The first sentence is a normal declarative sentence, the second is a fragment.

- Returning to England next spring will be the highlight of my year. (declarative sentence)
- Returning to England. (fragment—incomplete thought)

Imperative Sentences

These give commands or make requests. In normal circumstances, they are followed by a period, but a very strong command is followed by an exclamation point. Also, note that in commands or requests, the word "you" is understood, meaning you don't have to write it down; people already know you are talking to them. So you don't have to say, "You shut the door." You would say, "Shut the door." Look at the examples below:

- Write your name and address at the top of the card.
- Call the paramedics!

Exclamatory Sentences

These either express strong emotion or feeling or show excitement. These sentences are followed by an exclamation point. Review the samples below:

- Wow, look at that amazing display of awards!
- Watch out!

Interrogative Sentences

These sentences ask questions. They are *always*, *always* followed by a question mark. Review the examples below.

- What is your favorite movie?
- Where do you think you are going?

2. **Identify the following type of sentence: "In June, the city of Santa Barbara has a Summer Solstice Celebration."**
   A exclamatory
   B imperative
   C interrogative
   D declarative

Your Answer:

A ❑   B ❑   C ❑   D ❑

Analysis: The correct answer is D. This sentence makes a statement and ends with a period. It is definitely a declarative sentence. Exclamatory sentences exclaim something rather dramatically. Interrogative sentences interrogate or ask a question. Imperative sentences are fairly demanding.

The Subject and the Predicate

A sentence is divided into two parts. The subject and the predicate make up the two parts of a sentence. The subject tells whom or what the sentence is about; it includes the *noun*. The predicate, on the other hand, tells something about the subject; it is really the *verb* part or action part of the sentence. Usually, the subject comes before the predicate, but don't be surprised to find the subject somewhere else in the sentence. That's what's so exciting about English; there are always different ways to do things and there are always exceptions to the rules. But, if you will remember that the subject part is the *noun* part, and the predicate part is the *verb* part, this will be a piece of cake. In the examples below, the subjects are in boxes and the predicates are highlighted.

- **Simple Subject.** This is the *main word* in the **complete subject.** See the examples below;
  - My foot hurts. ("foot" is the simple subject)
  - A two-story building is being built. (building is the simple subject)
- **Complete Subject.** Basically, the complete subject is everything before the verb and includes the simple subject and all the words dealing with it.
  - Mota's home run tied the game.
  - The giant television screen replayed the run over and over.
- **Compound Subject.** This has two or more connected subjects that have the same verb. Usually, *and* or *or* connect the two subjects.
  - Neither snow nor wind will deter our postman from his rounds.
  - Vicky, Birgit, Ann, and Juli are the best friends in the world.
- **Simple Predicate.** This is the main word or group of words in the complete predicate, which is the part of the sentence that tells something about the subject.
  - My sister paints.
  - She is a well-respected artist.
- **Complete Predicate.** This is the group of words that tag along with the simple predicate. Basically, everything from the verb on is the complete predicate.
  - John has never played football before today.
  - The Peninsula Drama Club will sponsor the Southern Regional Drama Festival.
- **Compound Verbs.** Like the compound subject, the compound verb (notice it is not called "compound predicate") has two or more connected verbs that have the same subject. *And, or,* or *but* usually connect the verbs. See the examples below.
  - Alex and his dad leveled and planted a garden plot in the steep slope behind their house.
  - While we were home we washed the car, vacuumed the living room, and dusted the furniture.

3. **Identify the term that best describes the highlighted portion of the sentence. "During this century, guarding and protecting the environment is of the utmost importance."**
   A a simple subject
   B compound verbs
   C compound subjects
   D complete predicate

Your Answer:

A ☐   B ☐   C ☐   D ☐

Analysis: The correct answer is B. This is a tricky question, but it asks you to choose the *best* term that describes the sentence. Although this highlighted part is also a complete predicate, it nevertheless contains two verbs with one subject, thus making it compound verbs, which is the better answer. Answers **A** and **C** are completely wrong.

Subject-Verb Agreement

When you have a *singular* (meaning one) subject, you must have a *singular* verb. When you have a *plural* (meaning more than one) subject, you therefore must use a *plural* verb. It is said that the subject and the verb must agree in number which is another way of saying *singular* subject = *singular* verb, or *plural* subject = *plural* verb. The examples in the table below should help.

Singular Subject	Singular Verb	Example
chair	squeaks	The chair squeaks when you lean back on it.
book	falls	The book falls from the shelf, making a loud noise.
sun	fades	Silently, the sun fades off in the distance.
plant	grows	That large-leafed plant grows well in the shade.
star	shines	The star shines brightly in the desert sky.
vase	shatters	The vase shatters on the floor.
container	sour	A container of milk will sour without refrigeration.
veteran	recover	The injured veteran will recover from his injuries.
student	studies	That student studies in the library every day.
globe	turns	The globe turns hesitantly on its rusted stand.

Plural Subject	Plural Verb	Example
women	challenge	Women of the new millennium challenge men for jobs.
lights	sparkle	Neon lights seem to sparkle more after the rain.
senators	discuss	The senators on the floor discuss the proposed bill.
horses	gallop	The wild horses gallop freely on the island off the coast.
frogs	leap	Newly developed frogs leap uncontrollably at first.
license plates	are	Metal license plates are easily bent on a car's bumper.
neighbors	celebrate	Our neighbors like to celebrate occasions.
runners	struggle	Some marathon runners struggle in the last five miles.
pianists	memorize	Most pianists memorize their recital pieces.
peaches	reach	Peaches reach their peak of sweetness about mid-July.

Now, look what happens if you mix up the agreement of the subjects and verbs. Mixing and matching verbs and subjects from the lists above should allow you to see how funny, as in odd, things sound when the subject and verb don't agree.
- Student celebrate after the exam. (s. subject, pl. verb)
- Students celebrate after the exam. (pl. subject, pl. verb)
- Students celebrates after the exam. (pl. subject, s. verb)

Let's try another one:
- Horse gallop over the plains of Wyoming. (s. subject, pl. verb)
- Horses gallop over the plains of Wyoming. (pl. subject, pl. verb)
- Horses gallops over the plains of Wyoming. (pl. subject, s. verb)

Hopefully, after reading the sentences with the mixed-up agreements you understand the need to make certain that a singular subject has a singular verb; a plural subject has a plural verb. What confuses some people is the fact that we are taught that to make a singular noun plural we add an "s" or "es," but what seems odd is that the *singular verbs* have an "s" or an "es," but the plural verbs don't. How can they agree? Listening or hearing the way they sound together makes all the difference in the world. With all the rules and regulations in the game of English, sometimes all you can do is to listen carefully to the way its sounds, and then make a judgment call.

4. Select the sentence below whose subject and verb do NOT agree.
   A The baby coughs all night and all day long.
   B The highway leading out of town appears to be deteriorating.
   C The boys skates down the street.
   D The frogs jump into the pond with much excitement.

Your Answer:

A ❑   B ❑   C ❑   D ❑

Analysis: **The correct answer is C.** The subject-verb agreement of *boy-skates* is wrong. It should be *boys-skate*. The remaining answers have correct subject and verb agreement.

Double Negatives

We don't have no milk in the refrigerator. There is barely nothing to eat. There is hardly no soap in the shower. Ouch! Those are double negatives. The use of *two* negative words to express *one* negative idea is a double negative. Avoid them at all costs. Let's see if we can repair the damage we caused in the above sentences.
   • We don't have no milk in the refrigerator. ☹
   • We don't have any milk in the refrigerator. ☺
   • There is barely nothing to eat. ☹
   • There is nothing to eat.—or—There is hardly anything to eat. ☺
   • There is hardly no soap in the shower. ☹
   • There is hardly any soap in the shower. ☺
Review the following words; these are frequently used negative words and they are OK to use; just don't use more than one per sentence.

barely	never	none	nothing
hardly	no	no one	nowhere
neither	nobody	not	scarcely

5. Select the sentence from the list below that uses a double negative.
   A There never seems to be enough pencils to go around.
   B Nobody seemed to notice that I had a bad hair day today.
   C Not one of you said "thank you!"
   D Hardly none of them liked to swim.

Your Answer:

A ❑   B ❑   C ❑   D ❑

Analysis: **The correct answer is D.** The double negatives are "hardly" and "none." They don't belong in the same sentence. The correct way to write this sentence would be, "Hardly any of them like to swim." or "None of them liked to swim." Answers **A, B,** and **C** are correct.

Comparison of Modifiers

These are words, phrases, or clauses that describe or place a limit on the meaning of another word. *Adjectives* and *adverbs* are modifiers and they may be used to compare different things. There are three different degrees of modifiers; **positive, comparative,** and **superlative.**

How you use them depends upon how many things are being compared and how many syllables the modifier has.

> **NOTE: Use the comparative form when you are comparing two persons, places, or things.**
> **Use the superlative form to compare three or more persons, places, or things. The charts below should clarify this for you.**

POSITIVE	COMPARATIVE	SUPERLATIVE
bad	worse	worst
weak	weaker	weakest
well	better	best
bad	worse	worst
near	nearer	nearest
fast	faster	fastest
brave	braver	bravest
dry	drier	driest
simple	simpler	simplest
creative	more creative	most creative
happily	more happily	most happily
remorsefully	more remorsefully	most remorsefully
clearly	more clearly	most clearly
important	more important	most important
often	more often	most often
↓ These show decreasing comparison ↓		
safe	less safe	least safe
cautious	less cautious	least cautious
loyal	less loyal	least loyal
cute	less cute	least cute
serious	less serious	least serious

Review the sentences using the following three forms.
- He was **weak** when he first began weight training. (positive)
- He was **weaker** than anyone else in the gym. (comparative)
- He was the **weakest** person in Redondo Beach. (superlative)
- I thought the results of the game were **bad.** (positive)
- I thought the results of the game were **worse** than before. (comparative)
- I thought the results of the game were the **worst** I had ever seen. (superlative)

6. **In the sentences below, select the one whose modifier is used *incorrectly*.**
   A Steve believes he is bravest than his brother.
   B Steve believes he is braver than his brother.
   C Steve believes he is the bravest boy in town.
   D Steve believes he is brave.

Your Answer:

A ☐   B ☐   C ☐   D ☐

Analysis: **The correct answer is A.** The question asks for the *incorrectly* used modifier. The modifier in this sentence (bravest) is the superlative form, but it is being used with as a comparison. The correct way to write this sentence is the way it is written in Answer **C**.

Chapter Review and Quick Quizzes

Let's see how well you remember what we've reviewed in this chapter. The quizzes that follow should help to spark your memory. The answers are in the appendix in the back of the book.

SECTION I: CAPITALIZATION

DIRECTIONS: Using the word bank, complete the sentences by filling in the blanks with the word that best completes the sentence. Some words are repeated more than once, but they are listed more than once in the word bank.

> **Word Bank:** organization, capitalize, government bodies, associations, quotations, I, first, proper

Capitalize the _____ (1) word in every sentence, the pronoun _____ (2), the first word in a full-sentence _____, (3) and all _____ (4) nouns and adjectives. You must also _____ (5) words that name a particular section of the country, planets, stars, races, nationalities, language, and religions. _____ (6), _____ (7), and _____ (8) must also be capitalized.

SECTION II: SENTENCES

DIRECTIONS: Using the word bank, complete the sentences by filling in the blanks with the word that best completes the sentence. Some words are repeated more than once, but they are listed more than once in the word bank.

> **Word Bank:** imperative, declarative, exclamatory, sentence, interrogative

A _____ (1) is a group of words that expresses a complete thought. _____ (2) sentences make a statement. An _____ (3) sentence gives a command or makes requests. _____ (4) sentences express strong emotions or feelings. Sentences that ask questions are _____ (5) sentences.

SECTION III: SENTENCE STRUCTURE

DIRECTIONS: Using the word bank, complete the sentences by filling in the blanks with the word that best completes the sentence. Some words are repeated more than once, but they are listed more than once in the word bank.

> **Word Bank:** negative, verb, plural, subject, verb, superlative, comparative, verb, sentence, agreement, double, predicate

A _____ (1) is divided into two parts. One part, the _____ (2) tells whom or what the sentence is about. The _____ (3) tells something about the subject and contains the _____ (4) part of the sentence. When you have a singular noun you must have a singular_____ (5). When you have a _____ (6) noun, you must have a plural_____ (7). This is called subject-verb _____ (8). _____ (9) negatives happen when there are two _____ (10) words in the same sentence, such as "not" and "no." When you compare two persons, places, or things, you must use the_____ (11) form of the word. When three or more persons are compared you use the _____ (12) form of the word.

Chapter 10

Writing Strategies

This is where the fun begins! The CAHSEE offers two opportunities to write; one for each session of the test. The writing tasks will focus on anything from responding to a piece of literature or literary analysis to one of the many different writings that have been covered in the English-Language Arts Content Standards such as: expository, persuasive, biographical, or autobiographical, etc. What we will review in this chapter as well as in Chapter 11 are the skills you need to get through them successfully. Being able to write a well-thought, cohesive essay on the spot is challenging, but if you know specifically what they are looking for, the task seems less demanding. This chapter will get you through some of the nuts and bolts of writing, while Chapter 11 will focus more on the actual writing itself.

CHAPTER FOCUS: *Tips for Good Writing*
- *Sentence Beginnings*
- *Avoiding Word Repetition*
- *Word Choice*
- *Line Length*
- *Use of Sensory Imagery*
- *Audience/Tone/Focus*

                            Organization
- *The Prompt and How to Deal With It*
- *Prewriting/Brainstorming*
- *Rough Outline*
- *Introduction*
- *Body Paragraphs*
- *Conclusion*

                            Chapter Review and Guided Writing

Tips for Good Writing

Sentence Beginnings

When writing a paper of any length, **begin your sentences with different words.** There are a million and one words in the English language, so there is no need to repeat the word you use to begin your sentences. Again, *avoid repeating sentence beginnings*. It is OK to use prepositions (see list below as a reminder) at the beginning of your sentences, but it is frowned upon to use them at the end of your sentence. To avoid boring the reader, begin your sentences with something other than "The" or "I" over and over again. Use a different word to begin each sentence.

PREPOSITIONS—THOSE WITH MORE THAN ONE WORD ARE COMPOUND PREPOSITIONS

aboard	before	from	out
about	behind	in	over
above	below	in addition to	past
according to	beneath	in front of	since
across	beside	inside	through
after	besides	in spite of	throughout
against	between	instead of	to
along	beyond	into	toward
along with	but (except)	like	under
amid	by	near	underneath
among	concerning	next to	until
around	down	of	up
aside from	during	off	upon
as of	except	on	with
at			within
because of	for	on account of	without

Avoiding Word Repetition

Just as you would avoid repeating sentence beginnings over and over, avoid repeating the same words over and over throughout your writing. Some words have to be repeated (the, a, an), but most don't. When you write an autobiographical piece, avoid overusing "I"—especially at the beginning of a sentence. Certainly "I" needs to be used in an autobiographical piece, but there are many ways to write a sentence without using "I." Review the samples below.

- I went to the market and to the dry cleaners yesterday afternoon.
- Going to the market and to the dry cleaners were my goals yesterday afternoon.
- I believe that the drought will end long before October.
- From a personal perspective; the drought will end long before October.

> **NOTE:** If you maintain a rough objective of not repeating the same word more than twice (except in an autobiographical piece) in a paragraph, your writing will be more interesting.

Word Choice

Look at the words below and choose the words that sound better when you say them out loud:

drag	haul
rock to sleep	soothe
lucky	fortunate
begin	start
pest	nuisance
pick	select
big	enormous
a lot	numerous, many, infinite

(**NOTE:** a lot is *two words*!)

- **Words that sound better.** There are words that literally just sound better than others. Be conscious of the words you use. Choosing better-sounding words doesn't mean using *arrogant* or *haughty* words, or words that sound so intellectual or professional that it changes your natural style of writing. But words can make a difference.

- **Avoid colloquial language.** Being aware of your audience (the person reading the paper) is extremely important in writing for an exam. *Do not use colloquial language* or words that you would use with your friends such as *s'up*, or *ain't*, or *dude*. Colloquial language in a formal essay situation like the exit exam is definitely not appropriate.
- **Listen for the tone.** Words can alter the *sound* of your paper; keep that in mind when you write. When you want to sound *bold*, use bold-sounding words: *The time is now! We must be conscious of environmental needs; tomorrow will be too late.* When you want to sound *gentle*, use gentle-sounding words: *If one silently ponders the environmental issues at hand, one might conclude that the need for a more conditioned response to those issues are imminent.* Words make a difference, but choose them wisely.

Line Length

To avoid boring your reader to tears, try varying the lengths of your sentences; this means varying the number of words in them. For instance, in one paragraph with five sentences, you might have a sentence word count like this: sentence 1 = 8 words, sentence 2 = 5 words, sentence 3 = 12 words, sentence 4 = 7 words, sentence 5 = 10 words. The more you vary the lengths of your sentence, the more interesting your writing becomes to the reader. Even a one-word sentence is effective on occasion. A one-word sentence is bold and can add excitement, but you must be careful to do it at the right time. Imagine an essay or any paper for that matter, written with seven words in every sentence—it would become extremely tedious reading after awhile. Vary the lengths of your sentences!

Use of Sensory Imagery

Another way to put a spark into your writing is to use an occasional descriptive word. An occasional adjective will do wonders for a less exciting line of prose. Again, the key is to not overdo it. Too many adjectives or adverbs will have a negative effect. Look at the samples below to see the change a descriptive word or two can make; notice the difference between underdoing it and overdoing it.

1. Meredith likes ice cream sometimes.
2. Meredith enjoys chocolate ice cream on hot afternoons.
3. Meredith likes nothing more than to while away the hot, summer afternoon sitting in the shade of the weeping willow tree with a bowl of rich dark chocolate ice cream, savoring every morsel of tantalizing flavor.

Let's look closer at the samples. #1 is rather simple and lacks imagination. #2 is much better, and certainly more vivid than #1. Now, look at #3. We've gone from one extreme to another, obviously to make a point, but #3 is definitely overdone and a perfect example of what you *don't* want to do. Something between 1 and 3 is great. Remember to think of the *visualization* trick we learned in the reading comprehension chapter. Drawing a picture of the sentence in your mind might be an effective way to guide you. Remember, you are not writing a novel, just an essay.

Audience/Tone/Focus

We briefly touched upon the importance of audience earlier, but knowing who you are writing for (the audience), is important in that the style of your writing, the tone, and the focus of the paper will all be dependent upon just that. For the exit exam, your audience will be professionally trained readers who are judging the *skill level* of your writing. The importance of these writing tasks for your future is foremost on their mind and should be on yours as well. These essays should be formal in that you are writing for professional people, not your friends or family. That's your audience. Because they are professional doesn't mean that you should lose your natural style of writing or that they won't want to read a humorously written paper, it simply means that you, the writer, need to follow the rules of good writing. The tone of your paper depends on the topic and how it is approached. The tone can be serious, sarcastic, tongue-in-cheek, solemn, objective, enthusiastic, etc. Tone allows for creativity, but again, it all depends on the topic. Focusing on the specific topic or the subject matter gives it emphasis or clarity. Straying from the topic will cause the writing to become disjointed and you will lose the reader, and there in turn goes your score. What's important? Stay focused.

Organization

The Prompt and How to Deal with It

When you are writing for an examination like the CAHSEE, or any other in-class writing or impromptu essay, it is *vital* to understand the prompt or the topic. What **are** they asking you to write? Don't be surprised if the prompt is on a topic that arrives seemingly out of nowhere—something unusual—chances are good that it might be. If you are lucky, it will be a topic you are comfortable with, but be prepared for some major brainstorming if it isn't. Regardless of what the prompt is, this is what you are going to write about so read it over carefully. Reread it. Underline or jot down notes about the purpose of the essay. Reread it again. Ponder. Think. Reread the prompt. Get your mind *focused* on the task itself. Follow these steps; become very comfortable with the prompt.

- The Prompt: **American society has shifted from eating healthy food straight from the kitchen to prepackaged, ready-to-eat, or fast food from restaurants. Explain the benefits and the drawbacks for this shift in eating habits.**
- Read the prompt very carefully; take your time
- Underline the main ideas and what it is asking. For instance, you might jot down the following and then use them to jumpstart your brainstorm
  - Shift in eating habits
  - Fresh/healthy/from the kitchen
  - To prepackaged/quick/fast food
  - Drawbacks?
  - Benefits?
- Reread the prompt again.
- *Think/Ponder/Deliberate*/Focus.
- Reread yet again.
- Get ready to write.

Completing this little meditative exercise should help you concentrate and really focus on what you are being asked to write. It shouldn't take long—a couple of minutes, maybe five at the most. It is worth the time to get your mind going in the direction it needs to go.

Prewriting/Brainstorming

After reading and thoroughly understanding the prompt, the next step is the prewriting or brainstorming stage. Some people are anxious to jump into the writing and don't feel they need this step in the writing process, but I can guarantee that taking the few minutes that are needed to do this, is well worth the time and the people reading your paper will appreciate it as well. Your paper will be far more organized and *logical*, as opposed to just writing what comes to mind and taking a chance that your mind in all its greatness will do the job for you. Take time to brainstorm! There are many ways to brainstorm; use whatever you are comfortable with. Try one of these.

- **Webbing or clustering**
- **Notes or lists**

Most important to know about the brainstorming process is that you should immediately write down whatever comes into your mind about the topic. It doesn't have to be logical at this point, but the more you think and write, the more information you will have to draw from later. You will not use all of the information that accumulates on paper during the prewriting, but it is a great opportunity to get you thinking more concretely about the topic.

> **NOTE: In the back of your mind, think in threes. Most essays require five paragraphs and you will need three body paragraphs or three main topics to write about.**

- For webbing or clustering draw as many lines going in all directions off the main boxes as necessary.

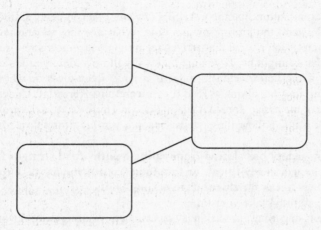

- When using lists, try bulleting (✸).
- After you have written all that has surfaced from your mind, look at the information and begin to organize what you have. This is where the next step, outlining, will come in.

Rough Outline

Many people panic when they are asked to outline. Outlining can be a challenging exercise at certain times, but do *not* panic about this outline. Basically, what you really want to accomplish with this outline is to set up your essay in a logical manner, drawing from the information you jotted down while brainstorming. Follow these steps in setting up your outline.

> Remember, you are the only one who is going to see this; it doesn't have to be a work of art, just a functional piece to help you write a good essay.

- INTRODUCTION
- TOPIC PARAGRAPH I
- TOPIC PARAGRAPH II
- TOPIC PARAGRAPH III
- CONCLUSION

✓ Spread these headings out, leaving four or five lines in between to write on, on one side of a piece of scratch paper.

✓ Looking at your brainstorm material, *select the three main topics first*. These should address the prompt directly. Most essays will require five paragraphs, so be sure you choose three strong topics that can be well supported.

✓ Once the main topics are chosen, begin listing or placing supporting evidence under each topic.

✓ For the introduction, you will need to decide on how you are going to hook the reader, either with a strong statement, a question, or a quote, and then introduce your three topics. We will discuss the writing of an introduction below.

✓ For the conclusion, you will need to summarize your writings and then end with a good line of writing. Again, we will discuss the ins and outs of conclusion writing later.

Introduction

The introduction to your essay, or your opening paragraph should do two things; *hook* your reader's attention and *identify the focus* of your writing, which is to explain, persuade, or entertain basically. How you write the introductory paragraph will affect the style, tone, and focus of the entire paper. Your opening paragraph is vital. First of all, you've got to get the reader's attention. There are many ways to do this; choose one that fits your style and go with it.

- Begin with a dramatic or "wow" (eye-opening) statement.
- Open with a funny anecdote or story to set a humorous tone.
- Start with an appropriate quote.
- Ask a thought-provoking question.
- List all of your main points in a straightforward, no-nonsense manner for a serious tone.

Once you have decided how you are going to begin, then begin. The introductory paragraph should include the following:

- The opening line or hook to get the reader's attention.
- A sentence detailing what each of the body paragraphs will be about. Write these details in a logical manner, as the body paragraphs that you write will follow the same order as they are listed in the introduction.
- A focus sentence or thesis statement of what you are going to *prove*. The thesis statement is usually found at the end of the introductory paragraph and is used as a concluding sentence, but it may be used as a boldly written statement right up front as well, serving two purposes: the hook and the thesis statement.

Thesis Statement Formula
=

A Specific Subject
+
A Specific Feature or Feeling
=
A Thesis Statement

Using the thesis statement formula above, let's look at the possibilities for the prompt that was given earlier.

- A Specific Subject = prepackaged, ready-to-eat, fast food
- + Specific Feeling or Feature = unhealthy
- = Thesis Statement = "Prepackaged, ready-to-eat foods, and fast foods so typical in the American diet today are unhealthy."

Body Paragraphs

From your introduction, you have laid out the plan for the body paragraphs. By writing a sentence about each of the body paragraph topics, you have prepared the writer for what's ahead. Each of the paragraphs should continue the tone and focus that you have started in the introduction and each paragraph should have about five sentences. Paragraphs typically are set up like this:

- Topic Sentence (see formula for topic sentence below).
- Supporting details that focus on the topic sentence to help make it clearer, explain, or describe the topic to the reader.
- Concluding or clincher sentence, which is used to summarize or restate the topic.

Topic Sentence Formula
=

A Limited or Focused Topic
+
A Specific Impression or Opinion
=
A Topic Sentence

Using this formula, let's work on a topic sentence for the prompt we were given earlier:
- Limited Topic = High fat content of convenience foods.
- Specific Impression = Causes obesity, heart disease, high blood pressure.
- = Topic Sentence = Obesity, heart disease, and high blood pressure are just a few of the health problems that plague the American public due to the high fat content of convenience foods.

Conclusion

Concluding paragraphs are intended to stress the important points, speculate the future outcome, suggest a solution, or raise further questions. Frequently, the concluding paragraph summarizes or briefly restates important facts and ties them all together, unifying the essay. It may then end with a thought-provoking statement or detail, giving the reader something to think about long after the reading is completed. Avoid preaching, worn-out endings like morals or clichés (see the brief list below). You don't want the reader to be turned off by something trite.

Avoid These: believe it or not, better late than never, calm before the storm, easier said than done, food for thought, grin and bear it, in the nick of time, last but not least, so far so good, and so on.

Final Hints for Concluding an Essay
Restate your main idea in a different manner, sum up your ideas and tie loose ends but not in a dull manner, close with a final thought that again allows the reader to take something away from your essay. Let the reader learn something from your efforts.

Chapter Review and Guided Writing

In getting you focused for writing, in this chapter we've gone over basic ideas and tips that will help you write an essay. We have looked at: avoiding the repetition of sentence beginnings, avoiding word repetition throughout the essay, varying the lengths of your sentences, paying attention to who is reading the essay (the audience), and to the words that you choose. We visited the structure and organization of the essay along with the steps of prewriting, which is brainstorming and outlining. Now, let's practice the prewriting aspect of essay writing; address each of the topics below as if they were going to be your essay topic on the exit exam. Practice these steps with each of them:

- Reading the prompt—over and over.
- Brainstorming—webbing, clustering, listing, etc.
- Outlining—roughly set up your paragraphs as you would if you were going to write the essay

Use a separate piece of paper for each topic. Practice having to think of something different, a topic you may not know much about, but are forced to come up with something to write. Try *all* of the topics, not just those you are comfortable with. In your prewriting, continue brainstorming until you have at least a main topic for three body paragraphs. Think of quotes or strong statements about the topic as you go along.

1. Music has a different meaning for everyone. It is a universal source of healing, comfort, and connection. Explain what music means to you.
2. Respond to the quote by Jacques Barzun: "History's most conspicuous feature is active change."
3. Being a hero or heroine or not being a hero or heroine is all about the difference in doing something or not doing something. Write about heroism.
4. Respond to Eleanor Roosevelt's statement from her speech to the United Nations in 1948 regarding the International Bill of Human Rights: "The unalienable right of all members of the human family is the foundation of freedom, justice, and peace in the world."
5. Physical fitness has been proven to be beneficial in many ways. Prove or disprove this statement.

Chapter 11

Writing Applications

As promised, this chapter will walk you through the process of writing essays for the examination. Following the English-Language Arts Content Standards for ninth and tenth grades, we will focus on the types of writing that could possibly be included on the exam. You will witness the writing process for each of the genres.

CHAPTER FOCUS: *Biographical or Autobiographical Narratives*

Response to Literature
  • *Integrating Quotations*

Expository Compositions

Persuasive Writing

Business Letters

Biographical or Autobiographical Narratives

A narrative is simply telling a story. In an exam situation, you might be asked to relay a personal experience in an autobiographical narrative or about someone else, a biographical narrative. Regardless of the type of paper, the process in getting to the finished product is the same: prewriting with a brainstorm and rough outline and then writing the essay. In a testing environment, chances are that there will be little time for revision, but if you do have time, by all means reread your writing and correct errors neatly. An autobiographical prompt might ask you to respond to one of these:

- an unforgettable or memorable experience
- memories of people
- memories of places
- memories of events
- memories of objects
- memories of family life

A biographical prompt might ask you to respond to:

- someone who has inspired you
- describing an experience through someone else's eyes
- an extraordinary person in your life
- a special person who is
  - helpful/kind
  - talented
  - patriotic
  - weird
  - happy
  - funny

Let's take a look at a prompt and begin the writing process.

The Prompt: In a narrative essay, relate the details of an unforgettable experience in your own life.

Prewriting: Brainstorm

walking on the street	listened to speaker
approached by a girl my age	felt uncomfortable
speaking in a familiar language	decided to get out quickly
asked to attend a meeting	invented a sudden and uncontrollable cough
invited to dinner	ran out coughing as fast as I could
there were lots of kids	never looked back

Prewriting: Informal Outline

Introduction: Attention Getting—Hook—Running
Body Par. I: Walking in a new town
Body Par. II: Meeting/Dinner
Body Par. III: Lecture
Conclusion: What you learned

Autobiographical Writing: Unforgettable Experience

Welcome to Your New Home!

My heart was racing, my lungs were aching, my legs exhausted, but there I was in the middle of a strange new town, running as fast as I could to get to my bicycle and then back home. What had just happened to me was an unforgettable incident that took me by complete surprise and when my thoughts return to the incident that occurred so long ago, it forces me to realize the value in trusting one's intuition. When something doesn't seem right, get out, get away as fast as you can, and never look back.

Just having moved to a new town, one that I was exploring by bicycle one sunny Saturday afternoon, I locked my bicycle onto a tree and began exploring on foot, the shops and side streets of my new hometown. The excitement and curiosity of exploring must have been visible on my face, because not three or four blocks from where my bicycle stood, I was approached by a girl who appeared to be my age. She asked if I was new in town and I confirmed her suspicion. Noticing that she had an accent, I asked her where she was from, and she said Germany. We had an immediate connection because I had just returned from spending some time there as an exchange student. During the course of our brief conversation, she asked if I would like to meet some local people, and trusting her I said "Sure."

The young woman gave me the address and directions to a house not far away and said that there would be quite a few people getting together at 3:00 and to come along then. Agreeing, we separated and I continued my exploration. As 3:00 arrived, I found my way to the house. Reaching the door, I heard friendly chatter and was greeted cheerfully and invited to come in. Entering the house, which wasn't a normal house with living room furniture, I saw that it was mostly empty, and that struck me as being rather odd. Hanging on the wall in the empty living room was a large portrait of someone I didn't recognize. I immediately had a very strange feeling. I was escorted into the dining room. There were about twenty young people gathered around a large wooden kitchen table that had plenty of room for everyone. We were offered bowls of chili, cornbread, salad, and milk. I declined the food, stating that I had just eaten, but in reality all sorts of suspicious thoughts were surfacing in my mind: "What if there's poison in the food?"

After everyone had finished eating, we were herded into another room of the house. It was filled with chairs and there was that portrait again. Who is this guy? I wondered, and again my suspicions were being challenged. A young man stood up and began to speak. He began talking about the man in the portrait. The speaker had such incredible charisma when he spoke that it would be mesmerizing, if not for the content of his speech. Listening for about ten minutes, I began to feel extremely uncomfortable. "How do I get out of here," I thought to myself. Not knowing how I arrived at this decision, I suddenly began coughing and choking, I stood up and headed for the door. The speaker questioned where I was going, but I shook my head and continued to cough and ran out of the room. Outside the door, there were two other men who also questioned me, but I continued my acting, motioned to my throat, continued the cough, and ran out the door.

And I ran! Breaking personal speed records, my bicycle was right where I left it. Hopping on, I pedaled as fast as I could. By the time my house was in sight, I was exhausted and out of breath. Sitting down in the comfort of my cozy little home, my thoughts spun around the unexpected incident. I was thankful for the fact that I was able to think quickly enough to get out of an uncomfortable situation, and even more thankful that I was safe at home. Reading the papers years later, I discovered who that man was in the portrait, and knowing what I know now, relying on my intuition was a good thing.

An autobiographical essay obviously will use the pronoun "I" frequently, but this writer manages to use "me" and "I" interchangeably, making the narrative flow easier. As a *hook*, the writer begins in the *middle of the action*. That is a good way to get the story going and the reader into it. Although this story was suspenseful, using this technique with humorous stories is also effective.

GOOD WRITING TIP REMINDERS:
- Vary lengths of sentence.
- Use different sentence beginnings (prepositions, *ing*-words, etc.).
- Watch word choice.

Response to Literature

In writing an essay about a piece of literature, on an exam, initially, the most important thing to do is to read the prompt. As instructed in the last chapter, make certain you thoroughly understand and absorb it before you complete the reading. Once you have sorted out what you need to focus on for the writing, the reading will be more focused as well. **Literary analysis** challenges you to present a *thoughtful* interpretation of a literary work. Your well-thought-out interpretation is going to depend upon how well you understand the work and this may take more than one reading. Remember, underline, take notes, do whatever you need to do to understand the reading and then proceed with the writing process. **NOTE:** *The example for this type of essay is going to be the literary analysis prompt that was actually given on the exam the first year.* Again, we will walk through the entire writing process, but know that this is the type of writing that will be expected of you.

The Prompt: In this essay about hummingbirds, the author describes many of the bird's characteristics. In each paragraph, she supports the purpose of her essay. What is the author's purpose for writing this essay about hummingbirds? What details does she give to support her purpose?

Write an essay in which you discuss the author's purpose for writing this essay on hummingbirds. What details and examples does she use to support the purpose of her essay?

Your response will be scored in two ways. One score will be given for how well you understand the selection and for the completeness of your response. A second score will be given for the overall quality of your writing.

Checklist for Your Writing

The following checklist will help you do your best work. Make sure you:
- ☐ Read the selection and the description of the task carefully.
- ☐ Use specific details and examples from the reading selection to demonstrate your understanding of the selections' main ideas and the author's purpose.
- ☐ Organize your writing with a strong introduction, body, and conclusion.
- ☐ Choose specific words that are appropriate for your audience and purpose.
- ☐ Vary your sentences to make your writing interesting to read.
- ☐ Use an appropriate tone and voice.
- ☐ Check for mistakes in grammar, spelling, punctuation, and sentence formation.

The Reading:

Hummingbirds

A flicker of color off to the side catches my eye as I walk along the back fence. It is a warm May morning, and I am outside early to see how the lettuce I've planted is doing. The wire mesh fence that edges my backyard is draped in blue and white morning glories just starting to open in the morning sun. The flicker of color off to my left becomes more pronounced, and I turn, expecting to see a butterfly hovering over the flowers. Instead, a tiny green bird with a red throat is hanging upside down above one of the morning glory blossoms. It is bigger than the butterfly and has a long bill protruding from its tiny head. The bird I have sighted above the morning glories is a male ruby-throated hummingbird, the most common species in the eastern United States.

The hummingbird is found only in the Western Hemisphere and belongs to the *Trochilidae* family, which contains more than 300 species of "hummers," as they are known among enthusiasts. Sporting an emerald green back with gray flanks and an iridescent ruby-red throat, this bird is also called *Joyas Voladoras* or "flying jewels" in Spanish because of its brilliant colors. With an average length of 3.5 inches and weighing only one eighth of an ounce, this hummingbird is incredibly quick, flying at speeds of 30 miles per hour and diving at speeds of up to 65 miles per hour. Hummingbirds' brains make up almost 2.5 percent of their overall weight, making them proportionately, the largest-brained in the bird kingdom, yet the flying muscles comprise some 30 percent of the bird's tiny weight. With these flying muscles, hummingbirds have the fastest wing rate of any bird, which helps them on their migratory paths that can cover up to 2,000 miles between Canada and Panama.

Hummingbirds use their speed to be aggressive feeders and become very territorial. They will fiercely fight one another for sources of food, diving and colliding in midair, and using their bills and claws as weapons. The tremendous speeds at which hummingbirds fly require that they feed constantly. One bird may visit a thousand flowers a day in search of food, munching on gnats, spiders, and sapsuckers, feeding every 10 minutes, and eating almost two thirds of its body weight every day. Like butterflies, they also feed on the pollen and nectar of flowers, sucking out this drink through a long tube-like tongue that absorbs the liquid through capillary action.

The most remarkable aspect of the hummingbirds' wing function is that the wings can rotate fully, making them the only birds that can fly forward, backward, up, down, sideways, or simply hover in space. This ability makes the tiny birds seem like magical creatures. They can hang poised over a blossom, or they can appear to stand still in midair. When hovering in this apparent stationary position, they are actually moving their wings in a figure-eight pattern, and from this position can move in any direction.

On this particular morning, I continue my stroll along the perimeter of the fence. I see two more hummingbirds: one a female that lacks the ruby iridescence at its throat, but that sports a white breast; the other, a male with the ruby gorget. Since it is spring, I wonder if the female is nesting or if her two eggs have hatched. I hope that each season brings more of the tiny, brilliant birds to my backyard, where I can enjoy their aerodynamic antics and their brilliant flashes of color.

Prewriting: Brainstorm
The prompt—what's the author's purpose?
To share her knowledge about the hummingbird
To share her love of the bird
Give details that support her purpose
Each paragraph supports her purpose

1ˢᵗ paragraph—all about body compositions
        hb found only in W. hemisphere. 300 + species
        Joyas Voladoras or flying jewels in Spanish—brightly colored
        3.5 inches weighs 1/8 of an ounce
        fast—flying speeds 30 mph diving speeds 65 mph
        hb brain 2.5% of body weight—largest-brained in bird kingdom
        flying muscles 30% of body weight
        fastest wing rate of any bird
2ⁿᵈ paragraph—all about feeding habits
        aggressive feeders—very territorial
        fight for food, diving, colliding use of bills/claws
        tremendous speed = need lots of food
        visit as many as 1,000 flowers/day—every 10 mins
        gnats, spiders, sapsuckers, pollen, nectar of flowers
        long tube-like tongue
3ʳᵈ paragraph—all about flying capability
        wing functions—can rotate fully
        only birds that can fly forward, backward, up, down, sideways, hover
        appear to be standing still in midair
        when hovering wings = figure 8 pattern

Prewriting: Informal Outline

Introduction: Hook—Attention Grabber—Did you know that hb can fly forward etc.
        Author's purpose is to share knowledge and interest
        Body composition, feeding habits, flying capabilities
Body Paragraph 1: Body composition—brain, weight, length,
Body Paragraph 2: Feeding habits—aggressive, 1,000 flowers, specific foods
Body Paragraph 3: Flying capabilities—all directions, wing functions
Conclusion: Amazing, unique, one-of-a-kind Superbird of the bird kingdom

Literary Analysis Essay:

Hummingbirds: The Superbird of the Species

Did you know that hummingbirds can fly forward, backwards, up, down, sideways, or hover in midair? This is one of many fascinating facts shared by the author who appears to be an expert on the subject. The author enthusiastically shares her knowledge of the hummingbird's body composition, its aggressive feeding habits, as well as its unique flying capabilities. From this article, we learn that the hummingbird is truly an amazing creature.

Found only in the Western Hemisphere, the hummingbird is not only one of the tiniest birds in the kingdom, but it is the largest brained and the one of the fastest as well. The hummingbird weighs only one eighth of an ounce and its average length is only 3.5 inches. That's tiny! As the largest-brained bird (proportionately) in the bird kingdom, the hummingbird's brain makes up about 2.5 percent of its body weight. Thirty percent of the hummingbird's body is flying muscles. These muscles allow the bird to have the fastest wing rate and to facilitate their 2,000-mile migration between Canada and Panama.

Considering the hummingbird is so tiny, it is remarkable that they are such aggressive feeders. Because they use up so much energy, they need to feed about every ten minutes and visit about a 1,000 flowers every day. These tiny birds use their bills and claws as weapons to get the food they need. They are extremely territorial. Eating roughly two thirds of its body weight in food every day, the hummingbird enjoys eating gnats, spiders, sapsuckers, pollen, and the nectar of flowers.

The hummingbird has a unique flying capability. It is the only bird that can fly in all directions and hover in midair as well. Its wings rotate fully, which is unusual in and of itself, but when the hummingbird hovers, its wings move in a figure-eight pattern. Flying forwards, backwards, up, down, sideways, and hovering is an incredible aspect of this bird.

After reading this article, it is easy to understand why the author is such a hummingbird enthusiast. This bird sets many records in the bird kingdom. From its speed and unique flying capabilities, to its aggressive and almost constant need to feed, and to its proportionately largest brain, the hummingbird is a fascinating creature. It is truly the Superbird of the bird kingdom.

After first reading the prompt—understanding it thoroughly—and then going on to the reading, it appears to be a fairly straightforward article. The author's tone is one of enthusiasm and therefore, the writer of this essay, carried that tone into her essay. The essayist's introduction *hook* was a question and the subsequent paragraphs supported the request of the *prompt* with *details from the article*. Although this essayist, did not use specific quotes, but reworded everything, she could have inserted an author's quote. Using quotes is a good way to use authentic information to support your writing. See the following to clarify the use of quotes.

- **Integrating quotations.** The use of quotes to support a point in question is valuable. Depending on the type of paper you are writing, the use of quotes will provide official legitimacy to your paper. In nonfiction writing, a quote from an expert in the field can be used to your advantage. In writing about fiction, a dialogue quote from a character that supports the issues you are writing about is advantageous as well. Follow these guidelines when using quotes in your writings:
- Make certain that the capitalization, punctuation, and spelling are the same as that found in the original work.
- Have a short quotation of four lines or fewer, which can be worked into the body of the paragraph that you are working on with quotation marks around it.
- Quotations that are long, five lines or more, should be set off from the rest of the writing. Indent ten spaces and double-space the material. Do not use quotation marks with these longer quotes.
- In using only part of the quote, use an ellipsis (. . .) in place of the words that you are removing from the quote. Use quotation marks as directed above.
- When you add anything to an author's quote use brackets [ ] to show exactly what you have added.

Expository Compositions

These explain or present information about a specific topic. They may give facts, directions, or explain an idea or define terms. The following are example topics for expository essays. On an exam, one will be chosen for you; it would be a topic broad enough that you should be able to spontaneously gather enough information to write about it.

- **The Causes of:** immigration, good grades, cheating, global warming, litter, water pollution, air pollution, dropouts, corporate greed, etc.
- **The Definition of:** a hero, rap, rock'n'roll, metric system, a conservative, a liberal, soul, the government, a disabled person, generation gap, friendship, loyalty, honesty, a good time, time, patriotism, etc.
- **How to:** operate a video system, grow vegetables, protect the environment, get in shape, impress your teacher, earn extra money, get a job, improve your memory, repair, etc.
- **Kinds of:** friends, dreams, neighbors, clouds, stereos, pain, vacations, heroes, compliments, happiness, censorship, chores, communication, etc.

> The Prompt: Define, in a thorough and thoughtful essay, the definition of a school.

Prewriting: The Brainstorm
School is a place to learn
A place to socialize
A place to participate in a club or sport
Study
Experience new things
Make new friends
Teachers, students, lockers, lunch period, classes, gym, sports
Library, offices, principal, counselors, career center
Benches, meeting place, the field
Cafeteria, snack shack, lunch carts—pizza, Chinese, sandwiches, Mexican, junk food
Different groups of people
Where you grow and develop physically, emotionally, and academically

Prewriting: The Informal Outline
Introduction: The hook, attention grabber—no more pencils, no more books
academic /emotional-social/ shaping future in participatory activities
Paragraph 1: academic
Paragraph 2: Character/social development
Paragraph 3: Shaping future
Conclusion: Not just an institution of learning

The Expository Essay:

"No more pencils, no more books, no more teachers' dirty looks." Superficially, when you think of school, something negative seems to surface in your mind. But if you honestly begin to consider school from a more philosophical standpoint, the definition you once had changes dramatically. Learning and academics is the foundation of education, but school not only builds intellect, it builds character and shapes your future as well. School is much more than pencils and books. School is where you begin to become who you are and school guides you to where you want to be.

Of course, you go to school to learn. School is English, science, mathematics, art, physical education, languages, history, social science, journalism, and the list goes on; this is what you "learn" at school. Teachers are there to instruct and to share their expertise. Each grade level builds upon the previous and as you move from one level to the next, your skills become more advanced. What you knew as a freshman seems elementary compared to what you know as a senior. And, that's the nature, the basic premise of school, academic learning.

But, there's more to school than academic learning, much more. School is where you develop as a person, socially and emotionally. Of course, each of us has a friend or group of friends that we socialize with, but socializing isn't all there is to it. When you bond with a few people, they often become confidants, sounding boards, and people to whom you are loyal. These friends help define you as a person. The people that you sit in class with day after day, also become a part of your social development. There are some people you laugh at because they are funny; there are some who are very quiet and seem difficult to get to know; there are others who are loud and boisterous and you only hope they can control themselves so that you won't get held after class. In classes, you meet a variety of people, and you begin to learn about yourself through these observations.

Participating in sports, clubs, and various activities is an indicator of your future as well. Specific interests that are discovered through school-sponsored activities and functions expand upon the depths of your personality. You are developing interests, and broadening your world. An interest in journalism could lead you to a career in that field. An interest in debate or MUN, could spark an interest in politics or diplomacy. The possibilities are almost endless. Participating in school activities really does have the possibility of shaping your future or at least providing guidance.

School is the beginning of your future. If you add together academic learning, social development, and participatory activities, that's the true definition of school. It is not just one-dimensional learning; school is an all-encompassing socially expanding experience that shapes your future, and what you get out of school is dictated by what you put into it. When you hear "No more pencils, no more books," think of all the opportunities to grow and not the one dimension of academics. School is growth.

The expository essay above, takes the three main points that the essayist came upon in his brainstorm and expands upon them. You can clearly see what he is attempting to get across to you, that school is much more than academics. His sentences begin with different words and he manages to develop his paragraphs quite thoroughly.

Persuasive Writing

This is one of the most common types of essays assigned, and is one that asks you to convince someone to come over to your side of thinking. In order to do this, you must first form your opinion, and then back it up with facts and details. In general, you must mention the opposing opinion and give details of its weakness without coming right out and saying something degrading or sarcastic. Most important in a persuasive essay is the *need* to be persuasive. Editorials, letters, cartoons, research papers, advertisements, pamphlets, and commercials are examples of persuasive writings.

Common topics for persuasive papers include something that needs improving, something that deserves support, something that everyone should see or do, something that is unfair, etc. Review the writing process below and the essay that follows.

> The Prompt: Choose a subject that you believe is unfair. In a well-written and well-thought-out essay, persuade the reader to believe as you do regarding the issue.

The Brainstorm: Wearing school uniforms is unfair
Because you lose self-identity
Lack of self-expression
Boring
Ho hummm
Everyone looks the same
Constitutional right

Opposing Argument: less comparison to others—less pressure to be cool
Less to worry about every morning—it is already decided.
Self-expression through shoes and hair.

> **The Informal Outline:**
>
> Introduction: Where are the founding fathers when we need them?
> Body Paragraph 1: Constitutional right of freedom of expression
> Body Paragraph 2: Lack of self-expression
> Body Paragraph 3: Opposing—safety issues/less competition, less pressure
> Conclusion:

The Persuasive Essay:

Freedoms Lost, Uniforms Gained

Help! Where are our founding fathers when we need them? The recent decree sent forth by the powers that be in our school that *all* students shall wear a white-collared shirt and dark navy pants or skirts should be abolished. Now! The First Amendment speaks of freedom of speech; choosing our own clothes is a freedom tied closely to that amendment and it is being denied us. We have lost our individuality; we have lost our freedom of expression—all in the name of safety. It is unconstitutional and we need to do something about it.

It used to be that getting up in the morning and deciding what to wear was fun. Wearing this with that or that with this, mixing, matching, rolling it up, rolling it down, blue socks, red socks, no socks. It was fun. Now, we get up, go to the closet, and choose a white-collared shirt and navy blue pants, no not the black pants or the jeans, the navy blue ones. Dressing for school has become boring, ho hummmmmmmmmmm. Yawn. We no longer are individuals, nor are we independent. All of that is lost, lost to the demands of those who would rather see us all look the same. There goes our individuality.

During lunch, when you look out over the field at everyone dressed in their white and blue, what do you see? A sea of similarity. Bobby looks like Fred, Fred looks like Steve, and Steve looks like Bobby. *Everyone looks the same!* It is as though we are being controlled by an academic big brother. This is much like the government in Ray Bradbury's book *Fahrenheit 451.* They didn't want anyone to think for themselves so they burned all the books so everyone would be on the same level. This is a similar idea; we have no freedom of expression, which is what being a teenager is all about. Freedom of expression is what we long for; conformity is what we live by. But no, oh no, we all look the same and this is not by our choice. We need to do something about it.

The adults who impose this ruling on us unsuspecting students believe that we will all be safe wearing our white and navy, being afraid that someone with an outside group affiliation will disturb the balance of things here at school. They also mistakenly believe that we will be less likely to be judgmental about what someone else is wearing or feel pressured to wear something because it is a fad. That's their argument, their rationale. Group affiliation or association should be under the control of parents and if necessary, the police. And, as far as fads go, that too is a need that teenagers need to fulfill on their own. Teenagers should be able to express themselves and that allows them to grow socially and emotionally. Developing self-expression is what being a teenager is all about.

Yes, without a doubt, our founding fathers would be disappointed in the restrictions and lack of choice that has been imposed upon us. Uniforms are boring. Uniforms deny us our freedom of expression. Uniforms have caused us to lose our identity. We are nothing but white and navy with legs—our minds are dormant—our lives, boring. We want to wear *real* clothes, we want to be normal teenagers, and we want to be free to express ourselves. It's all a part of growing up.

The essayist has a strong opinion, that's for certain. She doesn't like uniforms, but she manages to express herself boldly and not offensively. The topic paragraphs are supported with facts and arguments that are valid to someone her age. The writer also addresses the opposing opinion somewhat harshly, but validates her opposition with facts supporting the social and emotional needs of teenagers. Her conclusion is emotional without being offensive and it leaves the reader knowing her opinion and that was the point.

Business Letters

Business letters are intended to help you get information about something (letters of inquiry), to express an opinion about something (letter to an editor or official), and to order a product or to complain about one (a letter of complaint). Regardless of the type of letter you write, there is a formal format that should be followed. Most letters these days are formatted in a **full-block** style. This means that the left margins are lined up evenly. See the following sample.

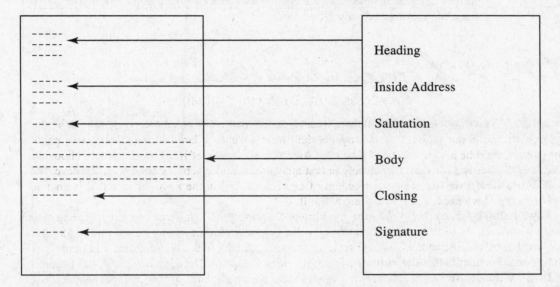

Identification of the parts of a letter:

- **Heading:** Includes the sender's address and the full date. The heading is placed about an inch down from the top of the page.

  2314 Hawthorne Blvd.
  Mayberry, CA 96722
  July 31, 2004

- **Inside Address:** Placed four to seven spaces below the heading. It should include the name and complete address of the person/company to whom the letter is being written. If the person has a title, place the title after his or her name.

  Darryl Scoffers, Director
  National Foundation for the Retired
  1413 18th Street SE
  Washington D.C. 20038

- **Salutation:** Placed two spaces or lines below the inside address, the salutation is for a specific person or persons. For an individual use: *Dear Mr. ——, Dear Ms. ——*, etc. For a company, a group, or an organization, use *Gentlemen, Dear Sirs, Dear Name of Company*, etc. Place a colon (:) at the end of the salutation.

  Dear Mr. Scoffers:

- **Body:** The body of the business letter is placed two lines below the salutation. The information written should be clear and concise, meaning to the point. Business-people, like almost everyone else, are busy, and prefer that the direction of the letter is matter of fact and not rambling. Do not indent, and leave a double space between paragraphs.

  It has come to my attention after visiting your establishment last week that your business could benefit from organization. What I observed was a variety of employees not focused on what they were doing and making mistakes because they were continually having to interrupt (or be interrupted) to locate a needed form or supply from a drawer that was being obstructed by something or someone else.

  My company, Time Savers, Inc., could be saving you time and money by organizing the way in which your office is set up and operated. Efficiency is our business. Let us help you make it yours. Please call (333) 566-7777 to discuss your options. We have been in business for over twenty years and have hundreds of satisfied customers as references. Let us make a difference in your office.

- **Closing:** Placed two spaces below the body and use *Yours truly*, *Sincerely*, or *Very Truly* for business letters, followed by a comma.

  Sincerely,

- **Signature:** Skip four lines after the closing and then *type* your name. Sign your name between the closing and your typed name.

Thomas Van Horne

Now, put it all together and you have a business letter.

2314 Hawthorne Blvd.
Mayberry, CA 96722
July 31, 2004

Darryl Scoffers, Director
National Foundation for the Retired
1413 18th Street SE
Washington D.C. 20038

Dear Mr. Scoffers:

It has come to my attention after visiting your establishment last week that your business could benefit from organization. What I observed was a variety of employees not focused on what they were doing and making mistakes because they were continually having to interrupt (or be interrupted) to locate a needed form or supply from a drawer that was being obstructed by something or someone else.

My company, Time Savers, Inc. could be saving you time and money by organizing the way in which your office is set up and operated. Efficiency is our business. Let us help you make it yours. Please call (333) 566-7777 to discuss your options. We have been in business for over twenty years and have hundreds of satisfied customers as references. Let us make a difference in your office.

Sincerely,

Thomas Van Horne

Thomas Van Horne

Chapter Review and Guided Writing

As you can see from the last two chapters, there is a lot of organization that goes into writing an essay. From prewriting to the final draft, essay writing takes preparation and thought. You will always find that some essays are easier to write than others. But, regardless of whether the topic is easy or challenging, knowing how to set it up and develop your thoughts in an organized manner is the important part. Being able to write a good essay doesn't happen overnight; it is a skill that has to be developed. Following the processes outlined in Chapter 10 and in this chapter will definitely help. But, you've got to continue to practice. Review the prewriting that you completed on the topics from Chapter 10. Using your brainstorms and outlines, begin writing the essays. Follow the suggestions below, which is a walk through the writing process. When you have finished each essay go back over it and look at your sentence beginnings, word choice, sensory imagery (added sparingly), sentence lengths, and structure of each of your paragraphs. Have someone else read them, if possible. Rewrite the essay until you are happy with the end product. You probably won't have time to rewrite the essay on the exit exam, but these essays are to help you achieve a passing score. Practice. Practice.

- Read topic thoroughly—over and over until you understand it well.
- Begin brainstorming—webbing, clustering, listing, etc.
- Circle main subtopics that are strong enough to be supported in a paragraph for the body of your essay.
- Make a rough outline of the essay, listing what is going where for each of the paragraphs, including a hook for the introduction.
- Begin writing the essay, being mindful of:
  - Sentence beginnings
  - Word choice
  - Avoiding repetition of words
  - Varying the lengths of your sentences
  - Adding an occasional adjective now and then
  - Staying with the topic in each paragraph
  - Making certain each topic is supported with facts or details and if possible, use a quote (if writing a literary analysis)
- Once the essay is complete with Introduction, Body Paragraphs, and Conclusion, reread it.
- Look at your paper and compare it to the list of things above to be mindful of. Rewrite sentences that repeat words, or change the structure of the sentence if you have been repetitious of sentence beginnings.
- Read the paper *aloud*! You can often catch errors in grammar or punctuation by reading it aloud. How does it sound?
- Repair what needs to be repaired.
- Rewrite the essay and reread; begin the process all over again, if necessary.
- Practice!

Chapter 12

Practice Exams

This is it! Your opportunity to practice taking the exam is now! The California Department of Education releases selected items from the test for this purpose. On the exam, there are a total of 94 multiple-choice questions and two essays to write. They are divided into two sessions. Following are two full-length exams. The testing material that is titled "California High School Exit Examination" at the top is part of the material that was given the first year of the exam; the remainder is simulated materials intended for practice purposes only. Good luck!

California High School Exit Examination

The following article discusses the sport of falconry. Read the article and answer questions <u>1</u> through <u>3</u>.

On Becoming a Falconer

Falconry, an ancient sport popular in the days of medieval royalty and jousting tournaments, is still practiced by dedicated enthusiasts around the world. Falconers work with predatory birds ranging from expert fliers, like the peregrine falcon, to less spectacular hawks, such as the redtail. Regardless of the species, training is the most important part of falconry. But it can be frustrating; so, you must be very patient.

The first step in training your falcon is to establish her trust in you. Initially, the falcon won't allow you near—she will "bate," or beat her wings wildly, as you approach. But gradually you will coax her to fly to you by offering food. The proud and cautious bird will be reluctant to fly to your hand, but she will want the food there and she will move back and forth on her perch, stamping her feet. Suddenly she will leave her perch.

She may land on your hand and bate off right away, frightened by her own bravery at first. Sooner or later, however, she will return to feed, and that will be her first careful step toward accepting you.

Why do falconers love this sport? To understand falconry, you must understand the special nature of the bond that forms between the falconer and the bird. The wild behavior and skills of the falcon are treasured by the falconer. The reward in working with a trained falcon is the companionship of a creature that can choose at any time to disappear over the horizon forever. You can join the honored tradition of falconers if you have patience and respect for wild creatures.

GO ON ▶

*Reprinted by permission, from *California High School Exit Exam (CAHSEE), English Language Arts, Practice Exam, Sessions 1 and 2*, California Department of Education, P.O. Box 271, Sacramento, CA 95812-0271.

This is a representative sample of items that were on the March and May, 2001 California High School Exit Examination. This is NOT an operational test form. Do NOT attempt to locate a passing score on these selected items.

SESSION 1 SESSION 1 SESSION 1 SESSION 1 SESSION 1

1. **What does the phrase *disappear over the horizon* mean in the following sentence?**

   > The reward in working with a trained falcon is the companionship of creatures that can choose at any time to disappear over the horizon forever.

   A return to the falconer
   B abandon the falconer
   C go behind some trees
   D fly very high

2. **According to the article, which of the following summarizes the main reason modern falconers love their sport?**
   F It allows them to work with a creature that is normally wild.
   G It was popular among royalty of the Middle Ages.
   H The falcon bates the falconer.
   J They like the reward money from the sport.

3. **Which of the following MOST accurately indicates the author's attitude toward the sport of falconry?**
   A It is not suited to modern times.
   B It can be frustrating.
   C It is best to work with a peregrine falcon.
   D It is a rewarding experience.

GO ON ▶

The following newspaper article is about electric cars. It is followed by a letter that responds to the article. Read the newspaper article and answer questions <u>4</u> through <u>6</u>.

Electric Cars Deserve a Second Look

As the world becomes increasingly populated, it is also becoming alarmingly polluted. We deplete more resources, produce more waste, and cause more cumulative environmental strain than ever before.

Fortunately, there are many ways that you can help counter the negative effects that we impose on the environment. One of these is driving an electric car. This benefits not only the environment, but also individual drivers.

Electric cars produce about 80 percent less pollution than cars with gas-powered motors. In fact, the only reason that electric cars produce any pollution at all is that their electric energy is generated by power plants; electric cars themselves emit no exhaust. When energy comes from large sources such as power plants, it's easier to regulate and monitor, so there's less waste than if the energy is generated by many smaller sources, such as the gas engines in individual cars. In addition, electric cars are simply more efficient than gas-powered cars for several reasons. First, electric cars have regenerative braking, which means that when you use the brakes in an electric car, the battery has a chance to recharge. Conversely, when you brake in a gas-powered car, you actually *use* energy.

Also, during the production of electric cars, more time and energy is spent making the design lighter and more aerodynamic so that there will be less drag from the wind. This allows them to travel farther using less energy than a gas-powered car would use to go the same distance.

In addition to the environmental benefits of driving electric cars, there are also financial and time-saving benefits for the drivers.

For one, they cost less to maintain. The cost of charging an electric car is about 20 percent of the cost of gas, and electric cars require far less maintenance than gas-powered cars. This is due, in part, to the fact that a lot of the things that go wrong with gas-powered cars simply aren't present in electric cars. Electric cars have no cooling system, fan belts, radiators, hoses, or oil—just a battery. There are fewer moving parts overall, so there are fewer potential problems. Also, electric motors have far greater longevity than combustion motors, so after the body of an electric car gives out, the engine can be reused in another body.

Furthermore, the federal government is encouraging electric car use by giving significant rebates for purchasing electric cars, and some states offer additional rebates. Electric cars can also save people time. While gas-powered cars require visits to a mechanic every few months, the only routine maintenance required by electric cars is replacing the battery every four years. And California, for example, recently passed a law making it legal for drivers of electric cars to use the carpool lanes any time—even if they are driving alone. This makes your trips much quicker and saves a considerable amount of time, especially in rush-hour traffic.

Overall, there are numerous benefits of driving an electric car. It may take a little getting used to, but in the long run, the use of electric cars can help preserve the environment and give people more time and money to be put to better use.

GO ON ▶

SESSION 1 SESSION 1 SESSION 1 SESSION 1 SESSION 1

4. **Read this sentence from the article.**

> Furthermore, the federal government is encouraging electric car use by giving significant rebates for purchasing electric cars, and some states offer additional rebates.

What is the meaning of the word *rebates* in Darrow's article?

F money returned
G tax credits
H awards
J additional guarantees

5. **Read this sentence from the article.**

> We deplete more resources, produce more waste, and cause more cumulative environmental strain than ever before.

What does the word *deplete* in Darrow's article mean?

A store away
B use up
C own
D ruin

6. **What is the purpose of Darrow's article?**

F to convince readers that their cars are using too much energy
G to show how to improve driving
H to convince people that electric cars are good
J to show how the environment can be saved

GO ON ▶

SESSION 1 SESSION 1 SESSION 1 SESSION 1 SESSION 1

The following selection is from the book *White Fang*. White Fang is about to make an important decision. Read the selection and answer questions 7 through 9.

White Fang

In the fall of the year when the days were shortening and the bite of the frost was coming into the air, White Fang got his chance for liberty. For several days there had been a great hubbub in the village. The summer camp was being dismantled, and the tribe, bag and baggage, was preparing to go off to the fall hunting. White Fang watched it all with eager eyes, and when the tepees began to come down and the canoes were loading at the bank, he understood. Already the canoes were departing, and some had disappeared down the river.

Quite deliberately he determined to stay behind. He waited his opportunity to slink out of the camp to the woods. Here in the running stream where ice was beginning to form, he hid his trail. Then he crawled into the heart of a dense thicket and waited. The time passed by and he slept intermittently for hours. Then he was aroused by Gray Beaver's voice calling him by name. There were other voices. White Fang could hear Gray Beaver's squaw taking part in the search, and Mitsah, who was Gray Beaver's son. White Fang trembled with fear, and though the impulse came to crawl out of his hiding-place, he resisted it. After a time the voices died away, and some time after that he crept out to enjoy the success of his undertaking. Darkness was coming on, and for awhile he played about among the trees, pleasuring his freedom. Then, and quite suddenly, he became aware of loneliness. He sat down to consider, listening to the silence of the frost and perturbed by it. That nothing moved nor sounded, seemed ominous. He felt the lurking of danger, unseen and unguessed. He was suspicious of the looming bulks of the trees and of the dark shadows that might conceal all manner of perilous things.

Then it was cold. Here was no warm side of a tepee against which to snuggle. The frost was in his feet, and he kept lifting first one forefoot and then the other. He curved his bushy tail around to cover them, and at the same time he saw a vision. There was nothing strange about it. Upon his inward sight was impressed a succession of memory-pictures. He saw the camp again, the tepees, and the blaze of fires. He heard the shrill voices of the women, the gruff basses of the men, and the snarling of the dogs. He was hungry, and he remembered pieces of meat and fish that had been thrown him. Here was no meat, nothing but a threatening and inedible silence.

His bondage had softened him. Irresponsibility had weakened him. He had forgotten how to shift for himself. The night yawned about him. His senses, accustomed to the hum and bustle of the camp, used to the continuous impact of sights and sounds, were now left idle. There was nothing to do, nothing to see nor hear. They strained to catch some interruption of the silence and immobility of nature. They were appalled by inaction and by the feel of something terrible impending.

He gave a great start of fright. A colossal and formless something was rushing across the field of his vision. It was a tree-shadow flung by the moon, from whose face the clouds had been brushed away. Reassured, he whimpered softly; then he suppressed the whimper for fear that it might attract the attention of the lurking dangers.

GO ON ▶

A tree, contracting in the cool of the night, made a loud noise. It was directly above him. He yelped in his fright. A panic seized him, and he ran madly toward the village. He knew an overpowering desire for the protection and companionship of man. In his nostrils was the smell of the camp smoke. In his ears the camp sounds and cries were ringing loud. He passed out of the forest and into the moonlit open where were no shadows nor darkness. But no village greeted his eyes. He had forgotten. The village had gone away.

Reprinted from *White Fang* by Jack London. (Troll Communications).

7. **This selection is BEST described as _____**
   A fiction.
   B a biography.
   C an article.
   D an essay.

8. **Which of the following BEST describes the relationship between Gray Beaver and White Fang?**
   F Gray Beaver is White Fang's owner.
   G Gray Beaver is White Fang's brother.
   H Gray Beaver and White Fang are members of the same tribe.
   J Gray Beaver and White Fang are father and son.

9. **Which of these sentences from the story BEST illustrates the wild side of White Fang's nature?**
   A "He knew an overpowering desire for the protection and companionship of man."
   B "Upon his inward sight was impressed a succession of memory-pictures."
   C "Here in the running stream where ice was beginning to form, he hid his trail."
   D "Then, and quite suddenly, he became aware of loneliness."

GO ON ▶

SESSION 1 SESSION 1 SESSION 1 SESSION 1 SESSION 1

The following poem is about the poet's inheritance. Read the poem and answer questions 10 through 12.

The Courage That My Mother Had

The courage that my mother had
Went with her, and is with her still:
Rock from New England quarried;
Now granite in a granite hill.

The golden brooch my mother wore
She left behind for me to wear;
I have no thing I treasure more:
Yet it is something I could spare.

Oh, if instead she'd left to me
The thing she took into the grave!—
That courage like a rock, which she
Has no more need of, and I have.

"The Courage That My Mother Had" by Edna St. Vincent Millay, from *Collected Poems*, Harper Collins. Copyright © 1954, 1982 by Norma Millay Ellis. All rights reserved. Reprinted by permission of Elizabeth Barnett, literary executor.

GO ON ▶

SESSION 1 SESSION 1 SESSION 1 SESSION 1 SESSION 1

10. **Which sentence BEST describes the theme of this poem?**
    F Personal strengths are more important than valuable objects.
    G Only a daughter can truly relate to her mother's feelings.
    H Having a golden brooch is better than nothing.
    J Unlike jewelry, traits such as courage are not valued.

11. **Which phrase from the poem creates a tone of sadness and regret?**
    A "Rock from New England quarried"
    B "Oh, if instead she'd left to me"
    C "The golden brooch my mother wore"
    D "That courage like a rock"

12. **Which pair of nouns BEST describes the mood of this poem?**
    F admiration and longing
    G distrust and jealousy
    H awe and amazement
    J anger and resentment

GO ON ▶

SESSION 1 SESSION 1 SESSION 1 SESSION 1 SESSION 1

The following article describes some of the many positive features of the state of California. Read the article and answer questions 13 through 15.

California: A Tribute

You do not have to travel to many other states to realize that California is a world unto itself. This is so widely recognized throughout the world that the state may as well be its own country. The Golden State is complete in itself, with a landscape ranging from desert to mountain to meadow to coastline. Snow-capped mountains rise up majestically before the ocean and golden deserts stretch over vast plains. Fragrant, fruit-scented breezes waft through valleys full of orange groves, apple orchards, and vineyards. Pacific Coast Highway, also known as Highway 1, charts a sometimes winding course, edging the rugged, sea-worn cliffs, curving through the mountains, and sailing by smooth beaches, past the white-capped waves of wild surf and the glassy blue waters of the bays. Pastoral scenes of cows grazing in pastures contrast with urban views of skyscrapers and city lights.

California's population is as diverse as its geography, including people from every race and ethnic background. This diversity intensifies the beauty of the state. Music, art, and dance from every country is widely performed in towns and cities throughout the state. Dragons lead parades for the Chinese and Vietnamese New Year celebrations, the music of guitars enlivens Cinco de Mayo festivals, and drumbeats quicken the heartbeat at Brazilian Samba and African dance performances in the parks. Music from summer jazz festivals drift over the communities while symphonies tune up for Bach festivals in the winter. All of these traditions and arts weave together to create an atmosphere of incredible intercultural beauty and richness.

The state's wealth is only increased by its eccentricities and its magic. In a small town north of San Francisco, there is a ranch populated with horses no bigger than large dogs. In the coastal city of Santa Cruz, a favorite tourist attraction is the Mystery Spot, a place where the rules of gravity don't seem to apply and objects actually roll uphill. The Monterey Bay region hosts hordes of regal black and orange Monarch butterflies during their annual migration. Swallows return yearly to San Juan Capistrano, perhaps because, like anyone who has traveled to California, they cannot bear to leave the Golden State forever.

13. What does the word *eccentricities* mean in the following sentence?

> The state's wealth is only increased by its eccentricities and its magic.

A unusual characteristics
B large population
C diverse climate
D famous beauty

GO ON ▶

SESSION 1 SESSION 1 SESSION 1 SESSION 1 SESSION 1

14. **Which of the following lines from the article BEST supports its theme?**
   F "Fragrant, fruit-scented breezes waft through valleys full of orange groves."
   G "The state's wealth is only increased by its eccentricities and its magic."
   H "You don't have to travel to many other states to realize that California is a world unto itself."
   J "California's population is as diverse as its geography."

15. **Which of the following strategies does the author use MOST frequently to describe California?**
   A imagery
   B statistics
   C expert opinion
   D historical fact

GO ON ▶

SESSION 1 SESSION 1 SESSION 1 SESSION 1 SESSION 1

The following is a story about two friends on a journey through the woods. Read the story and answer questions 16 through 18.

Out of the Woods

There was a strange silence in the woods. As they walked, Gabriel and Marie could hear birds chirping, pine needles crunching under their feet, the snapping of twigs, even the slight thump of the occasional pinecone landing softly.

They had been hiking as part of a project with their natural sciences class, a group that included thirteen other students and two teachers. As the trail became steeper, the others had started to fall behind. Mr. Davis had kept up with Gabriel and Marie most of the way, but had turned around to make sure the others were on the right track. Oblivious to the group, Gabriel and Marie had climbed and climbed as the trail narrowed and twisted and peaked.

"It's the soccer legs," said Gabriel, who was a forward on the varsity team. "I could climb forever."

"You'll be sore tomorrow," said Marie. "I, on the other hand, have the stamina. I'm used to logging miles and miles." Marie ran cross-country.

"Miles of flat land. We'll see who's sore tomorrow."

They thought they had been following a straight course, but when they finally turned back to find the group, they discovered that the trail had actually split.

"Are we lost?" Marie asked.

"How could we be lost? They were all here just a few minutes ago."

The sheer silence, the absence of other human voices, was overwhelming.

"Let's go back that way." Marie pointed at the trail leading in the opposite direction.

The trail led nowhere. Gabriel and Marie soon found themselves at a precipice, looking down into a canyon. Realizing that they were lost, they panicked. Every snap of a twig was a mountain lion stalking them; every twitch of a branch behind them was a bear getting ready to charge. They ran. They ran wildly, blindly into the forest ahead, slipping on pine needles, leaping over fallen branches, and looking—they later agreed, laughing—like complete idiots.

"You should have seen yourself," said Marie. She mimicked a terrified face.

"Me? You're the one who ran into a tree," said Gabriel.

"I tripped!"

"Okay, you just keep saying that." Gabriel looked around. "We can't be too far from everyone."

GO ON ▶

SESSION 1 SESSION 1 SESSION 1 SESSION 1 SESSION 1

"Then why can't we hear them?"

They followed the trail back and began to make their way down the mountain. Surely they could find their way to the beginning of the trail. As they hiked down, the landscape looked unfamiliar. "Hey, this doesn't look right," said Gabriel, stopping. "Look how the trail slopes up again."

"We didn't come this way."

"Let's go back," said Gabriel.

No, wait. Listen." Both were quiet. They heard a sound, a new sound.

"It's a creek!" The first trail had crossed over a creek!

The sound of water led them to the creek. Following the direction of the running water, they hiked along the creek bed until they reached another trail crossing.

"This is it!"

"I knew we'd find it," said Marie. They jumped the creek and ran down the trail. As the trail widened, they ran even faster, propelled by relief. Nearing the road where the bus was parked, they heard the sounds they had been longing to hear.

"Come on," yelled Gabriel. "Race!"

16. **What is the author's purpose in writing this story?**
    F to entertain the reader with a lesson about paying attention to the surroundings when hiking
    G to teach the reader a moral about the importance of listening to your leader
    H to present factual information about the best places in nature to hike
    J to give an explanation of what to take when preparing to go for a hike

17. **Read this sentence from the selection. What does the author convey in the sentence?**

> Every snap of a twig was a mountain lion stalking them; every twitch of a branch behind them was a bear getting ready to charge.

    A Although the woods had been strangely silent at first, now they were full of deafening noises.
    B The strange noises Gabriel and Marie heard were being made by different animals.
    C Every strange noise they heard was frightening to Gabriel and Marie.
    D The woods were full of dangerous animals that were stalking Gabriel and Marie.

18. **Read this sentence from the selection. In this sentence, the author is referring to the sounds of _____**

> Nearing the road where the bus was parked, they heard the sounds they had been longing to hear.

    F the voices of the other hikers.
    G the water in the creek
    H the pine needles crunching under their feet
    J he noises of other cars on the road where the bus was parked.

GO ON ▶

SESSION 1 SESSION 1 SESSION 1 SESSION 1 SESSION 1

The following article provides information about a potentially fatal source of food that koalas were given in zoos. Read the article and answer questions 19 through 21.

Deadly Leaves

Koalas, native to the Australian wilds, initially proved difficult to keep alive in zoos. Because koalas eat nothing but the leaves of the eucalyptus tree, zoos provided them with an unlimited supply of eucalyptus leaves. One zoo even planted eucalyptus trees in a special grove to ensure that the koalas had a continual supply of fresh leaves. However, koalas kept in captivity always died within a year of their arrival at the zoo.

Eventually it was discovered that eucalyptus trees that are less than five years old sometimes generate hydrocyanic acid in their leaves. Taking in small quantities of this acid is fatal to the koala. In their natural habitat, the koalas' senses tell them which eucalyptus trees have dangerous leaves, and they simply move on to other trees until they find leaves that are safe to eat. But in captivity, when their keepers unknowingly were giving them leaves contaminated with acid, the koalas were left with only two options: eat the poisonous leaves or starve. Either option was fatal to the trapped koalas.

Fortunately, today's zoos use special tests to distinguish between poisonous eucalyptus leaves and safe ones, and now koalas are eating well and thriving in zoos.

19. **What does the word** *contaminated* **mean in the following phrase?**

> But in captivity, when their keepers unknowingly were giving them leaves contaminated with acid, the koalas were left with only two options: eat the poisonous leaves or starve.

A carried with
B polished with
C poisoned with
D grown from

20. **What is the purpose of this article?**
F to inform
G to persuade
H to entertain
J to express opinion

21. **What tone does the author establish in the article?**
A critical
B hopeful
C straightforward
D humorous

GO ON ▶

SESSION 1 SESSION 1 SESSION 1 SESSION 1 SESSION 1

The following document is from a training manual for new employees at a restaurant. Read the document and answer questions 22 through 25.

Staff Responsibilities

Greeter

Your job as restaurant greeter requires that you greet every guest graciously and promptly. Upon greeting our early Sunset diners°, be sure to provide them with the regular dinner menu as well as the special Sunset menu. In addition, every evening the chef posts daily specials on the chalkboard at the entrance. Be sure to remind the customers of those dishes too, although those are not eligible for the early Sunset dinner price. (Diners who are seated after the early Sunset period should not receive the special Sunset menu.)

You will be working with a team of three additional members: the person who sets the table and provides the water and place settings (in some restaurants referred to as the busboy or busgirl), the waiter/waitress who actually takes each order to the exact specification of each diner, and the cashier who will accept the diners' payments upon their way out the door after dining. Your job is to ensure that the diners feel welcomed, informed, and served pleasantly in every possible way. For example, if their coats are draped across the back of their chairs, creating a potential floor hazard, please suggest that you would be happy to hang them in the closet at the rear of the restaurant.

Our goal is satisfied, happy customers who will return to visit us again and will recommend our establishment to their friends. Each employee plays an important role in ensuring that our goal is met. If you smile, greet diners pleasantly, seat them as soon as possible, and provide them with the full range of dinner options, you should have every reason to believe that you have done your job well. When customers have been unhappy in the past with the quality of service by the person who filled your position, it was generally because of one of the following reasons:

- Customers were left standing in the foyer as the entry greeter continued a personal phone call, ignoring them.
- Customers were not told of their eligibility or ineligibility for the early Sunset dinner.
- Customers' seating preferences were not honored.
- Early Sunset definition: a choice from one of five set-price, three-course meals available to diners seated before 6:00 P.M., Monday through Friday. Note: One of those choices is always vegetarian.

°Early Sunset definition: a choice from one of five set-price, three-course meals available to diners seated before 6:00 PM, Monday through Friday. Note: One of those choices is always vegetarian.

GO ON ▶

---

22. What is the purpose of this selection?

F to notify customers of Sunset dinner rules

G to describe the layout of the restaurant and kitchen

H to explain the duties of the greeter

D to make new employees aware of meal prices

23. The document provides the MOST information on _____

A how to satisfy diners.

B how to get along with coworkers.

C the restaurant's special offers.

D the restaurant's payment policy.

24. Read this sentence from the selection. According to this sentence, what must greeters do?

> Your job as a restaurant greeter requires that you greet each guest graciously and promptly.

F Welcome customers warmly as they arrive.

G Quickly list the specials for the customers.

H Ask the customers what they would like to drink.

J Seat customers as soon as possible.

25. The document provides the LEAST information on _____

A Sunset specials.

B food preparation.

C greeter responsibilities.

D customer dissatisfaction.

GO ON ▶

SESSION 1 SESSION 1 SESSION 1 SESSION 1 SESSION 1

The following is a brochure provided for new volunteers at a pet hospital. Read the brochure and answer questions 26 through 29.

Pet Hospital

Being a volunteer pet-aide in the Community Pet Hospital should be lots of fun! You were selected among many other applicants; so, you should feel proud that we recognize that you have something special to offer—a passion for helping pets in need. We also hope that over your eight-week assignment with us you will develop useful skills that will serve you well when you seek employment in the future. Who knows? Perhaps you will want to become a veterinarian too some day!

The pets who come to Community Pet Hospital are experiencing some level of illness, injury, or behavioral distress. Since we limit our practice to reptiles and birds, we can somewhat predict the activity in our waiting room on a typical day.

Frankly, we have more problems with pet owners than with the pets themselves. You will notice that we have signs prominently hanging around the office asking that owners should not release their pets from their pens or cages while in the office. Yet, nearly every day some owner will permit his or her pet to crawl or fly about the office anyway. As a volunteer pet-aide, we ask you to discourage owners from this practice. But if and when it happens, we appreciate your assistance in helping to retrieve the escaped pet.

When pets and their owners are being seated, we ask your assistance in separating, when possible, the birds from the reptiles. This can help prevent a noisy, distressing climate in the waiting room. Also, it is our experience that small birds need separation from large birds who tend to be aggressive and dominate the "chatter."

While we have only a few snakes in our practice, their visits can provoke upsetting responses in the waiting room. Both pets and owners seem to respond poorly to the presence of snakes in the waiting room, even if they are caged. So our receptionist tries very hard to arrange snake appointments at the end of the day when most of our other patients have been seen and are gone. We encourage your interest in every pet that comes through the door! However, there are a few basic rules in engaging with any pet patient that are essential for you to apply at all times:

1. The pet owner should be politely asked first if it is acceptable to interact with his or her pet.
2. Don't assume that a pet wants to interact with anyone except his or her owner. You may like the pet but it may not like you (or anyone else).
3. Refrain from physically handling any pet except as absolutely necessary. Pets that come to us are in distress, so additional handling by strangers may exacerbate their fragile condition.
4. Pets in distress may lash out in self-defense and could injure you with a bite or a painful scratch.
5. Excessive attention paid to one pet may make an owner of another pet somewhat jealous on the other side of the room.

GO ON ▶

6. Sometimes it seems that paying attention to a pet causes an owner to feel it is all right to open the pen or cage in order to demonstrate pet tricks. We don't want that!

7. In the event you do handle any pet in any way, immediately wash your hands well with disinfectant soap in the washroom. *Absolutely never* touch one pet immediately after handling another unless your hands are thoroughly cleaned between interactions.

Helping a pet in distress and its owner is a very rewarding experience. We're sure you will come to feel the satisfaction of your contributions to the harmony of our waiting room here at the Community Pet Hospital.

26. What does *retrieve* mean as used in following sentence?

> But if and when it happens, we appreciate your assistance in helping to retrieve the escaped pet.

F help take care of the pet
G help the owners take care of the pet
H help the pet escape and leave the office
J help catch the pet and put it back into its cage

27. Which of the following is NOT a correct rewording of the following sentence?

> Additional handling by strangers may exacerbate its fragile condition.

A A stranger handling a pet may worsen its condition.
B A stranger handling a pet may improve its condition.
C A stranger handling a pet may intensify its condition.
D A stranger handling a pet may aggravate its condition.

28. The main purpose of this brochure is _____
F to explain to veterinarians how to care for hurt animals.
G to explain to pet owners how to care for reptiles and birds.
H to explain why pet owners should use the Community Pet Hospital.
J to explain how volunteers should interact with pet patients and their owners.

29. Which of the following is NOT discussed in this brochure?
A how snake appointments are made by the receptionist
B how to release pets from their pens or cages while in the office
C why small birds need separating from large birds
D why the hospital can predict the activity in the waiting room on a typical day

GO ON ▶

SESSION 1 SESSION 1 SESSION 1 SESSION 1 SESSION 1

The following article offers information on hummingbirds. Read the article and answer questions 30 through 31.

Hummingbirds

A flicker of color off to the side catches my eye as I walk along the back fence. It is a warm May morning, and I am outside early to see how the lettuce I've planted is doing. The wire mesh fence that edges my back yard is draped in blue and white morning glories just starting to open in the morning sun. The flicker of color off to my left becomes more pronounced, and I turn, expecting to see a butterfly hovering over the flowers. Instead, a tiny green bird with a red throat is hanging upside down above one of the morning glory blossoms. It is bigger than the butterfly and has a long bill protruding from its tiny head. The bird I have sighted above the morning glories is a male ruby-throated hummingbird, the most common species in the eastern United States.

The hummingbird is found only in the Western Hemisphere and belongs to the *Trochilidae* family, which contains more than 300 species of "hummers," as they are known among enthusiasts. Sporting an emerald green back with gray flanks and an iridescent ruby-red throat, this bird is also called *Joyas Voladoras* or "flying jewels" in Spanish because of its brilliant colors. With an average length of 3.5 inches and weighing only one eighth of an ounce, this hummingbird is incredibly quick, flying at speeds of 30 miles per hour and diving at speeds of up to 65 miles per hour. Hummingbirds' brains make up almost 2.5 percent of their overall weight, making them proportionately, the largest brained in the bird kingdom, yet the flying muscles comprise some 30 percent of the bird's tiny weight. With these flying muscles, hummingbirds have the fastest wing rate of any bird, which helps them on their migratory paths that can cover up to 2,000 miles between Canada and Panama.

Hummingbirds use their speed to be aggressive feeders and become very territorial. They will fiercely fight one another for sources of food, diving and colliding in midair, and using their bills and claws as weapons. The tremendous speeds at which hummingbirds fly require that they feed constantly. One bird may visit a thousand flowers a day in search of food, munching on gnats, spiders, and sapsuckers, feeding every 10 minutes, and eating almost two thirds of its body weight every day. Like butterflies, they also feed on the pollen and nectar of flowers, sucking out this drink through a long tube-like tongue that absorbs the liquid through capillary action.

The most remarkable aspect of the hummingbirds' wing function is that the wings can rotate fully, making them the only birds that can fly forward, backward, up, down, sideways, or simply

GO ON ▶

SESSION 1 SESSION 1 SESSION 1 SESSION 1 SESSION 1

hover in space. This ability makes the tiny birds seem like magical creatures. They can hang poised over a blossom, or they can appear to stand still in midair. When hovering in this apparent stationary position, they are actually moving their wings in a figure eight pattern, and from this position can move in any direction.

On this particular morning, I continue my stroll along the perimeter of the fence. I see two more hummingbirds: one a female who lacks the ruby iridescence at its throat, but who sports a white breast; the other, a male with the ruby gorget. Since it is spring, I wonder if the female is nesting or if her two eggs have hatched. I hope that each season brings more of the tiny, brilliant birds to my backyard, where I can enjoy their aerodynamic antics and their brilliant flashes of color.

NOTE: You will be writing an essay based upon this reading, and you will be referring back to this reading.

30. **What does the word *pronounced* mean in the following sentence?**

> The flicker of color off to my left becomes more pronounced, and I turn, expecting to see a butterfly hovering over the flowers.

   F spoken
   G proclaimed
   H uttered
   J noticeable

31. **In the second paragraph, the phrase *largest brained* suggests that hummingbirds are _____**
   A monsterlike.
   B the largest bird species.
   C intelligent despite their small size.
   D top heavy in flight.

GO ON ▶

SESSION 1 SESSION 1 SESSION 1 SESSION 1 SESSION 1

The following article is a story about a dog lost at sea. Read the story and answer questions **32** through **35**.

Seafaring Dog Rescue

A two-year-old white terrier dog named Forgea, that lived aboard an Indonesian tanker since she was a puppy, was rescued by the crew of a tugboat from the decks of the abandoned ship, hundreds of miles off the coast of Hawaii after spending 24 days alone. She seems to be in good condition and is eating and drinking well.

The eleven-member crew was rescued from the ship when a fire broke out in the engine room, but Forgea had not been seen for several days since she had scampered below the decks of the tanker when fishermen from Honolulu attempted to coax her off the ship.

An earlier rescue attempt funded by the Hawaiian Humane Society costing approximately $48,000 was abandoned when it was believed that the ship had sunk with Forgea aboard. But, much to the relief of those people following the story, a happy ending occurred when the dog was coaxed into a portable kennel with food by the tugboat crew and brought to shore.

32. The first paragraph of this article, which might appear in a newspaper, is
    called a _____
    F sentence.
    G lead.
    H quote.
    J word.

33. A news article usually includes information that answers _____
    A who, what, where, when, why, and how.
    B a question about the paragraph.
    C the 5 Hs and a W.
    D ten facts.

34. The dog was _____ years old.
    F two
    G seven
    H eleven
    J one

35. The definition of the word *portable* in the last sentence of the article is _____
    A built to be permanent or stationary.
    B used in a harbor or port.
    C able to be carried.
    D constructed of metal.

GO ON ▶

SESSION 1 SESSION 1 SESSION 1 SESSION 1 SESSION 1

For questions <u>36</u> and <u>37</u> place the events of the following scenarios in the order that they most likely occurred.

        a. rivers and lakes rising above normal levels
        b. heavier and more frequent snowfall during winter
        c. severe water damage and people displaced from homes
        d. rapid thawing with heavy rainfall

36. Which of the following, places the events listed above in the correct sequence?
    F d b a c
    G d a c b
    H b d a c
    J b a c d

---

        a. an area brightened by neon light
        b. an area brightened by moon light
        c. an area brightened by incandescent light
        d. an area brightened by candlelight

37. Which of the following places the events listed above in the correct sequence?
    A a b c d
    B b d c a
    C b c a d
    D c a b d

GO ON ▶

SESSION 1 SESSION 1 SESSION 1 SESSION 1 SESSION 1

Indicate the reference tool that you would use to find the information listed in questions <u>38</u> through <u>41</u>.

38. The most direct highway route from Los Angeles to San Francisco
   F almanac
   G globe
   H thesaurus
   J map

39. Synonyms for the word *pedantic*
   A almanac
   B globe
   C thesaurus
   D map

40. The names of United States presidents
   F almanac
   G globe
   H thesaurus
   J map

41. The longitude and latitude of the continent of Australia
   A almanac
   B globe
   C thesaurus
   D dictionary

GO ON ▶

SESSION 1 SESSION 1 SESSION 1 SESSION 1 SESSION 1

For questions <u>42</u> through <u>47</u> read the groups of words listed and decide whether they are synonyms, antonyms, homonyms, or root words.

42. cover—conceal
    F synonyms
    G antonyms
    H homonyms
    J root words

43. hear—here
    A synonyms
    B antonyms
    C homonyms
    D root words

44. their—there
    F synonyms
    G antonyms
    H homonyms
    I root words

45. elegant—shabby
    A synonyms
    B antonyms
    C homonyms
    D root words

46. pedal—pedestrian
    F synonyms
    G antonyms
    H homonyms
    I root words

47. prosecute—defend
    A synonyms
    B antonyms
    C homonyms
    D root words

GO ON ▶

SESSION 1 SESSION 1 SESSION 1 SESSION 1 SESSION 1

Writing Task 1: Refer to Essay on Pages 192 and 193.

In this essay about hummingbirds, the author describes many of the bird's characteristics. In each paragraph, she supports the purpose of her essay. What is the author's purpose for writing this essay about hummingbirds? What details does she give to support her purpose?

Write an essay in which you discuss the author's purpose for writing this essay on hummingbirds. What details and examples does she use to support the purpose of her essay?

Your response will be scored in two ways. One score will be given for how well you understand the selection and for the completeness of your response. A second score will be given for the overall quality of your writing.

Checklist for Your Writing

The following checklist will help you do your best work. Make sure you:
- ☐ Read the selection and the description of the task carefully.
- ☐ Use specific details and examples from the reading selection to demonstrate your understanding of the selection's main ideas and the author's purpose.
- ☐ Organize your writing with a strong introduction, body, and conclusion.
- ☐ Choose specific words that are appropriate for your audience and purpose.
- ☐ Vary your sentences to make your writing interesting to read.
- ☐ Use an appropriate tone and voice.
- ☐ Check for mistakes in grammar, spelling, punctuation, and sentence formation.

STOP ●

*This is a representative sample of items that were on the March and May, 2001 California High School Exit Examination. This is NOT an operational test form. Do NOT attempt to locate a passing score on these selected items.

**THIS IS THE END OF
SESSION 1**

STOP

The following essay discusses the early years of the film industry. Read the essay and answer questions 48 through 50.

On Screen

The lights go down and flickering images appear on the big screen. Suddenly, the engaging grins of two small boys emerge in black and white. The tow-headed boys are dressed in coveralls and are sitting on a porch with their dusty bare feet propped on a wooden step below them. A long-eared hound lies listlessly at their feet. Catcalls and giggles fill the theater. "Hey, look. It's George and Roy. And there's old Tige snoozin' away at their feet." Applause and more giggles break out in the small movie house in eastern Tennessee.

It is early in the twentieth century, and movie houses are springing up all over the country. During this time, nickelodeons were being replaced by a new industry. The emerging movie houses were given regal names such as the "Majestic," the "Imperial," and the "Plaza." Patrons were happy to pay the price of a movie ticket, usually 10 cents, to see the latest moving picture show. At first, single reels of film were projected onto the big screen. By 1907, multiple reels of film were spliced together and presented as feature films. Early audiences were lured into the movie houses not only by the western feature shown every Saturday but also by the promise of seeing still shots of themselves up on the big screen.

Traveling photographers earned a living, moving from town to town, taking photos of local people—especially children—and nearby scenes of interest to show on the screen of the local movie house. The photographers were paid not only by the movie house owner who knew that local shots would be popular attractions, but they were also paid by the parents for the children's photographs. Eventually, these still shots of local people and places were replaced by newsreels of current news events, such as the world wars in Europe. These newsreels, precursors of the evening news now watched nightly, showed flickering images of real men going off to battle. The reels played before the main feature and were eagerly awaited reports of current events in the world.

The early features shown every Saturday and occasionally during the week were silent films. A local, talented pianist usually sat in the front of the theater supplying a musical backdrop for the action. Chords were pounded out as the western film star Tom Mix rode his horse up to the latest, staged train robbery or as the Keystone Cops investigated another caper. Soon, the feature films were no longer silent; recorded sound was now possible, and the feature films were now referred to as "talkies" and became even more popular. The films were all in black and white, with color films not appearing until the late 1930s.

With the invention of air conditioning, movie theaters became cool retreats in the midst of summer's sultriest weather. The Rivoli Theater in New York heavily advertised the cool comfort of the interior, and summer ticket sales soared. Eager patrons slipped in out of the heat and humidity and enjoyed the cooled air and watched the latest feature film.

GO ON ▶

---

*Reprinted by permission, from *California High School Exit Exam (CAHSEE), English Language Arts, Practice Exam, Sessions 1 and 2*, California Department of Education, P.O. Box 271, Sacramento, CA 95812-0271.

This is a representative sample of items that were on the March and May, 2001 California High School Exit Examination. This is NOT an operational test form. Do NOT attempt to locate a passing score on these selected items.

SESSION 2 SESSION 2 SESSION 2 SESSION 2 SESSION 2

Today, movie theaters remain cool havens of sight and sound entertainment. Popcorn and sodas are served in every theater—multiplexes showing several different features at once. Missing are the still photographs of local children or scenes. The only remaining clues as to their part in the development of the industry are faded copies of the original photographs now tucked away in dusty family albums.

48. **According to the passage, the reason the sound of Tom Mix's horse was accompanied by a piano was because _____**
   F viewers were making too much noise.
   G the horse made snorting noises that needed to be masked by the music.
   H films were silent since audio technology was not invented then.
   J Tom Mix preferred pianos to violins.

49. **The main idea of this essay is that movies _____**
   A are popular because theaters are air conditioned.
   B provide audiences with world news.
   C give parents an opportunity to entertain children.
   D have been entertaining audiences for many years.

50. **Which of the following sentences from the essay helps describe the setting of the opening paragraph?**
   F "Nickelodeons were being replaced by a new industry."
   G "The films were all in black and white, with color films not appearing until the late 1930s."
   H "Patrons were happy to pay the price of a movie ticket, usually ten cents, to see the latest moving picture show."
   J "The lights go down and flickering images appear on the big screen."

GO ON ▶

SESSION 2 SESSION 2 SESSION 2 SESSION 2 SESSION 2

The following article tells of children seining for minnows while also offering some general information on the fish. Read the article and answer questions 51 through 54.

Seining for Minnows

There was a time when hot summer days brought children outdoors to local creeks and streambeds to seine for minnows. Catching the small, silver fish was a fun, refreshing opportunity to wade in cool, rushing water on a sultry summer's day. Before setting out for the creek in their neighborhood, however, children first had to locate a burlap bag to use for a seine. Girls as well as boys loved this outdoor activity.

Upon reaching the creek bank, the children pulled off their socks and shoes and plunged feet first into the cold, sparkling water. Wading carefully over the pebbly bottom, they looked for the right spot where the minnows flashed. Seining for minnows was easiest if two children worked together. Grasping two corners of the bag, each child would stand in shallow water and slowly lower the bag until it was flat on the bottom of the streambed. Then, standing very still, the children would wait for the dirt and silt to settle and for the fish life in the stream to resume normal activity. The children would bend over and again grasp a corner of the bag in each hand and quickly and smoothly raise the bag straight up, keeping it as level as possible. A flutter and flicker of silver shades would glimmer all over the soaked burlap bag. Dozens of tiny silver fish almost too small to have been seen in the stream would now cover the rough bag. Tiny little fish bodies, startled by being thrust into the open air, would wiggle and turn, seeking an outlet back into the cold, clear water of their creek.

The joy of seining for minnows is that, once caught, the fish are thrown back into the water to continue their natural lives, perhaps to be scooped up by other children and then returned again to their watery home. So the net is swiftly lowered back into the stream, and the small fish swim off. Then the whole process is repeated once more as more minnows are scooped up and then released.

The small silver fish that children call minnows are really any small fish, regardless of species. Fish called *minnows* actually belong to the *cyprindae* family of fish. Members of the *cyprindae* family, including carp and goldfish among several dozen species, can be found in lakes and streams throughout the United States and much of the world.

Minnows often serve as primary consumers in a streambed, sometimes as bottom feeders to suck up ooze or eat algae. Others, as secondary consumers, ingest zooplankton, crustaceans, insects, worms, and other minnows. Some become food for tertiary consumers, being the prey of birds, mammals, and other fish. Those of a larger size are used as bait for sport fishing. Still others are used as food additives in livestock feeds.

GO ON ▶

This is a representative sample of items that were on the March and May, 2001 California High School Exit Examination. This is NOT an operational test form. Do NOT attempt to locate a passing score on these selected items.

SESSION 2 SESSION 2 SESSION 2 SESSION 2 SESSION 2

Their role as prey and their use as bait and food additives are not the only dangers that minnows face in the world today. The child with a burlap sack who goes out to seine for minnows on a summer's day now will find fewer glittering fish on the bag when it is lifted out of the stream. The destruction and alteration of the minnows' habitat due to land treatment and watercourse alteration threaten the future of this beautiful, hardy family of fish. If the children of tomorrow are to have the joy of seining for minnows on a hot summer's day, the natural habitats of our lakes and streams must be preserved.

51. What does the word *consumers* mean in the following sentence?

> Minnows often serve as primary consumers in a streambed, sometimes as bottom feeders to suck up ooze or eat algae.

    A those who shop
    B those who eat
    C those who occupy
    D those who serve

52. Which of the following questions about minnows could be BEST answered by further research?
    F What do minnows taste like to other species of fish?
    G Why do minnows prefer the taste of algae over minnows?
    H Have minnows ever been caught and released more than once?
    J How has land treatment affected the existence of minnows in the last decade?

53. This article suggests that minnows face which of the following dangers?
    A being used as prey or bait
    B eating poisonous food
    C lack of food
    D children playing in the water

54. What information supports the idea that minnows play an important role in the food chain?
    F Minnows do not eat algae.
    G Minnows only eat worms and insects.
    H Birds avoid eating minnows.
    J Birds and other minnows eat minnows.

GO ON ▶

SESSION 2 SESSION 2 SESSION 2 SESSION 2 SESSION 2

The following article discusses the inspiring efforts of Esther Morris in her crusade for women's suffrage. Read the article and answer questions 55 through 57.

A One-Woman Campaign

In the territory of Wyoming on September 6, 1870, for the first time anywhere in the United States, women went to the polls to cast their ballots. By 1870, the women's suffrage movement had battled unsuccessfully for 30 years on the East Coast. The big surprise to everyone was that the first victory for women's right to vote occurred in Wyoming, where there had been no public speeches, rallies, or conventions for the women's suffrage movement. Instead, there had been just one remarkable woman: Esther Morris. Her one-woman campaign is a classic example of effective politics. She managed to persuade both rival candidates in a territorial election to promise that, if elected, they would introduce a bill for women's suffrage. She knew that, as long as the winner kept his word, women's suffrage would score a victory in Wyoming. The winning candidate kept his promise to Esther Morris, which led to this historic Wyoming voting event in 1870.

55. According to the article, why is it surprising that Wyoming was the first state to allow women to vote?
A Few people knew about formal elections.
B There was a small population of women in the state.
C The community showed no obvious interest in the issue.
D The efforts on the East Coast were moving ahead quickly.

56. Which statement below BEST illustrates the time sequence of the events in the article?
F It begins in the present and then goes back in time to explain the preceding events.
G It begins on September 6, 1870 and then goes back in time to explain the preceding events.
H It begins in 1865 and moves to September 6, 1870 and then goes back to 1865.
J It all takes place on the same day—September 6, 1870.

57. Which sentence from the article explains specifically how Esther Morris succeeded in providing the women of Wyoming with the right to vote?
A "The big surprise to everyone was that the first victory for women's right to vote occurred in Wyoming, where there were no public speeches, rallies, or conventions for the women's suffrage movement."
B "In the territory of Wyoming in September 6, 1870, for the first time anywhere in the United States, women went to the polls to cast their ballots."
C "She managed to persuade both rival candidates in a territorial election to promise that, if elected, they would introduce a bill for women's suffrage."
D "She knew that, as long as the winner kept his word, women's suffrage would score a victory in Wyoming."

GO ON ▶

SESSION 2 SESSION 2 SESSION 2 SESSION 2 SESSION 2

The following is a rough draft of an essay discussing how opposite sides of the writer's brain might influence her personality and behavior. It may contain errors in grammar, punctuation, sentence structure, and organization. Some of the questions may refer to underlined or numbered sentences or phrases within the text. Read the essay and answer questions 58 through 59.

My Brain

Sometimes I think I am probably more right-brained, but other times I feel more left-brained. I love to play music and I especially like to make it up as I go along. For <u>anybody else to hear my music, they might think it sounds like noise</u>. My brother, for one, always complains about it.
(1)

I also like to write poetry. It is a way for me to put down on paper how I am really feeling. I write things in my poetry I would probably never tell anyone else. I am also pretty good at giving prepared speeches in my English class. Because I really like to do these kinds of things, I feel that I must be right-brained.

But there are other times I am not so sure about it. For example, I am really pretty good at math and other things that require me to be logical. <u>I also think I am pretty good at writing essays
(2)
about technical things, like explaining how things work. And I'm good at remembering things too.</u>

Though I guess I prefer right-brained activities and can do them more easily, I can do left-brained things pretty well if I have to. I like doing math problems. So I am not sure what that makes me!

---

58. **Which of the following sentences does NOT fit well in the paragraph in which it is found?**
    F "I love to play music and I especially like to make it up as I go along." (first paragraph)
    G "I also like to write poetry." (second paragraph)
    H "I like doing math problems." (fourth paragraph)
    J "For example, I am really pretty good at math and other things that require me to be logical." (third paragraph)

59. **What is the BEST way to combine the underlined sentences labeled 2?**
    A I am good at writing technical essays explaining how things work, and I also have a good memory.
    B Writing technical essays, I am good at explaining how things work and have a good memory.
    C I am good at explaining how things work by writing technical essays and remembering things too.
    D Explaining how things work and technical things are things I am good at writing essays about, and I have a good memory.

GO ON ▶

SESSION 2 SESSION 2 SESSION 2 SESSION 2 SESSION 2

The following is a rough draft of an article suggesting that water may have flowed (or does flow) on the planet Mars. It may contain errors in grammar, punctuation, sentence structure, and organization. Some of the questions may refer to numbered sentences or phrases within the text. Read the article and answer questions 60 through 61.

Water on Mars

(1) For a long time, people have considered the possibility that life may have once existed (or may still exist) on the planet Mars. (2) In 1910, Percival Lowell wrote a book suggesting that a large system of "canals" was built on Mars by a civilization that has since disappeared. (3) The "canals" were grooves on the planet's surface which Lowell saw through a telescope he believed had been built by Martians. (4) We now know that Lowell was wrong—there is no evidence of construction on Mars. (5) However, recent photos from the Mars Orbiter Camera suggest that, until very recently, liquid water flowed on the surface of the planet. (6) And some scientists believe that liquid water might still be found beneath the planet's surface. (7) Why is this important? (8) Well, scientists think that water is necessary for life to develop. (9) If there was (or is) water on Mars, it's quite possible that the planet may have supported life at some point during its history. (10) And if there was once life on Mars, the odds that there is life elsewhere in the Universe become much greater. (11) Scientists warn that it's too early to tell for sure, but maybe we Earthlings are not alone after all.

60. **What is the correct way to quote the sentence labeled 9?**
   F "If there was (or is) water on Mars, the author writes, it's quite possible that the planet may have supported life at some point during its history."
   G "If there was (or is) water on Mars," the author writes, it's quite possible that the planet may have supported life at some point during its history."
   H "If there was (or is) water on Mars," the author writes, "it's quite possible that the planet may have supported life at some point during its history."
   J Leave as is.

61. **What is the correct way to express the ideas in the sentence labeled 3?**
   A When the "canals" were observed by Lowell, he believed that they had been built by Martians through his telescope.
   B The "canals" were grooves on the planet's surface that, when observed by Lowell, appeared to have been built by Martians.
   C Through a telescope, Martians were those who Lowell believed had built the "canals."
   D Leave as is.

GO ON ▶

SESSION 2 SESSION 2 SESSION 2 SESSION 2 SESSION 2

The following is a rough draft of an essay that discusses the future of the human race in light of the Earth's history. It may contain errors in grammar, punctuation, sentence structure, and organization. Some of the questions may refer to underlined or numbered sentences or phrases within the text. Read the essay and answer questions <u>62</u> through <u>65</u>.

Killer Asteroids

People tend to think that the human race will be around forever. After all, we have been here for thousands of years and, many would argue, we dominate our planet in a way that no other species ever has. However, before we get too cocky, it would be wise to review the history of the Earth. Many species before us have enjoyed great success only to fall victim to changes in climate, <u>competing of</u> (1) other species, or other factors beyond their control. Could the same thing happen to human beings?

Just as humans do today, dinosaurs once walked the Earth in great numbers. Then, about 65 million years ago, an asteroid about 5 to 10 miles across hit the Earth and everything changed. The asteroid produced a deadly fireball, threw huge amounts of dust into the atmosphere, and caused tidal waves, fires, and terrible storms. With their world so <u>interestingly</u> (2) changed, the dinosaurs were helpless. And most scientists agree that it is only a matter of time before another asteroid hits the Earth, causing similar <u>trouble</u> (3).

Of course, humans might have a better chance of survival than the dinosaurs did. We can adapt to a wide range of climates, and <u>even underground living is something we can do if we have to</u>. (4) We might even be able to use our technology to locate the asteroid and destroy it before it strikes the Earth. However, there is one thing about which everyone can agree. If human beings ever have to face a killer asteroid from space, it is our brains rather than our brawn that will give us a fighting chance.

---

62. **Which phrase would BEST replace the underlined phrase labeled (1)?**
    F competed by
    G competition from
    H compete by
    J Leave as is.

63. **To more accurately describe how the impact of the asteroid changed the dinosaurs' world, the underlined word labeled (2) should be changed to** _____
    A dramatically.
    B strangely.
    C mysteriously.
    D thrillingly.

GO ON ▶

SESSION 2 SESSION 2 SESSION 2 SESSION 2 SESSION 2

64. **In order to achieve more precise meaning, the underlined word labeled (3) should be changed to _____**

    F danger.

    G worry.

    H destruction.

    J hassle.

65. **Which change to the underlined clause labeled (4) would make it more consistent with the first part of the sentence?**

    A even underground living can be done by us if we have to.

    B even we can live underground if we have to.

    C we can even live underground if we have to.

    D Leave as is.

GO ON ▶

SESSION 2 SESSION 2 SESSION 2 SESSION 2 SESSION 2

For questions <u>66</u> through <u>71</u>, choose the answer that is the most effective substitute for each <u>underlined</u> part of the sentence. If no substitution is necessary, choose "Leave as is."

66. When Tom <u>arrived at school he</u> was carrying all his books with him.
    F arrived at school, he
    G arrived, at school he
    H arrived at school he,
    J Leave as is.

67. <u>After, the volcano erupted, the</u> tiny tropical
    A After the volcano erupted, the
    B After the volcano erupted the
    C After the volcano erupts, the
    D Leave as is.

68. Responsibilities of the job include <u>greeting customers, escorting them to a table, and offering beverages</u>.
    F greeting customers, escort them to a table and offer a beverage.
    G to greet customers, escorting them to tables and offering a beverage.
    H to greet customers, escorting them to a table, and to offer a beverage.
    J Leave as is.

69. <u>A dog bit Tom's ankle while riding a bicycle.</u>
    A Riding a bicycle, a dog bit Tom's ankle.
    B While riding a bicycle, a dog bit Tom's ankle.
    C While Tom was riding a bicycle, a dog bit his ankle.
    D Leave as is.

70. <u>When the money was stolen by the bandits, the owner</u> of the store felt betrayed.
    F When the bandits stole the money, the owner
    G The money was stolen by the bandits. The owner
    H By the bandits the money was stolen. The owner
    J Leave as is.

71. <u>The poetry of Langston Hughes combining</u> the idioms of African-American speech and the rhythms of the blues.
    A The poetry of Langston Hughes will combine
    B The poetry of Langston Hughes combines
    C Langston Hughes' poetry combining
    D Leave as is.

GO ON ▶

SESSION 2 SESSION 2 SESSION 2 SESSION 2 SESSION 2

For questions 72 through 76, choose the word or phrase that best completes the sentence.

72. "We should _____ without the captain," the coach said impatiently.
   F proceeds
   G precede
   H precedent
   J proceed

73. _____ is a book written by Harper Lee.
   A To Kill A Mockingbird
   B "To Kill a Mockingbird"
   C To Kill a Mockingbird
   D "To Kill a Mockingbird"

74. The legendary goddess was the _____ of all the Greek deities.
   F beautifulest
   G more beautiful
   H most beautiful
   J most beautifying

75. The frightened pilot's face was ashen as he gingerly lowered the plane onto the Smiths' private _____ that time was running out for his ailing friend.
   A runway: he knew
   B runway, he knew
   C runway. He knew
   D runway but he knew

76. "Which of the three Olympic runners is the _____?" the spectator asked the judge.
   F more fast
   G fastest
   H most fastest
   J most faster

GO ON ▶

SESSION 2 SESSION 2 SESSION 2 SESSION 2 SESSION 2

Read the following story about three children exploring an abandoned house and then answer questions 77 through 80.

An Unexpected Adventure

Wanda, Buddy, and Allen, out for a leisurely afternoon walk in the forest near their home, suddenly came upon an abandoned old home. Questioning whether or not they should explore the inside, the three agreed to go ahead, vowing that they would not separate from each other.

The three friends walked cautiously up the steps of the steep front porch. Allen, being the bravest, carefully pushed the door until it opened with a loud rusty screeching sound, causing all of them to jump about a foot. Stepping inside the doorway, the shadowy room they entered with the towering ceilings was filled with cobwebs and broken furniture. Anxiously whispering their concerns, the three hesitantly continued their exploration.

Wanda led the way into the next room, which was equally as dark and menacing if you let your imagination go, when all of a sudden Crash! there was a loud unforgiving sound and directly behind her; Allen and Buddy had fallen through the cracked wooden floor.

"Help!" They both screamed. "Wanda, you've got to help!" "Who knows what's lurking down here? It's dark and musty and there are probably all kinds of rats and other creatures too frightening to mention just waiting to attack their next meal" shouted Allen. "Hurry! Wanda. Find a ladder to get us out," yelled Buddy. But Wanda, who was beginning to panic, wasn't sure what she could do to help.

77. **What problem needs to be solved before Wanda can rescue the boys?**
   A She needs to find a hammer and nails
   B She needs to locate a ladder
   C Wanda needs to stop laughing
   D She needs to pretend nothing happened.

78. **Which of the following BEST describes the general mood of the story?**
   F regretful
   G hopeful
   H humorous
   J suspenseful

79. **The *setting* of the story is _____**
   A in the forest.
   B at school.
   C at the beach.
   D in the mountains.

80. **The word *leisurely* in the first sentence means**
   F fast paced.
   G after awhile.
   H without hurry.
   J flowered.

GO ON ▶

SESSION 2 SESSION 2 SESSION 2 SESSION 2 SESSION 2

Read the following paragraph about a humanitarian and answer questions 81 through 82.

In 1929, Sister Teresa, who was born in Albania, arrived in India. Watching India struggle with foreign and domestic problems that brought suffering to the poor, she was disturbed by the suffering that surrounded her. One day as she traveled from Calcutta to a neighboring rural area, Sister Teresa had a vision. She realized that her mission in life was to aid the poorest citizens of Calcutta who were living in the slums of the city. That was in 1946 and by 1950 the Missionaries of Charity began their work. Sister Teresa became the spiritual leader of the group to whom she dedicated her life. Soon she became known as Mother Teresa and in 1979, was awarded the esteemed Nobel Peace Prize.

81. The main idea of this paragraph is _____
   A that Mother Teresa was born in Albania.
   B that Mother Teresa was a nun.
   C that Mother Teresa won the Nobel Prize.
   D that Mother Teresa dedicated her life to helping the poor.

82. The word *esteemed* in the last sentence of the paragraph means _____
   F to be highly regarded.
   G earning disrespect.
   H regretting the past.
   J fulfilling a dream.

GO ON ▶

SESSION 2 SESSION 2 SESSION 2 SESSION 2 SESSION 2

Read the following paragraph about Lyme disease and then answer questions 83 through 84.

A tick is a bloodsucking insect that lives on deer. This little mite burrows into your skin and can cause a serious illness if left untreated. This insect is the cause of a disease called Lyme disease. Although the disease is most commonly found in North America, it is now found all over the world. Lyme disease was originally discovered in Connecticut in the early 1970s, but now the disease is found in nearly every state in the United States. Within the first 3–32 days of the illness, or the first stage, a rash might appear along with a fever, headache, and pain in the muscles and joints. The rash may last as long as four weeks. If untreated, the disease can progress into chronic arthritis. Later stages involve disorders linked to the nervous system, heart, liver, or kidneys. The disease is treated with antibiotics in its early stage.

83. After reading the paragraph above, you may conclude that _____
  A the disease will go away on its own.
  B left untreated the rash will turn black.
  C late-stage Lyme disease will not affect you.
  D people believe they are cured if the rash disappears, but most likely they are not.

84. The word *chronic* found in the paragraph means _____
  F previously thought.
  G joint pains.
  H a time-keeping device.
  J affecting a person all the time.

GO ON ▶

SESSION 2 SESSION 2 SESSION 2 SESSION 2 SESSION 2

Read the following passage about a Japanese ceremony. Answer questions 85 through 87.

The Japanese tea ceremony can be a very elaborate occasion (1). Japanese tea is usually green (2). The tea ceremony is performed on special occasions in a very quiet and simply decorated room set aside especially for this purpose (3). Guests sit on floor cushions placed around a table (4). The tea master who is specially trained in this art prepares the tea (5). He or she follows precise rules in serving the tea (6). The ceremony is based on ancient Zen Buddhist beliefs that we should create beauty and serenity in the ordinary events of our everyday lives (7).

85. **Which sentence in the paragraph above is irrelevant or wouldn't change the story if it were removed?**
    A Sentence 5
    B Sentence 3
    C Sentence 1
    D Sentence 2

86. **From reading this passage you would conclude that _____**
    F the tea ceremony is not a serious occasion.
    G the tea is served with dessert.
    H the tea ceremony is a meaningful and respectful occasion.
    J the tea is black.

87. **The word *elaborate* in the first sentence of the passage means _____**
    A boring and tedious.
    B elongated.
    C with many parts or details.
    D simple, uncomplicated.

GO ON ▶

SESSION 2 SESSION 2 SESSION 2 SESSION 2 SESSION 2

For the following groups of words in questions <u>88</u> through <u>94</u>, determine if they are synonyms, antonyms, homonyms, or root words.

88. **geriatrics—gerontology**
   F synonyms
   G antonyms
   H homonyms
   J root words

89. **congregate—gather**
   A synonyms
   B antonyms
   C homonyms
   D root words

90. **abbreviate—expand**
   F synonyms
   G antonyms
   H homonyms
   J root words

91. **weight—wait**
   A synonyms
   B antonyms
   C homonyms
   D root words

92. **doldrums—hyperactive**
   F synonyms
   G antonyms
   H homonyms
   J root words

93. **face—visage**
   A synonyms
   B antonyms
   C homonyms
   D root words

94. **ocular—binocular**
   F synonyms
   G antonyms
   H homonyms
   J root words

GO ON ▶

SESSION 2 SESSION 2 SESSION 2 SESSION 2 SESSION 2

Writing Task 2:

By the time students enter high school, they have learned about many moments in history that have influenced our world today. Think about a moment in history you studied and consider its importance.

Write a composition in which you discuss a moment in history. Share its importance in today's world. Be sure to support the moment with details and examples.

Checklist for Your Writing

The following checklist will help you do your best work. Make sure you:
- ☐ Read the description of the task carefully.
- ☐ Use specific details and examples to fully support your ideas.
- ☐ Organize your writing with a strong introduction, body, and conclusion.
- ☐ Choose specific words that are appropriate for your audience and purpose.
- ☐ Vary your sentences to make your writing interesting to read.
- ☐ Check for mistakes in grammar, spelling, punctuation, and sentence formation.

STOP ●

**THIS IS THE END OF
SESSION 2**

STOP

In the following excerpt from a story by Edgar Allan Poe about a brother and sister who are cursed with a dreaded family disease, answer questions 1 through 5.

The Fall of the House of Usher   by Edgar Allan Poe

DURING the whole of a dull, dark, and soundless day in the autumn of the year, when the clouds hung oppressively low in the heavens, I had been passing alone, on horseback, through a singularly dreary tract of country; and at length found myself, as the shades of the evening drew on, within view of the melancholy House of Usher. I know not how it was—but, with the first glimpse of the building, a sense of insufferable gloom pervaded my spirit. I say insufferable; for the feeling was unrelieved by any of that half-pleasurable, because poetic, sentiment, with which the mind usually receives even the sternest natural images of the desolate or terrible. I looked upon the scene before me—upon the mere house, and the simple landscape features of the domain— upon the bleak walls—upon the vacant eye-like windows—upon a few rank sedges—and upon a few white trunks of decayed trees—with an utter depression of soul which I can compare to no earthly sensation more properly than to the after-dream of the reveler upon opium—the bitter lapse into everyday life—the hideous dropping off of the veil. There was an iciness, a sinking, a sickening of the heart—an unredeemed dreariness of thought which no goading of the imagination could torture into aught of the sublime. What was it—I paused to think—what was it that so unnerved me in the contemplation of the House of Usher? It was a mystery all insoluble; nor could I grapple with the shadowy fancies that crowded upon me as I pondered. I was forced to fall back upon the unsatisfactory conclusion, that while, beyond doubt, there are combinations of very simple natural objects which have the power of thus affecting us, still the analysis of this power lies among considerations beyond our depth. It was possible, I reflected, that a mere different arrangement of the particulars of the scene, of the details of the picture, would be sufficient to modify, or perhaps to annihilate its capacity for sorrowful impression; and, acting upon this idea, I reined my horse to the precipitous brink of a black and lurid tarn that lay in unruffled luster by the dwelling, and gazed down—but with a shudder even more thrilling than before—upon the remodeled and inverted images of the gray sedge, and the ghastly tree-stems, and the vacant and eye-like windows.

Nevertheless, in this mansion of gloom I now proposed to myself a sojourn of some weeks. Its proprietor, Roderick Usher, had been one of my boon companions in boyhood; but many years had elapsed since our last meeting. A letter, however, had lately reached me in a distant part of the country—a letter from him—which, in its wildly importunate nature, had admitted of no other than a personal reply. The MS. gave evidence of nervous agitation. The writer spoke of acute bodily illness—of a mental disorder which oppressed him—and of an earnest desire to see me, as his best, and indeed his only personal friend, with a view of attempting, by the cheerfulness of my society, some alleviation of his malady. It was the manner in which all this, and much more, was said—it was the apparent *heart* that went with his request—which allowed me no room for hesitation; and I accordingly obeyed forthwith what I still considered a very singular summons.

GO ON ▶

SESSION 1 SESSION 1 SESSION 1 SESSION 1 SESSION 1

1. **The tone of this excerpt is** _____
   A chivalric.
   B ecstatic.
   C melancholy.
   D bold and energetic.

2. **Read the following sentence from the excerpt.**

   > I looked upon the scene before me—upon the mere house, and the simple landscape features of the domain—upon the bleak walls—upon the vacant eye-like windows—upon a few rank sedges—and upon a few white trunks of decayed trees—

   Of the following, identify the example of personification.
   F upon the mere house
   G upon the bleak walls
   H upon the vacant eye-like windows
   J upon a few white trunks of decayed trees

3. **From the excerpt you can conclude that the narrator** _____
   A felt compelled to visit his childhood friend.
   B had no desire to see the friend.
   C was excited to see the friend.
   D was lost and found the wrong house.

4. **The word _oppressively_ in the sentence below means** _____

   > DURING the whole of a dull, dark, and soundless day in the autumn of the year, when the clouds hung _oppressively_ low in the heavens.

   F gently and very lightly
   G happily
   H logically and rhythmically
   J weighed down with cares or unhappiness

5. **From the title _The Fall of the House of Usher_ you might conclude that**
   _____
   A the Usher Family has a tendency to fall.
   B the house was haunted.
   C the house will no longer be standing
   D Roderick Usher wants to own the house.

GO ON ▶

The following is a primary source document of Abraham Lincoln's *The Emancipation Procla-mation*. Answer questions 6 through 9 regarding the document.

The Emancipation Proclamation

A Proclamation by the
President of the United States of America
Done at the City of Washington,
this first day of January,
in the year of our Lord
one thousand eight hundred and sixty three,
and of the Independence of the
United States of America the eighty-seventh.

By the President: ABRAHAM LINCOLN
WILLIAM H. SEWARD, Secretary of State.

Whereas, on the twenty-second day of September, in the year of our Lord one thousand eight hundred and sixty-two, a proclamation was issued by the President of the United States, containing, among other things, the following, to wit:

"That on the first day of January, in the year of our Lord one thousand eight hundred and sixty-three, all persons held as slaves within any State or designated part of a State, the people whereof shall then be in rebellion against the United States, shall be then, thenceforward, and forever free; and the Executive Government of the United States, including the military and naval authority thereof, will recognize and maintain the freedom of such persons, and will do no act or acts to repress such persons, or any of them, in any efforts they may make for their actual freedom.

"That the Executive will, on the first day of January aforesaid, by proclamation, designate the States and parts of States, if any, in which the people thereof, respectively, shall then be in rebellion against the United States; and the fact that any State, or the people thereof, shall on that day be, in good faith, represented in the Congress of the United States by members chosen thereto at elections wherein a majority of the qualified voters of such State shall have participated, shall, in the absence of strong countervailing testimony, be deemed conclusive evidence that such State, and the people thereof, are not then in rebellion against the United States."

Now, therefore I, Abraham Lincoln, President of the United States, by virtue of the power in me vested as Commander-in-Chief, of the Army and Navy of the United States in time of actual armed rebellion against the authority and government of the United States, and as a fit and necessary war measure for suppressing said rebellion, do, on this first day of January, in the year of our Lord one thousand eight hundred and sixty-three, and in accordance with my purpose so to do publicly proclaimed for the full period of one hundred days, from the day first above mentioned, order and designate as the States and parts of States wherein the people thereof respectively, are this day in rebellion against the United States, the following, to wit:

Arkansas, Texas, Louisiana, (except the Parishes of St. Bernard, Plaquemines, Jefferson, St. John, St. Charles, St. James Ascension, Assumption, Terrebonne, Lafourche, St. Mary, St. Martin, and Orleans, including the City of New Orleans) Mississippi, Alabama, Florida, Georgia, South Carolina, North Carolina, and Virginia, (except the forty-eight counties designated as West Virginia, and also the counties of Berkley, Accomac, Northampton, Elizabeth City, York, Princess Ann, and

GO ON ▶

SESSION 1 SESSION 1 SESSION 1 SESSION 1 SESSION 1

Norfolk, including the cities of Norfolk and Portsmouth[)], and which excepted parts, are for the present, left precisely as if this proclamation were not issued.

And by virtue of the power, and for the purpose aforesaid, I do order and declare that all persons held as slaves within said designated States, and parts of States, are, and henceforward shall be free; and that the Executive government of the United States, including the military and naval authorities thereof, will recognize and maintain the freedom of said persons.

And I hereby enjoin upon the people so declared to be free to abstain from all violence, unless in necessary self-defense; and I recommend to them that, in all cases when allowed, they labor faithfully for reasonable wages.

And I further declare and make known, that such persons of suitable condition, will be received into the armed service of the United States to garrison forts, positions, stations, and other places, and to man vessels of all sorts in said service.

And upon this act, sincerely believed to be an act of justice, warranted by the Constitution, upon military necessity, I invoke the considerate judgment of mankind, and the gracious favor of Almighty God.

In witness whereof, I have hereunto set my hand and caused the seal of the United States to be affixed.

6. **A primary source document is** _____
   F   a copy or imitation.
   G   an unauthorized document.
   H   an unbelievable and unrealistic document.
   J   an original document.

7. **The author of *The Emancipation Proclamation* is** _____
   A   Frederick Douglas.
   B   Abraham Lincoln.
   C   Mary Todd Lincoln.
   D   John Wilkes Booth.

8. **President Lincoln declared** _____ **to be the defenders of this new freedom of all repressed citizens of the United States.**
   F   the executive, military, and naval authorities
   G   private citizens throughout the country
   H   Britain and France
   J   primarily the southern states

9. **In the following sentence, what does the word *abstain* mean?**

   > And I hereby enjoin upon the people so declared to be free to abstain from all violence, unless in necessary self-defense;

   A   to continue in the same manner
   B   to follow the rules
   C   to interject laws without force
   D   to keep oneself from some action

GO ON ▶

Read the following excerpt from Guy de Maupassant's short story "The Necklace." Answer questions 10 through 12.

The Necklace   by Guy de Maupassant

The girl was one of those pretty and charming young creatures who sometimes are born, as if by a slip of fate, into a family of clerks. She had no dowry, no expectations, no way of being known, understood, loved, married by any rich and distinguished man; so she let herself be married to a little clerk of the Ministry of Public Instruction.

She dressed plainly because she could not dress well, but she was unhappy as if she had really fallen from a higher station; since with women there is neither caste nor rank, for beauty, grace and charm take the place of family and birth. Natural ingenuity, instinct for what is elegant, a supple mind are their sole hierarchy, and often make of women of the people the equals of the very greatest ladies.

Mathilde suffered ceaselessly, feeling herself born to enjoy all delicacies and all luxuries. She was distressed at the poverty of her dwelling, at the bareness of the walls, at the shabby chairs, the ugliness of the curtains. All those things, of which another woman of her rank would never even have been conscious, tortured her and made her angry. The sight of the little Breton peasant who did her humble housework aroused in her despairing regrets and bewildering dreams. She thought of silent antechambers hung with Oriental tapestry, illumined by tall bronze candelabra, and of two great footmen in knee breeches who sleep in the big armchairs, made drowsy by the oppressive heat of the stove. She thought of long reception halls hung with ancient silk, of the dainty cabinets containing priceless curiosities and of the little coquettish perfumed reception rooms made for chatting at five o'clock with intimate friends, with men famous and sought after, whom all women envy and whose attention they all desire.

When she sat down to dinner, before the round table covered with a tablecloth in use three days, opposite her husband, who uncovered the soup tureen and declared with a delighted air, "Ah, the good soup! I don't know anything better than that," she thought of dainty dinners, of shining silverware, of tapestry that peopled the walls with ancient personages and with strange birds flying in the midst of a fairy forest; and she thought of delicious dishes served on marvelous plates and of the whispered gallantries to which you listen with a sphinx-like smile while you are eating the pink meat of a trout or the wings of a quail.

She had no gowns, no jewels, nothing. And she loved nothing but that. She felt made for that. She would have liked so much to please, to be envied, to be charming, to be sought after.

She had a friend, a former schoolmate at the convent, who was rich, and whom she did not like to go to see any more because she felt so sad when she came home.

But one evening her husband reached home with a triumphant air and holding a large envelope in his hand.

"There," said he, "there is something for you."

She tore the paper quickly and drew out a printed card which bore these words:

"The Minister of Public Instruction and Madame Georges Ramponneau request the honor of M. and Madame Loisel's company at the palace of the Ministry on Monday evening, January 18th."

Instead of being delighted, as her husband had hoped, she threw the invitation on the table crossly, muttering:

"What do you wish me to do with that?"

GO ON ▶

"Why, my dear, I thought you would be glad. You never go out, and this is such a fine opportunity. I had great trouble to get it. Everyone wants to go; it is very select, and they are not giving many invitations to clerks. The whole official world will be there."

She looked at him with an irritated glance and said impatiently: "And what do you wish me to put on my back?"

10. **The character Matilde can best be described as** _____
  F bold.
  G energetic.
  H content.
  J unhappy.

11. **Matilde envied** _____
  A those who were more intelligent.
  B those who were more wealthy.
  C those who gave freely to charity.
  D those who were clerks.

12. **Her reaction to her husband's pride in obtaining an important invitation was** _____
  F genuine sincerity.
  G much excitement.
  H anger.
  J hesitation.

GO ON ▶

SESSION 1 SESSION 1 SESSION 1 SESSION 1 SESSION 1

Read the following paragraph about a leader from the Mexican state of Oaxaca and then answer questions 13 through 15.

Eight-Deer was an important leader of the Mixtec people in southern Mexico from 1030 until the time of his death at age 52. His story is recorded on seven colorful codices. Codices are picture books without words that describe the lives of the people in the area.

Each of the seven codices describe Eight-Deer's rule and he was known for the many battles he fought against neighboring peoples. With each victory, Eight-Deer would murder the opposing leader, marry their wives and adopt their children. By the end of his rule, he had acquired a very large family with many wives and endless children.

One of Eight-Deer's fight for victory lasted over eight years. It was with the rulers of a town called Xipe-Bundle. This battle, which was eventually won by Eight-Deer, is described in many of the codices. Eventually there was a personal challenge between the two rulers, and although Eight-Deer won, he offered a wonderful funeral for the defeated ruler.

After a 33-year rule, Eight-Deer was finally captured and sacrificed as he had done so many times before.

13. **The purpose of this story is** _____
   A to tell about codices.
   B to demonstrate the power of pictures.
   C to tell the story of a powerful leader.
   D to provide historic facts about Mexico.

14. **From reading the paragraph, you can conclude that the author believes that Eight-Deer is** _____
   F a legendary leader and fighter of the Mixtec people.
   G a religious figure.
   H a man who took advantage of people.
   J a man who was not well liked by his people.

15. **There are _____ codices that describe the life of Eight-Deer.**
   A 52
   B 7
   C 2
   D 19

GO ON ▶

SESSION 1 SESSION 1 SESSION 1 SESSION 1 SESSION 1

Read the following Aesop Fable about a wily wolf and then answer questions 16 through 19.

The Wolf in Sheep's Clothing

A wolf found great difficulty in getting at the sheep owing to the vigilance of the shepherd and his dogs. But one day it found the skin of a sheep that had been thrown aside. The wolf put the skin on over his own pelt and sauntered cavalierly down among the sheep. The lamb of the sheep to which the skin belonged recognized the scent and began to follow the wolf in the sheep's clothing. Leading the lamb away from the others, the wolf soon made a meal of her and for some time he succeeded in deceiving the sheep, and enjoyed hearty meals.

Appearances are deceptive.

16. **In most fables, there is a moral to the story. The moral to this story is** _____
   F it pays to be clever.
   G it pays to be a wolf.
   H do not rely of outward appearances.
   J it doesn't pay to be a sheep.

17. **The word *vigilance* in the following sentence means** _____

   > A wolf found great difficulty in getting at the sheep owing to the vigilance of the shepherd and his dogs.

   A watchful, on the lookout for danger.
   B stubborn, unforgiving.
   C intelligent and crafty.
   D frightened.

18. **In the following sentence, what does the word *cavalierly* mean?**

   > The wolf put the skin on over his own pelt and sauntered *cavalierly* down among the sheep.

   F enthusiastically
   G with arrogance
   H shyly with hesitation
   J fiercely

19. **In the sentence above, what word might help you to define the word *cavalierly*?**
   A put
   B pelt
   C down
   D sauntered

GO ON ▶

SESSION 1 SESSION 1 SESSION 1 SESSION 1 SESSION 1

Read the following poem by Emily Dickinson and answer questions 20 through 23.

Dear March, Come In!
by Emily Dickinson

Dear March, come in!
How glad I am!
I looked for you before.
Put down your hat—
You must have walked—
How out of breath you are!
Dear March, how are you?
And the rest?
Did you leave Nature well?
Oh, March, come right upstairs with me,
I have so much to tell!

I got your letter, and the bird's;
The maples never knew
That you were coming,—I declare,
How red their faces grew!
But, March, forgive me—
And all those hills
You left for me to hue;
There was no purple suitable,
You took it all with you.

Who knocks? That April!
Lock the door!
I will not be pursued!
He stayed away a year, to call
When I am occupied.
But trifles look so trivial
As soon as you have come,
That blame is just as dear as praise
And praise as mere as blame.

20. **The narrator of the poem seems to be talking to March. The literary device used in this poem is called _____**
    F onomatopoeia.
    G simile.
    H personification.
    J metaphor.

GO ON ▶

SESSION 1 SESSION 1 SESSION 1 SESSION 1 SESSION 1

21. The narrator states:

> *"You must have walked—*
> *Look how out of breath you are!*

What is meant by these two lines?
A that with March comes wind
B that March walked upstairs with her
C that March has respiratory problems
D that there is nothing to fear

22. These lines reference a human trait. What trait is it?

> The maples never knew
> That you were coming,—I declare,
> How red their faces grew!

F greediness
G embarrassment
H arrogance
J mischievousness

23. From this poem you can conclude that the poet _____
A would like to change the world.
B prefers winter.
C resents the coming of spring.
D is happy to see the spring.

GO ON ▶

SESSION 1 SESSION 1 SESSION 1 SESSION 1 SESSION 1

For questions <u>24</u> through <u>29</u> select the correct answer for each.

24. Mrs. Smith gave us <u>explicit</u> directions to the meeting. <u>Explicit</u> means
    F incomplete.
    G strange.
    H confusing.
    J specific.

25. The principal was prepared to <u>adjourn</u> the meeting. <u>Adjourn</u> means
    A to prepare for.
    B to discontinue.
    C to lead.
    D to question.

26. The third-period class approached the project with much <u>zeal</u>. <u>Zeal</u> means
    F a soap product.
    G enthusiasm.
    H questioning.
    J shyness.

27. The team had <u>qualms</u> about attending the banquet without the coach. <u>Qualms</u> means
    A confusion.
    B avoidance.
    C hesitation.
    D aggravation.

28. There is a <u>consequence</u> for not completing your homework. <u>Consequence</u> means
    F estimation.
    G legalization.
    H realize.
    J result.

29. We all appreciate the <u>diligent</u> efforts of our teaching staff. <u>Diligent</u> means
    A destructive.
    B carefree.
    C summarize.
    D hard-working.

GO ON ▶

SESSION 1 SESSION 1 SESSION 1 SESSION 1 SESSION 1

Read the following paragraph and answer questions 30 through 32.

Have you ever seen a street performer singing, playing an instrument, dancing or doing magic tricks? These street performers are similar to troubadours who entertained people on the streets during the Middle Ages. They told stories and were often accompanied by a lute, which is an instrument similar to a guitar. The tradition of the troubadours began in 11th century France. But, at that time, troubadours were nobles and kings who wrote poems that were set to music. Originally, they did their own singing, but by the 13th century, these noblemen hired traveling performers to do it for them. It was through these singers that the French citizens heard news of war, love, and politics.

30. **The tradition of troubadour singing began in the _____ century.**
    F 11th
    G 12th
    H 13th
    J 14th

31. **Troubadours are similar to the _____ of today.**
    A hobos
    B pilots
    C street performers
    D bakers and chefs

32. **A lute is _____**
    F what robbers steal from victims.
    G a guitarlike instrument of old.
    H a wooden toy made for sailing.
    J a string tied between two trees.

GO ON ▶

Read the following excerpt from Edgar Allan Poe's poem about an unusual bird and answer questions <u>33</u> through <u>36.</u>

The Raven
by Edgar Allan Poe

Once upon a midnight dreary, while I pondered, weak and weary,
Over many a quaint and curious volume of forgotten lore—
While I nodded, nearly napping, suddenly there came a tapping,
As of some one gently rapping, rapping at my chamber door.
"'Tis some visitor," I muttered, "tapping at my chamber door—
Only this and nothing more."

Ah, distinctly I remember it was in the bleak December,
And each separate dying ember wrought its ghost upon the floor.
Eagerly I wished the morrow;—vainly I had sought to borrow
From my books surcease of sorrow—sorrow for the lost Lenore—
For the rare and radiant maiden whom the angels name Lenore—
Nameless here for evermore."

And the silken sad uncertain rustling of each purple curtain
Thrilled me—filled me with fantastic terrors never felt before;
So that now, to still the beating of my heart, I stood repeating,
"'Tis some visitor entreating entrance at my chamber door—
Some late visitor entreating entrance at my chamber door;
This it is and nothing more."

Presently my soul grew stronger; hesitating then no longer,
"Sir," I said, "or Madam, truly your forgiveness I implore;
But the fact is I was napping, and so gently you came rapping,
And so faintly you came tapping, tapping at my chamber door,
That I scarce was sure I heard you"—here I opened wide the door;—
Darkness there and nothing more.

Deep into that darkness peering, long I stood there wondering, fearing,
Doubting, dreaming dreams no mortal ever dared to dream before;
But the silence was unbroken, and the stillness gave no token,
And the only word there spoken was the whispered word "Lenore!"
This I whispered, and an echo murmured back the word "Lenore"—
Merely this and nothing more.

GO ON ▶

33. The line *Doubting, dreaming dreams no mortal ever dared to dream before;* demonstrates the use of _____
   A alliteration.
   B onomatopoeia.
   C simile.
   D personification.

34. What is most noticeable about each six-line stanza?
   F Each stanza uses personification.
   G All stanzas contain the name Lenore.
   H The first line of each stanza contains references to weather.
   J The last three lines of each stanza rhyme.

35. The tone of the poem seems to be _____
   A dark and mysterious.
   B lively and full of vigor.
   C respectful.
   D arrogant.

36. From reading the excerpt, the visitor at the narrator's door is most likely _____
   F a neighbor needing to borrow sugar.
   G a tree brushing against it in the wind.
   H the raven.
   J a creature from the unknown.

GO ON ▶

SESSION 1 SESSION 1 SESSION 1 SESSION 1 SESSION 1

The following passage contains many capitalization and punctuation errors. Answer questions <u>37</u> through <u>40</u> regarding the correct punctuation and capitalization of the paragraph.

the nine muses were the children of zeus and mnemosyne (1). Originally they were goddesses of memory but it is told that zeus was asked to create the muses to sing the great deeds of the gods (2). traditionally authors invoked a particular muse for inspiration for their work (3). The names of the muses are: calliope the chief muse associated with epic poetry poetic inspiration and eloquence clio is the muse of history and heroic exploits euterpe is the muse of music and lyric poetry thalia is the muse of gaity comedy and pastoral life melpomene is the muse of tragedy terpisichore the muse of dancing choral son and lyric poetry erato the muse of erotic and love poetry miming and geometry polhymnia the mus of chant and inspired hymn and urania the muse of astronomy (4).

37. **The correct capitalization of sentence (1) is:**
    A The nine Muses were the children of zeus and Mnemosyne.
    B the nine muses were the children of Zeus and Mnemosyne.
    C The nine Muses were the children of Zeus and Mnemosyne.
    D The nine muses were the children of Zeus and Mnemosyne.

38. **The correct punctuation of sentence (2) is**
    F a comma after the word *memory* and a period at the end of the sentence.
    G a period at the end of the sentence.
    H a comma after the word *memory.*
    J a comma after the word *memory* and an exclamation point at the end.

39. **The two words that need to be capitalized in sentence (3) are**
    A Muse and Work.
    B Traditionally and Authors.
    C Traditionally.
    D Traditionally and Muse.

40. **The two most common errors in sentence (4) is the need for**
    F commas and semicolons.
    G commas.
    H periods and colons.
    J exclamation points and colons.

GO ON ▶

SESSION 1 SESSION 1 SESSION 1 SESSION 1 SESSION 1

**In the following passage there are words missing from each sentence. In answering questions
41 through 44, select the word that best completes the sentences in the passage.**

Gabriel Daniel Fahrenheit was a German born in Poland. He was _____ (1) at the age
of 15, but lived most of his life in Holland and England. Fahrenheit _____ (2) and then
manufactured the first practical mercury-in-glass thermometer. He also invented the scale for measuring temperature that is named after him. Although Galileo, an Italian inventor, _____ (3)
a airthermoscope long before this, Fahrenheit's was the first of the most accurate instruments of its
kind. Today only two of his reference points are in use on the Fahrenheit scale used for measuring
_____ (4) pressure; 32 degrees (freezing) and 212 degrees (boiling). Fahrenheit was elected
to Britain's Royal Society before his death in 1736. He was 50 years old.

41. **Which word below BEST completes the sentence marked (1)?**
    A arrogant
    B orphaned
    C ignorant
    D athletic

42. **Which word below BEST completes the sentence marked (2)?**
    F ate
    G stole
    H broke
    J perfected

43. **Which word below BEST completes sentence marked (3)?**
    A invented
    B watched
    C staged
    D destroyed

44. **Which word below BEST completes the sentence marked (4)?**
    F atmospheric
    G English
    H critical
    J elongated

GO ON ▶

SESSION 1 SESSION 1 SESSION 1 SESSION 1 SESSION 1

Read the following letter from the blind and deaf Helen Keller to the poet John Greenleaf Whittier. Answer questions 45 through 47 in regards to the poem.

TO JOHN GREENLEAF WHITTIER
Nov. 27, 1889.

Dear Poet,

    I think you will be surprised to receive a letter from a little girl whom you do not know, but I thought you would be glad to hear that your beautiful poems make me very happy. Yesterday I read "In School Days" and "My Playmate," and I enjoyed them greatly. I was very sorry that the poor little girl with the browns and the "tangled golden curls" died. It is very pleasant to live here in our beautiful world. I cannot see the lovely things with my eyes, but my mind can see them all, and so I am joyful all the day long.

    When I walk out in my garden I cannot see the beautiful flowers but I know that they are all around me; for is not the air sweet with their fragrance? I know too that the tiny lily-bells are whispering pretty secrets to their companions else they would not look so happy. I love you very dearly, because you have taught me so many lovely things about flowers, and birds, and people. Now I must say, good-bye. I hope [you] will enjoy the Thanksgiving very much.

From your loving little friend,
HELEN A. KELLER.

45. The letter above is an example of a _____
    A poem.
    B short fiction.
    C primary source document.
    D a contract.

46. The letter indicates the author's _____ of Whittier's poems.
    F appreciation
    G dislike
    H ambivalence
    J distrust

47. The author's outlook on life despite her disabilities appears to be _____
    A glamorous.
    B pessimistic.
    C mournful and sad.
    D enthusiastic and upbeat.

GO ON ▶

SESSION 1 SESSION 1 SESSION 1 SESSION 1 SESSION 1

Writing Task 1:

In your community there is a need to improve something—whether it is adding more parks for recreation, a better library, or an improved litter program; there is always something that can be made better.

In a formal letter to your city councilperson, write about the need you feel strongest about in your community. Describe the problem and how it can be improved. Provide a solution, not merely a letter of complaint. Be proactive in the letter.

Checklist for Your Writing

The following checklist will help you do your best work. Make sure you:
- ☐ Read the description of the task carefully.
- ☐ Use specific details and examples to fully support your ideas.
- ☐ Use a block letter format with all items lined up correctly on the left of the page.
- ☐ Organize your writing with a strong introduction, body, and conclusion.
- ☐ Choose specific words that are appropriate for your audience and purpose.
- ☐ Vary your sentences to make your writing interesting to read.
- ☐ Check for mistakes in grammar, spelling, punctuation, and sentence formation.

STOP ●

**THIS IS THE END OF
SESSION 1**

STOP

Read the following passage about O.K. and then answer questions 48 through 50.

Have you ever wondered where the word O.K. comes from? Most word aficionados believe that it comes from the nickname of Martin Van Buren who rose from a tavern potboy to the president of the United States. Elected in 1836, Van Buren became an eponym, which is a person whose name is taken for a people, place, or institution, etc. in 1840 when he ran for reelection against General William Henry Harrison. It was a tight race, and with this race came the first modern political campaign, but mostly to the disadvantage of the incumbent, Van Buren.

Harrison's followers attempted to identify Van Buren with the aristocracy and tagged him as "Little Van the Used Up Man," and "the Kinderhook Fox" among many other derogatory names. Harrison meanwhile was being christened as the "log cabin and hard cider candidate." But, to Van Buren's supporters, "Old Kinderhook," a title bestowed upon the president from the name of his birthplace, Kinderhook, New York, sounded better to them than any other title they could invent. In order to even things out a bit in the campaign, supporters in New York started the Democratic O.K. Club, taking their initials from "Old Kinderhook." These initials became the rallying cry of the Democratic party at the time and their use spread rapidly and before long the word became defined as all right, correct. As well known as the word became, it didn't do much for the president's reelection bid; he lost to Harrison. But the word honoring his name lives on and many claim that O.K. is one of the best Americanisms ever invented.

48. **O.K. are the initials that stand for _____**
   F Okalahoma.
   G Okinawa.
   H Old Kinderhook.
   J Old Kennebunkport.

49. **President Martin Van Buren ran for _____ against General William Henry Harrison.**
   A reelection
   B corporate sponsor
   C chief executive officer
   D governor

50. **In the following sentence, what does the word *incumbent* mean?**

   It was a tight race, and with this race came the first modern political campaign, but mostly to the disadvantage of the incumbent, Van Buren.

   F a person seeking to move from an area
   G a person seeking to be elected
   H a person waiting to surrender
   J a person who currently holds an office

GO ON ▶

Read the following excerpt from Mark Twain's novel *The Adventures of Huckleberry Finn* **and then answer questions 51 through 55.**

The Adventures of Huckleberry Finn   by Mark Twain

Chapter 1

YOU don't know about me without you have read a book by the name of The Adventures of Tom Sawyer; but that ain't no matter. That book was made by Mr. Mark Twain, and he told the truth, mainly. There was things which he stretched, but mainly he told the truth. That is nothing. I never seen anybody but lied one time or another, without it was Aunt Polly, or the widow, or maybe Mary. Aunt Polly—Tom's Aunt Polly, she is—and Mary, and the Widow Douglas is all told about in that book, which is mostly a true book, with some stretchers, as I said before.

Now the way that the book winds up is this: Tom and me found the money that the robbers hid in the cave, and it made us rich. We got six thousand dollars apiece—all gold. It was an awful sight of money when it was piled up. Well, Judge Thatcher he took it and put it out at interest, and it fetched us a dollar a day apiece all the year round—more than a body could tell what to do with. The Widow Douglas she took me for her son, and allowed she would sivilize me; but it was rough living in the house all the time, considering how dismal regular and decent the widow was in all her ways; and so when I couldn't stand it no longer I lit out. I got into my old rags and my sugar-hogshead again, and was free and satisfied. But Tom Sawyer he hunted me up and said he was going to start a band of robbers, and I might join if I would go back to the widow and be respectable. So I went back.

The widow she cried over me, and called me a poor lost lamb, and she called me a lot of other names, too, but she never meant no harm by it. She put me in them new clothes again, and I couldn't do nothing but sweat and sweat, and feel all cramped up. Well, then, the old thing commenced again. The widow rung a bell for supper, and you had to come to time. When you got to the table you couldn't go right to eating, but you had to wait for the widow to tuck down her head and grumble a little over the victuals, though there warn't really anything the matter with them,—that is, nothing only everything was cooked by itself. In a barrel of odds and ends it is different; things get mixed up, and the juice kind of swaps around, and the things go better.

51. **In reading the beginning of this novel, what do you detect in the voice of the narrator?**
    A a dialect
    B that he is highly educated
    C that he is from New Guinea
    D an aged tone

GO ON ▶

52. Identify the double negative in the following sentence.

> The widow she cried over me, and called me a poor lost lamb, and she called me a lot of other names, too, but she never meant no harm by it.

    F called me a poor lost lamb
    G The widow she cried over me
    H she called me a lot of other names, too,
    J but she never meant no harm by it.

53. What made Tom and Huck wealthy?
    A the money they found, $6,000.00 apiece
    B being loved by their aunts
    C their friendship
    D luck

54. Select the sentence below that is written correctly.
    F I couldn't stand it no longer.
    G She put me in them new clothes again.
    H The Widow Douglas adopted me as her son.
    J But Tom Sawyer he hunted me up.

GO ON ▶

SESSION 2 SESSION 2 SESSION 2 SESSION 2 SESSION 2

For questions 55 through 59, select the correct source for each.

55. **Where can you find up-to-date articles on Myanmar?**
    A the card catalog
    B an almanac
    C *The Reader's Guide to Periodical Literature*
    D an encyclopedia

56. **In a book about Brazil, where would you look to find the page numbers for information about the economic and political systems of Brazil?**
    F the preface
    G the table of contents
    H the glossary
    J the title page

57. **In a book about Guatemala, where would you look if you needed to have a term defined or translated for you?**
    A the preface
    B the table of contents
    C the glossary
    D the title page

58. **Which of the following is NOT seen on the title page?**
    F the title
    G the author's name
    H the publisher
    J the index

59. **To find the name of a book written by a specific author you would look in**
    A the card catalog.
    B an almanac.
    C *The Reader's Guide to Periodical Literature.*
    D an encyclopedia.

GO ON ▶

SESSION 2 SESSION 2 SESSION 2 SESSION 2 SESSION 2

For questions <u>60</u> through <u>63</u>, select the correct syllabication for the words given.

60. **audible**
   F aud ible
   G aud i ble
   H aud ib le
   J au di ble

61. **courtesy**
   A cour te sy
   B cou r tesy
   C cour tesy
   D court e sy

62. **intangible**
   F in tan gi ble
   G int an gi ble
   H in tang i ble
   J in tangible

63. **transference**
   A tran sfer ence
   B tra nsf er ence
   C trans fer ence
   D transfer ence

GO ON ▶

SESSION 2 SESSION 2 SESSION 2 SESSION 2 SESSION 2

Read the poem "Fog" by Carl Sandburg and answer questions 64 and 65.

Fog
by Carl Sandburg

The fog comes
on little cat feet.

It sits looking
over harbor and city
on silent haunches
and then moves on.

64. The _____ in this poem appeals to the sense of sight.
   F hyperbole
   G onomatopoeia
   H rhyme scheme
   J imagery

65. A literary device that is used in the poem is called
   A hyperbole.
   B onomatopoeia.
   C rhyme scheme.
   D personification.

GO ON ▶

SESSION 2 SESSION 2 SESSION 2 SESSION 2 SESSION 2

Read the following passage about the real Romeo and Juliet and then answer questions 66 through 69.

Although there is not much known about Romeo and Juliet, it is known that they were real lovers who lived in Verona, Italy, and died for each other in 1303. The Capulet and the Montague families lived in the town at the time, and as Shakespeare demonstrates in his play, Romeo and Juliet were victims of the rivalry between their parents. Although Shakespeare made the story famous, there were several versions of the story written before he wrote the play. The tale can be traced to the year 1476 in Masuccio's *Novelle* and to Arthur Brooke's poem *The Tragical Historye of Romeus and Juliet* written in the year 1562. Today, the name Romeo often refers to a male who is fond of the ladies, but *Romeo and Juliet*, as the Bard of Avon wrote, means a pair of youthful, often helpless lovers.

66. The real Romeo and Juliet lived in the city of _____
   F Cambria.
   G Los Angeles.
   H Vera Cruz.
   J Verona.

67. From the passage you can conclude that Shakespeare _____
   A liked tragedies that originated in Italy.
   B was destined to write the story of the two lovers.
   C heard or read of the original story of Romeo and Juliet from one of several sources.
   D knew Romeo and Juliet personally.

68. Romeo and Juliet lived in the _____ century.
   F 14th
   G 15th
   H 13th
   J 16th

69. The families that were feuding were the _____
   A Veronans and the Romans.
   B Martins and the Carlsons.
   C Montagues and the Capulets.
   D Johnsons and the Frenchs.

GO ON ▶

SESSION 2 SESSION 2 SESSION 2 SESSION 2 SESSION 2

Read the following excerpt of a literary work and answer questions 70 and 71.

THERE was once upon a time a poor miller who had a very beautiful daughter. Now it happened one day that he had an audience with the King, and in order to appear a person of some importance he told him that he had a daughter who could spin straw into gold. "Now that's a talent worth having," said the King to the miller; "if your daughter is as clever as you say, bring her to my palace to-morrow, and I'll put her to the test." When the girl was brought to him he led her into a room full of straw, gave her a spinning-wheel and spindle, and said: "Now set to work and spin all night till early dawn, and if by that time you haven't spun the straw into gold you shall die." Then he closed the door behind him and left her alone inside.

70. **The excerpt above is an example of what genre of literature?**
   F poem
   G nonfiction
   H novel
   J fairy tale

71. **Works in this genre usually end** _____
   A happily.
   B tragically.
   C resentfully.
   D logically.

GO ON ▶

SESSION 2 SESSION 2 SESSION 2 SESSION 2 SESSION 2

In questions <u>72</u> through <u>77</u>, read each of the sentences and select which of the words is spelled incorrectly or used incorrectly.

72. My friend Peter is going to <u>appreciate</u> seeing the <u>knew</u> <u>film</u> without a <u>doubt</u>. _____
                                    F   G   H   J

73. There will be <u>plenty</u> of <u>professional</u> jobs waiting <u>for</u> us when we <u>gradiate</u>. _____
                A   B   C   D

74. The <u>principle</u> called a <u>meeting</u> of all <u>teachers</u> to tell them about a <u>new</u> policy. _____
        F   G   H   J

75. Yesterday the <u>typhoon</u> struck the <u>eastern</u> coast of <u>japan</u> during the <u>early</u> morning. _____
                 A   B   C   D

76. My <u>family</u> spent the day driving <u>for</u> a hundred miles to <u>see</u> our <u>relatives</u> in Cerritos. _____
   F   G   H   J

77. The main <u>character</u> in the novel <u>seemed</u> to be a <u>pathetic</u>, lost <u>sole</u> destine for failure. _____
         A   B   C   D

GO ON ▶

Read the following story about a famous American and answer questions 78 through 80.

Sequoyah—Sequoia: Standing Tall

The largest and tallest of all living things on earth are the giant sequoias of California and Oregon. Their name is derived from the exalted Indian leader Sequoyah. Sequoyah is responsible for inventing the Cherokee syllabify. Not only did this alphabet make an entire people literate in a short period of time, it formed the basis for many Indian languages. It is believed that Sequoyah was born in 1770. He was the son of a white trader named Nathaniel Gist. His mother was related to the great king Oconostota. Using the name George Guess, Sequoyah had little contact with whites. He worked as a silversmith and trader in the Cherokee country of Georgia until a hunting accident left him lame. Unable to hunt, Sequoyah became fascinated with the white man's written pages and set his mind at discovering this secret of these written pages for his own people.

Over a period of twelve years, Sequoyah endured the ridicule of his family and friends. During this time he completed a table of characters representing all 86 sounds of the Cherokee spoken language by listening to the speech of those around him. In 1821, Sequoyah's alphabet system was adopted by the Cherokee. It is told that his young daughter helped in winning over the favor of the council by reading aloud a message that they secretly gave to her father to write. Because of Sequoyah's alphabet, thousands of Indians would learn to read and write.

The following year, Sequoyah joined the Arkansas Cherokee. After helping negotiate in Washington D.C. for more land, he moved with the Cherokee to Oklahoma in 1828. The remainder of his life was spent on his alphabet and studying the common elements in the Indian language. Sequoyah translated part of the Bible into Cherokee and initiated a weekly newspaper as well. Astute at avoiding bloodshed, he was instrumental in forming the Cherokee Nation. This was the result of the federal government relocating the Alabama and Tennessee Cherokee from their ancestral homes in 1839.

Sequoyah is believed to have died in 1843 while searching for a lost band of Cherokee who were rumored to have moved to Mexico at the time of his birth. He and his party of horsemen found their lost brothers and taught them to read and write. A legend in his own time, Sequoyah, is one of a few men to invent an entire alphabet and then have it adopted by a people.

Not long after Sequoyah's death, a Hungarian botanist named Stephan Endlicher gave the name Sequoia sempervirens to the redwood tree. Although it is not known for certain, it is generally assumed, that he had the great Cherokee leader in mind when he selected the name.

78. It is believed that the sequoia tree is named after the legendary Indian from the _____ tribe.

    F Chippewa

    G Nisqually

    H Navaho

    J Cherokee

GO ON ▶

SESSION 2 SESSION 2 SESSION 2 SESSION 2 SESSION 2

79. Sequoyah invented the Cherokee alphabet over a period of _____ years.
   A twelve
   B six
   C nine
   D eleven

80. There are a total of _____ sounds in the spoken language of the Cherokee.
   F 97
   G 86
   H 41
   J 56

81. From this passage you are able to infer that Sequoyah was _____
   A bored to tears.
   B lazy and always sleeping.
   C legendary and well respected.
   D an underachiever.

GO ON ▶

SESSION 2 SESSION 2 SESSION 2 SESSION 2 SESSION 2

Read the following poem about Abraham Lincoln by American poet Walt Whitman and then answer questions 82 through 85.

O Captain! My Captain!
by Walt Whitman

O Captain! my Captain! our fearful trip is done,
The ship has weathered every rack, the prize we sought is won,
The port is near, the bells I hear, the people all exulting,
While follow eyes the steady keel, the vessel grim and daring;
But O heart! heart! heart!
O the bleeding drops of red,
Where on the deck my Captain lies,
Fallen cold and dead!

O Captain! my Captain! rise up and hear the bells;
Rise up -for you the flag is flung -for you the bugle trills,
For you bouquets and ribboned wreaths -for you the shores a-crowding,
For you they call, the swaying mass, their eager faces turning;
Here Captain! dear father!
This arm beneath your head!
It is some dream that on the deck
You've fallen cold and dead.

My Captain does not answer, his lips are pale and still,
My father does not feel my arm, he has no pulse nor will,
The ship is anchored safe and sound, its voyage closed and done,
From fearful trip the victor ship comes in with object won:
Exult, O shores! and ring, O bells!
But I with mournful tread
Walk the deck my Captain lies,
Fallen cold and dead.

82. The use of the words "captain" and "ship" are _____, a literary device used in the poem to represent the assassination of Abraham Lincoln.
   F metaphorical
   G prosaic
   H personification
   J alliteration

GO ON ▶

SESSION 2 SESSION 2 SESSION 2 SESSION 2 SESSION 2

83. **Read the following line and interpret its meaning from the following.**

> The ship has weathered every rack, the prize we sought is won

  A After enduring the Civil War, the freedom fought for was won.
  B The ship survived the storm and manages to catch the largest fish
  C After weathering the storm, the ship won the prize at the fair
  D The racks at the farm were destroyed from the storm

84. **In the following passage, the narrator does not want to believe that his "Captain" is dead.**

> Here Captain! dear father!
> This arm beneath your head!
> It is some dream that on the deck
> You've fallen cold and dead.

  He wants to believe that it is all a _____.
  F fairy tale
  G dream
  H novel
  J lie

85. **Select the line that BEST confirms the death of the "Captain."**
  A But I with mournful tread
  B My father does not feel my arm, he has no pulse nor will,
  C Exult, O shores! and ring, O bells!
  D My Captain does not answer.

GO ON ▶

SESSION 2 SESSION 2 SESSION 2 SESSION 2 SESSION 2

Complete questions <u>86</u> through <u>89</u> by identifying the literary genre the name given represents.

86. Hercules
 F tale
 G fable
 H legend
 J myth

87. The Tortoise and the Hare
 A tale
 B fable
 C legend
 D myth

88. Johnny Appleseed
 F tale
 G fable
 H legend
 J myth

89. Hansel and Gretel
 A tale
 B fable
 C legend
 D myth

GO ON ▶

SESSION 2 SESSION 2 SESSION 2 SESSION 2 SESSION 2

For questions <u>90</u> through <u>94</u>, read the following pairs of words and identify whether they are synonyms, antonyms, acronyms, or homonyms.

90. FBI—CIA
    F synonym
    G antonym
    H acronym
    J homonym

91. hew—hue
    A synonym
    B antonym
    C acronym
    D homonym

92. bastion—fortress
    F synonym
    G antonym
    H acronym
    J homonym

93. hoard—squander
    A synonym
    B antonym
    C acronym
    D homonym

94. logical—irrational
    F synonym
    G antonym
    H acronym
    J homonym

GO ON ▶

SESSION 2 SESSION 2 SESSION 2 SESSION 2 SESSION 2

Writing Task 2:

Write a comparison/contrast essay in which you find things that are similar and things that are different about two objects, events, people, or ideas. Choose your topic wisely. Make certain that you are able to both compare them (find similarities) as well as contrast them (find differences). Your essay should have an introduction, two body paragraphs, and a conclusion.

Suggestions for writing: two restaurants, two characters in a play, movie, or book, two types of music, political parties, two means of travel, etc.

Checklist for Your Writing

The following checklist will help you do your best work. Make sure you:
- ☐ Read the description of the task carefully.
- ☐ Use specific details and examples to fully support your ideas.
- ☐ Organize your writing with a strong introduction, body, and conclusion.
- ☐ Choose specific words that are appropriate for your audience and purpose.
- ☐ Vary your sentences to make your writing interesting to read.
- ☐ Check for mistakes in grammar, spelling, punctuation, and sentence formation.

STOP ●

**THIS IS THE END OF
SESSION 2**

STOP

Appendix

- **Vocabulary Foursquares Page**
- **Answers to Chapter Quizzes**
- **Answers to Exam Questions**
- **Answer Documents for Practice Exams**
- **Scoring Guide to the Essays**

Vocabulary Foursquares

Chapter Review Answers: Chapter 1

DEFINITION REVIEW

1. literal
2. idiom
3. connotative
4. idiom
5. simile/figurative
6. figurative
7. personification
8. denotative/connotative (or vice versa)
9. metaphor
10. simile

VOCABULARY REVIEW I-A

1. e
2. a
3. g
4. i
5. b
6. j
7. c
8. h
9. d
10. f

VOCABULARY REVIEW I-B

1. curious
2. incentive
3. tinker
4. curiosity
5. impressed
6. darning
7. protest
8. intended
9. carriages
10. immigrants
11. variety
12. journey
13. mechanical

VOCABULARY REVIEW II-A

1. d
2. k
3. g
4. c
5. a
6. b
7. f
8. j
9. l
10. h
11. i
12. e

VOCABULARY REVIEW II-B

1. d
2. b
3. a
4. c
5. d
6. b
7. a
8. c
9. b
10. a
11. d
12. b
13. c
14. a
15. a
16. c
17. d
18. b

VOCABULARY REVIEW III-A

1. undertaking
2. frost
3. intermittently
4. impulse
5. eager
6. liberty
7. hubbub
8. dismantled
9. thicket
10. aroused
11. dense
12. slink
13. deliberately
14. trembled

VOCABULARY REVIEW III-B

1. i
2. a
3. b
4. j
5. c
6. m
7. k
8. f
9. e
10. l
11. g
12. h

13. d
14. n

VOCABULARY REVIEW IV-A

1. a
2. c
3. d
4. b
5. a
6. c
7. d
8. c
9. a
10. b
11. b
12. a
13. c
14. d

VOCABULARY REVIEW IV-B

1. iridescent
2. applicant
3. draped
4. ensure
5. perimeter
6. prominently
7. dominate
8. distress
9. foyer
10. receptionist
11. graciously
12. promptly
13. aggressive
14. protruding
15. pronounced

Chapter Review Answers: Chapter 2

SECTION I

1. u
2. m
3. i
4. c
5. n
6. q
7. v
8. b
9. j
10. k
11. p
12. o

13. g
14. f
15. e
16. a
17. t
18. s
19. r
20. d
21. h
22. l

SECTION II

1. c
2. b
3. f
4. e
5. a
6. d

SECTION III

1. c
2. u
3. y
4. z
5. a
6. p
7. f
8. r
9. u
10. k
11. m
12. e
13. b
14. o
15. r
16. v
17. i
18. aa
19. h
20. q
21. w
22. s
23. l
24. d
25. x
26. n
27. g

SECTION IV

1. d
2. k
3. h
4. f

5. b
6. d
7. l
8. i
9. e
10. a
11. j
12. n
13. c
14. g

SECTION V

1. b
2. d
3. g
4. e
5. a
6. f
7. c

SECTION VI

1. e
2. j
3. c
4. i
5. m
6. f
7. b
8. h
9. l
10. a
11. g
12. k
13. d

SECTION VII

1. junc
2. hom
3. gen
4. grad
5. hes
6. id
7. inter
8. intra
9. ject
10. grand
11. grat
12. jur
13. hetero
14. hyper

SECTION VIII

1. monit
2. man
3. lect
4. mut
5. mater
6. lev
7. morph
8. min
9. mort
10. mal
11. log
12. lus
13. mit
14. mag

SECTION IX

1. omni
2. path
3. nom
4. phone
5. nov
6. nat
7. plac
8. pater
9. port
10. pac
11. nox
12. par
13. pod
14. post
15. ped
16. pro
17. pre
18. pan
19. pug
20. pen
21. nym
22. pro
23. pen
24. para
25. peri

SECTION X

1. h
2. m
3. a
4. d
5. k
6. f
7. i
8. j

9. l
10. b
11. c
12. g
13. e

SECTION XI

1. e
2. b
3. j
4. g
5. a
6. c
7. k
8. i
9. f
10. d
11. h

SECTION XII

1. k
2. g
3. b
4. d
5. i
6. l
7. a
8. e
9. j
10. c
11. f
12. h

SECTION XIII

1. g
2. k
3. c
4. i
5. n
6. d
7. a
8. l
9. e
10. b
11. o
12. m
13. j
14. h
15. f

SECTION XIV

1. g
2. f
3. b
4. a
5. j
6. c
7. e
8. d
9. h
10. i

SECTION XV

1. f
2. i
3. c
4. a
5. h
6. j
7. b
8. d
9. g
10. e

SECTION XVI

1. c
2. a
3. b
4. a
5. c
6. b
7. a
8. b
9. c
10. b

SECTION XVII

1. c
2. c
3. a
4. a
5. b
6. a
7. a
8. a
9. b
10. a
11. a
12. b
13. a

SECTION XVIII

1. b
2. a
3. a
4. c
5. b
6. c
7. c
8. a
9. a
10. b
11. c
12. a
13. c

SECTION XIX

1. a
2. a
3. c
4. b
5. c
6. a
7. c
8. a
9. b
10. c

SECTION XX

1. c
2. c
3. b
4. a
5. c
6. a
7. a
8. c
9. c

SECTION XXI

1. a
2. c
3. b
4. a
5. c
6. b
7. a

Chapter Review Answers: Chapter 3

1. ad
2. aide
3. heir
4. aisle
5. awl
6. aweigh
7. bale
8. bawled
9. banned
10. bear
11. bass
12. beech
13. bow
14. bin
15. berth
16. block
17. bored
18. bow
19. brake
20. bred
21. bridle
22. brooch
23. cache
24. capital
25. carat
26. caste
27. ceded
28. scent
29. serial
30. coral
31. chute
32. cite
33. claws
34. course
35. kernel
36. pare
37. squeak
38. due
39. dough
40. urn
41. yew
42. fare
43. phase
44. feat
45. fur
46. flare
47. flee
48. flue
49. flour
50. forward
51. foul
52. gait
53. jeans

54. gourd
55. grate
56. grisly
57. groan
58. hare
59. haul
60. halve
61. heel
62. herd
63. idol
64. its
65. knight
66. knot
67. lead
68. leek
69. lyre
70. lynx
71. loan
72. lox
73. mane
74. meddle
75. minced
76. moor
77. mousse
78. mourning
79. naval
80. ore
81. pare
82. palette
83. patience
84. piece
85. piqued
86. pie
87. pistil
88. pleas
89. plumb
90. poll
91. pore
92. presence
93. principal
94. profit
95. wracked
96. razed
97. wrap
98. rapt
99. reed
100. read
101. wreak
102. wrest
103. wretched
104. rite
105. wry
106. sale
107. seam

108. seize
109. sow
110. sheared
111. sighed
112. sigh
113. slaying
114. soar
115. sword
116. staring
117. stake
118. stationary
119. suite
120. taut
121. tear
122. tents
123. tern
124. they're
125. threw
126. throne
127. thyme
128. tide
129. too
130. tow
131. toad
132. veil
133. vane
134. vial
135. wail
136. waste
137. weight
138. weighed
139. wee
140. weak
141. we'd
142. whine
143. would
144. yolk
145. yore

SECTION V

1. h
2. c
3. k
4. a
5. m
6. d
7. f
8. l
9. b
10. i
11. e
12. g
13. j

SECTION VI

1. d
2. h
3. a
4. j
5. b
6. k
7. c
8. l
9. e
10. f
11. g
12. i

Chapter Review Answers: Chapter 4

Answers:

Question 1 asks what the story is "mainly about." You will be looking for an answer that provides the **main idea** of the story. **The correct answer to Question 1 is B**—main idea. This means you must read the passage carefully; visualize and understand thoroughly.

Question 2 is asking for a date of some sort; this is a **detail** that is easily found in the reading—scanning the reading quickly will help you answer this question. **The correct answer to Question 2 is A**—details.

Question 3 asks what a certain paragraph is about. **The correct answer to Question 3 is B**—main idea.

Question 4 asks something that you need to think about or **infer.** You really don't know what was going on inside the mind of the people who were stuck on a Ferris wheel for hours, but you can imagine what was going through their minds. You must therefore infer. **The correct answer to Question 4 is C.**

Question 5 is asking for details of Clarence Smith's idea. Don't let the word "idea" fool you into thinking this is a question about the main idea—it isn't. The question makers simply want to find out what his idea is. **The correct answer to Question 5 is A.**

Chapter Review Answers: Chapter 5

1. C
2. B
3. D
4. A
5. D
6. A
7. D
8. A
9. B
10. A

11. B
12. A
13. D
14. C
15. A

Chapter Review Answers: Chapter 6

1. h
2. l
3. aa
4. q
5. a
6. ee
7. v
8. o
9. p
10. d
11. f
12. n
13. g
14. bb
15. y
16. i
17. b
18. dd
19. u
20. r
21. e
22. k
23. cc
24. z
25. t
26. m
27. j
28. s
29. x
30. c

Chapter Review Answers: Chapter 7

1. q
2. f
3. l
4. a
5. r
6. n
7. o
8. d
9. b
10. k
11. s

12. g
13. j
14. i
15. c
16. e
17. h
18. t
19. p
20. m

Chapter Review Answers: Chapter 8

SECTION I: CLAUSES

1. clause
2. subject
3. predicate
4. subject
5. verb
6. two
7. independent
8. subordinate
9. independent
10. subordinate
11. adjective
12. adverb
13. noun

SECTION II: PHRASES

1. phrase
2. subject
3. verb
4. prepositional
5. verbal
6. participial
7. gerund
8. infinitive
9. prepositional
10. noun
11. pronoun
12. adjective
13. phrase
14. adjective
15. adverb
16. Verbal
17. adjective
18. -ing
19. nouns
20. Infinitive
21. Appositive

SECTION III: PUNCTUATION

The word Machiavellian has become synonymous (a synonym) for political immorality. Niccolo Machiavelli, who lived from 1469–1527, wrote a book titled *The Prince*, which is remembered for its insistence that while his subjects are bound by conventional or the normal moral obligations, a ruler may use any means necessary to maintain power and it doesn't matter how unscrupulous. Therefore, Machiavellian has come to mean cynical political scheming, which is characterized by deceit and bad faith. Evidently, Niccolo was a thin-lipped man who was very hyperactive and sarcastic. Isn't it amazing how the memory of one man with a theory of political morality can be so appropriate to modern times?

Chapter Review Answers: Chapter 9

SECTION I: CAPITALIZATION

1. first
2. I
3. quotation
4. proper
5. capitalize
6. Organizations
7. associations
8. government bodies

SECTION II: SENTENCES

1. sentence
2. Declarative
3. imperative
4. Exclamatory
5. interrogative

SECTION III: SENTENCE STRUCTURE

1. sentence
2. subject
3. predicate
4. verb
5. verb
6. plural
7. verb
8. agreement
9. Double
10. negative
11. comparative
12. superlative

Answers: Chapter 12 Practice Exam 1

Answers: Practice Exam 1

SESSION 1

1. B
2. F
3. D
4. F
5. B
6. H
7. A
8. F
9. C
10. F
11. B
12. F
13. A
14. H
15. A
16. F
17. C
18. F
19. C
20. F
21. C
22. H
23. A
24. F
25. B
26. J
27. B
28. J
29. B
30. J
31. C
32. G
33. A
34. F
35. C
36. H
37. B
38. J
39. C
40. F
41. B
42. F
43. C
44. H
45. B
46. L
47. B

SESSION 2

48. H
49. D
50. J
51. B
52. J
53. A
54. J
55. C
56. H
57. B
58. J
59. C
60. H
61. B
62. G
63. A
64. H
65. C
66. F
67. A
68. J
69. C
70. F
71. B
72. J
73. C
74. H
75. C
76. G
77. B
78. J
79. A
80. H
81. D
82. F
83. D
84. J
85. D
86. H
87. C
88. J
89. A
90. G
91. C
92. G
93. A
94. J

Answers: Practice Exam 2

SESSION 1

1. C
2. H
3. A
4. J
5. C
6. J
7. B
8. F
9. D
10. J
11. B
12. H
13. C
14. F
15. B
16. H
17. A
18. G
19. D
20. H
21. A
22. G
23. D
24. J
25. B
26. G
27. C
28. J
29. D
30. F
31. C
32. G
33. A
34. J
35. A
36. H
37. C
38. F
39. D
40. F
41. B
42. J
43. A
44. F
45. C
46. F
47. D

Answers: Practice Exam 2

SESSION 2

48. H
49. A
50. J
51. A
52. J
53. A
54. H
55. C
56. G
57. C
58. J
59. A
60. J
61. A
62. F
63. C
64. J
65. D
66. J
67. C
68. F
69. C
70. J
71. A
72. G
73. D
74. F
75. C
76. G
77. D
78. J
79. A
80. G
81. C
82. F
83. A
84. G
85. B
86. J
87. B
88. H
89. A
90. H
91. D
92. F
93. B
94. G

English-Language Arts—Session 1 Practice Exam 1

USE ONLY A NO. 2 PENCIL TO COMPLETE THIS FORM

1. Ⓐ Ⓑ Ⓒ Ⓓ	11. Ⓐ Ⓑ Ⓒ Ⓓ	21. Ⓐ Ⓑ Ⓒ Ⓓ	31. Ⓐ Ⓑ Ⓒ Ⓓ	41. Ⓐ Ⓑ Ⓒ Ⓓ
2. Ⓕ Ⓖ Ⓗ Ⓙ	12. Ⓕ Ⓖ Ⓗ Ⓙ	22. Ⓕ Ⓖ Ⓗ Ⓙ	32. Ⓕ Ⓖ Ⓗ Ⓙ	42. Ⓕ Ⓖ Ⓗ Ⓙ
3. Ⓐ Ⓑ Ⓒ Ⓓ	13. Ⓐ Ⓑ Ⓒ Ⓓ	23. Ⓐ Ⓑ Ⓒ Ⓓ	33. Ⓐ Ⓑ Ⓒ Ⓓ	43. Ⓐ Ⓑ Ⓒ Ⓓ
4. Ⓕ Ⓖ Ⓗ Ⓙ	14. Ⓕ Ⓖ Ⓗ Ⓙ	24. Ⓕ Ⓖ Ⓗ Ⓙ	34. Ⓕ Ⓖ Ⓗ Ⓙ	44. Ⓕ Ⓖ Ⓗ Ⓙ
5. Ⓐ Ⓑ Ⓒ Ⓓ	15. Ⓐ Ⓑ Ⓒ Ⓓ	25. Ⓐ Ⓑ Ⓒ Ⓓ	35. Ⓐ Ⓑ Ⓒ Ⓓ	45. Ⓐ Ⓑ Ⓒ Ⓓ
6. Ⓕ Ⓖ Ⓗ Ⓙ	16. Ⓕ Ⓖ Ⓗ Ⓙ	26. Ⓕ Ⓖ Ⓗ Ⓙ	36. Ⓕ Ⓖ Ⓗ Ⓙ	46. Ⓕ Ⓖ Ⓗ Ⓙ
7. Ⓐ Ⓑ Ⓒ Ⓓ	17. Ⓐ Ⓑ Ⓒ Ⓓ	27. Ⓐ Ⓑ Ⓒ Ⓓ	37. Ⓐ Ⓑ Ⓒ Ⓓ	47. Ⓐ Ⓑ Ⓒ Ⓓ
8. Ⓕ Ⓖ Ⓗ Ⓙ	18. Ⓕ Ⓖ Ⓗ Ⓙ	28. Ⓕ Ⓖ Ⓗ Ⓙ	38. Ⓕ Ⓖ Ⓗ Ⓙ	
9. Ⓐ Ⓑ Ⓒ Ⓓ	19. Ⓐ Ⓑ Ⓒ Ⓓ	29. Ⓐ Ⓑ Ⓒ Ⓓ	39. Ⓐ Ⓑ Ⓒ Ⓓ	
10. Ⓕ Ⓖ Ⓗ Ⓙ	20. Ⓕ Ⓖ Ⓗ Ⓙ	30. Ⓕ Ⓖ Ⓗ Ⓙ	40. Ⓕ Ⓖ Ⓗ Ⓙ	

1   WRITING TASK 1—PRACTICE EXAM 1   **1**
USE ONLY A NO. 2 PENCIL TO WRITE YOUR RESPONSE

**ENGLISH-LANGUAGE ARTS—*SESSION 1*
CONTINUE WRITING YOUR RESPONSE FOR
PRACTICE EXAM 1—WRITING TASK 1 ONLY**

**ENGLISH-LANGUAGE ARTS—*SESSION 1*
CONTINUE WRITING YOUR RESPONSE FOR
PRACTICE EXAM 1—WRITING TASK 1 ONLY**

END OF WRITING TASK 1

English-Language Arts—Session 2 Practice Exam 1

USE ONLY A NO. 2 PENCIL TO COMPLETE THIS FORM

1. Ⓐ Ⓑ Ⓒ Ⓓ	11. Ⓐ Ⓑ Ⓒ Ⓓ	21. Ⓐ Ⓑ Ⓒ Ⓓ	31. Ⓐ Ⓑ Ⓒ Ⓓ	41. Ⓐ Ⓑ Ⓒ Ⓓ
2. Ⓕ Ⓖ Ⓗ Ⓙ	12. Ⓕ Ⓖ Ⓗ Ⓙ	22. Ⓕ Ⓖ Ⓗ Ⓙ	32. Ⓕ Ⓖ Ⓗ Ⓙ	42. Ⓕ Ⓖ Ⓗ Ⓙ
3. Ⓐ Ⓑ Ⓒ Ⓓ	13. Ⓐ Ⓑ Ⓒ Ⓓ	23. Ⓐ Ⓑ Ⓒ Ⓓ	33. Ⓐ Ⓑ Ⓒ Ⓓ	43. Ⓐ Ⓑ Ⓒ Ⓓ
4. Ⓕ Ⓖ Ⓗ Ⓙ	14. Ⓕ Ⓖ Ⓗ Ⓙ	24. Ⓕ Ⓖ Ⓗ Ⓙ	34. Ⓕ Ⓖ Ⓗ Ⓙ	44. Ⓕ Ⓖ Ⓗ Ⓙ
5. Ⓐ Ⓑ Ⓒ Ⓓ	15. Ⓐ Ⓑ Ⓒ Ⓓ	25. Ⓐ Ⓑ Ⓒ Ⓓ	35. Ⓐ Ⓑ Ⓒ Ⓓ	45. Ⓐ Ⓑ Ⓒ Ⓓ
6. Ⓕ Ⓖ Ⓗ Ⓙ	16. Ⓕ Ⓖ Ⓗ Ⓙ	26. Ⓕ Ⓖ Ⓗ Ⓙ	36. Ⓕ Ⓖ Ⓗ Ⓙ	46. Ⓕ Ⓖ Ⓗ Ⓙ
7. Ⓐ Ⓑ Ⓒ Ⓓ	17. Ⓐ Ⓑ Ⓒ Ⓓ	27. Ⓐ Ⓑ Ⓒ Ⓓ	37. Ⓐ Ⓑ Ⓒ Ⓓ	47. Ⓐ Ⓑ Ⓒ Ⓓ
8. Ⓕ Ⓖ Ⓗ Ⓙ	18. Ⓕ Ⓖ Ⓗ Ⓙ	28. Ⓕ Ⓖ Ⓗ Ⓙ	38. Ⓕ Ⓖ Ⓗ Ⓙ	
9. Ⓐ Ⓑ Ⓒ Ⓓ	19. Ⓐ Ⓑ Ⓒ Ⓓ	29. Ⓐ Ⓑ Ⓒ Ⓓ	39. Ⓐ Ⓑ Ⓒ Ⓓ	
10. Ⓕ Ⓖ Ⓗ Ⓙ	20. Ⓕ Ⓖ Ⓗ Ⓙ	30. Ⓕ Ⓖ Ⓗ Ⓙ	40. Ⓕ Ⓖ Ⓗ Ⓙ	

2   PRACTICE EXAM 1—WRITING TASK 2   **2**
USE ONLY A NO. 2 PENCIL TO WRITE YOUR RESPONSE

**ENGLISH-LANGUAGE ARTS—*SESSION 2*
CONTINUE WRITING YOUR RESPONSE FOR
PRACTICE EXAM 1—WRITING TASK 2 ONLY**

ENGLISH-LANGUAGE ARTS—*SESSION 2*
CONTINUE WRITING YOUR RESPONSE FOR
PRACTICE EXAM 1—WRITING TASK 2 ONLY

END OF WRITING TASK 2

English-Language Arts—Session 1 Practice Exam 2

USE ONLY A NO. 2 PENCIL TO COMPLETE THIS FORM

1. Ⓐ Ⓑ Ⓒ Ⓓ	11. Ⓐ Ⓑ Ⓒ Ⓓ	21. Ⓐ Ⓑ Ⓒ Ⓓ	31. Ⓐ Ⓑ Ⓒ Ⓓ	41. Ⓐ Ⓑ Ⓒ Ⓓ
2. Ⓕ Ⓖ Ⓗ Ⓙ	12. Ⓕ Ⓖ Ⓗ Ⓙ	22. Ⓕ Ⓖ Ⓗ Ⓙ	32. Ⓕ Ⓖ Ⓗ Ⓙ	42. Ⓕ Ⓖ Ⓗ Ⓙ
3. Ⓐ Ⓑ Ⓒ Ⓓ	13. Ⓐ Ⓑ Ⓒ Ⓓ	23. Ⓐ Ⓑ Ⓒ Ⓓ	33. Ⓐ Ⓑ Ⓒ Ⓓ	43. Ⓐ Ⓑ Ⓒ Ⓓ
4. Ⓕ Ⓖ Ⓗ Ⓙ	14. Ⓕ Ⓖ Ⓗ Ⓙ	24. Ⓕ Ⓖ Ⓗ Ⓙ	34. Ⓕ Ⓖ Ⓗ Ⓙ	44. Ⓕ Ⓖ Ⓗ Ⓙ
5. Ⓐ Ⓑ Ⓒ Ⓓ	15. Ⓐ Ⓑ Ⓒ Ⓓ	25. Ⓐ Ⓑ Ⓒ Ⓓ	35. Ⓐ Ⓑ Ⓒ Ⓓ	45. Ⓐ Ⓑ Ⓒ Ⓓ
6. Ⓕ Ⓖ Ⓗ Ⓙ	16. Ⓕ Ⓖ Ⓗ Ⓙ	26. Ⓕ Ⓖ Ⓗ Ⓙ	36. Ⓕ Ⓖ Ⓗ Ⓙ	46. Ⓕ Ⓖ Ⓗ Ⓙ
7. Ⓐ Ⓑ Ⓒ Ⓓ	17. Ⓐ Ⓑ Ⓒ Ⓓ	27. Ⓐ Ⓑ Ⓒ Ⓓ	37. Ⓐ Ⓑ Ⓒ Ⓓ	47. Ⓐ Ⓑ Ⓒ Ⓓ
8. Ⓕ Ⓖ Ⓗ Ⓙ	18. Ⓕ Ⓖ Ⓗ Ⓙ	28. Ⓕ Ⓖ Ⓗ Ⓙ	38. Ⓕ Ⓖ Ⓗ Ⓙ	
9. Ⓐ Ⓑ Ⓒ Ⓓ	19. Ⓐ Ⓑ Ⓒ Ⓓ	29. Ⓐ Ⓑ Ⓒ Ⓓ	39. Ⓐ Ⓑ Ⓒ Ⓓ	
10. Ⓕ Ⓖ Ⓗ Ⓙ	20. Ⓕ Ⓖ Ⓗ Ⓙ	30. Ⓕ Ⓖ Ⓗ Ⓙ	40. Ⓕ Ⓖ Ⓗ Ⓙ	

1   PRACTICE EXAM 2—WRITING TASK 1   **1**
USE ONLY A NO. 2 PENCIL TO WRITE YOUR RESPONSE

ENGLISH-LANGUAGE ARTS—*SESSION 1*
CONTINUE WRITING YOUR RESPONSE FOR
PRACTICE EXAM 2—WRITING TASK 1 ONLY

ENGLISH-LANGUAGE ARTS—*SESSION 1*
CONTINUE WRITING YOUR RESPONSE FOR
PRACTICE EXAM 2—WRITING TASK 1 ONLY

END OF WRITING TASK 1

English-Language Arts—Session 2 Practice Exam 2

USE ONLY A NO. 2 PENCIL TO COMPLETE THIS FORM

1. Ⓐ Ⓑ Ⓒ Ⓓ	11. Ⓐ Ⓑ Ⓒ Ⓓ	21. Ⓐ Ⓑ Ⓒ Ⓓ	31. Ⓐ Ⓑ Ⓒ Ⓓ	41. Ⓐ Ⓑ Ⓒ Ⓓ
2. Ⓕ Ⓖ Ⓗ Ⓙ	12. Ⓕ Ⓖ Ⓗ Ⓙ	22. Ⓕ Ⓖ Ⓗ Ⓙ	32. Ⓕ Ⓖ Ⓗ Ⓙ	42. Ⓕ Ⓖ Ⓗ Ⓙ
3. Ⓐ Ⓑ Ⓒ Ⓓ	13. Ⓐ Ⓑ Ⓒ Ⓓ	23. Ⓐ Ⓑ Ⓒ Ⓓ	33. Ⓐ Ⓑ Ⓒ Ⓓ	43. Ⓐ Ⓑ Ⓒ Ⓓ
4. Ⓕ Ⓖ Ⓗ Ⓙ	14. Ⓕ Ⓖ Ⓗ Ⓙ	24. Ⓕ Ⓖ Ⓗ Ⓙ	34. Ⓕ Ⓖ Ⓗ Ⓙ	44. Ⓕ Ⓖ Ⓗ Ⓙ
5. Ⓐ Ⓑ Ⓒ Ⓓ	15. Ⓐ Ⓑ Ⓒ Ⓓ	25. Ⓐ Ⓑ Ⓒ Ⓓ	35. Ⓐ Ⓑ Ⓒ Ⓓ	45. Ⓐ Ⓑ Ⓒ Ⓓ
6. Ⓕ Ⓖ Ⓗ Ⓙ	16. Ⓕ Ⓖ Ⓗ Ⓙ	26. Ⓕ Ⓖ Ⓗ Ⓙ	36. Ⓕ Ⓖ Ⓗ Ⓙ	46. Ⓕ Ⓖ Ⓗ Ⓙ
7. Ⓐ Ⓑ Ⓒ Ⓓ	17. Ⓐ Ⓑ Ⓒ Ⓓ	27. Ⓐ Ⓑ Ⓒ Ⓓ	37. Ⓐ Ⓑ Ⓒ Ⓓ	47. Ⓐ Ⓑ Ⓒ Ⓓ
8. Ⓕ Ⓖ Ⓗ Ⓙ	18. Ⓕ Ⓖ Ⓗ Ⓙ	28. Ⓕ Ⓖ Ⓗ Ⓙ	38. Ⓕ Ⓖ Ⓗ Ⓙ	
9. Ⓐ Ⓑ Ⓒ Ⓓ	19. Ⓐ Ⓑ Ⓒ Ⓓ	29. Ⓐ Ⓑ Ⓒ Ⓓ	39. Ⓐ Ⓑ Ⓒ Ⓓ	
10. Ⓕ Ⓖ Ⓗ Ⓙ	20. Ⓕ Ⓖ Ⓗ Ⓙ	30. Ⓕ Ⓖ Ⓗ Ⓙ	40. Ⓕ Ⓖ Ⓗ Ⓙ	

2   **WRITING TASK 2**   **2**
USE ONLY A NO. 2 PENCIL TO WRITE YOUR RESPONSE

**ENGLISH-LANGUAGE ARTS—*SESSION 1*
CONTINUE WRITING YOUR RESPONSE FOR
PRACTICE EXAM 2—WRITING TASK 2 ONLY**

ENGLISH-LANGUAGE ARTS—*SESSION 1*
CONTINUE WRITING YOUR RESPONSE FOR
PRACTICE EXAM 2—WRITING TASK 2 ONLY

END OF WRITING TASK 2

Response to Literary/Expository Text

Scoring Guide

4

The response —

- demonstrates a *thorough and thoughtful*, comprehensive grasp of the text.
- accurately and coherently provides *specific* textual details and examples to support the thesis and main ideas.
- demonstrates a *clear* understanding of the ambiguities, nuances, and complexities of the text.
- provides a variety of sentence types and uses *precise, descriptive* language.
- contains *few, if any, errors* in the conventions of the English language. (Errors are generally first-draft in nature.)*

Response to informational passages:

- *thoughtfully* anticipates and addresses the reader's potential misunderstandings, biases, and expectations.

Response to literary passages:

- clearly demonstrates an awareness of the author's use of literary and/or stylistic devices.

3

The response —

- demonstrates a comprehensive grasp of the text.
- accurately and coherently provides *general* textual details and examples to support the thesis and main ideas.
- demonstrates a *general* understanding of the ambiguities, nuances, and complexities of the text.
- provides a variety of sentence types and uses *some descriptive* language.
- contains *some errors* in the conventions of the English language. (Errors do not interfere with the reader's understanding of the essay.)*

Response to informational passages:

- anticipates and addresses the reader's potential misunderstandings, biases, and expectations.

Response to literary passages:

- demonstrates an awareness of the author's use of literary and/or stylistic devices.

2

The response —

- demonstrates a *limited* comprehensive grasp of the text.
- provides *few, if any,* textual details and examples to support the thesis and main ideas.
- demonstrates a *limited, or no,* understanding of the ambiguities, nuances, and complexities of the text.
- provides *few, if any,* types of sentences and uses *basic, predictable* language.
- contains *several errors* in the conventions of the English language. (Errors may interfere with the reader's understanding of the essay.)*

Response to informational passages:

- *may* address the reader's potential misunderstandings, biases, and expectations, but in a limited manner.

Response to literary passages:

- *may* demonstrate an awareness of the author's use of literary and/or stylistic devices.

1

The response —

- demonstrates *little, if any,* comprehensive grasp of the text.
- provides *no* textual details and examples to support the thesis and main ideas.
- demonstrates *no* understanding of the ambiguities, nuances, and complexities of the text.
- provides *no* sentence variety and uses *limited* vocabulary.
- contains *serious errors* in the conventions of the English language. (Errors interfere with the reader's understanding of the essay.)*

Response to informational passages:

- does *not* address the reader's potential misunderstandings, biases, and expectations.

Response to literary passages:

- does *not* demonstrate any awareness of the author's use of literary and/or stylistic devices.

Non-scorable

B = Blank

T = Off-topic

L = Written in a language other than English

I = Illegible/Unintelligible

Conventions of the English language refer to grammar, punctuation, spelling, capitalization, and usage.

Index

LOOKING FOR STUDY STRATEGIES THAT WORK? HAVE WE GOT SECRETS FOR YOU!

Study Tactics
$8.95, Canada *$11.95*
(0-8120-2590-3)
An easy-to-follow plan for sound study habits. Included are pointers for improving writing skills, increasing reading speed, reviewing for exams and taking them, developing good working habits, and much more.

Student Success Secrets, 5th Edition
$8.95, Canada *$12.50*
(0-7641-2007-7)
These sure-fire strategies can increase every student's test scores and raise their grades. Advice covers methods for forming good study habits, retaining information from reading, and taking useful classroom notes. There are also tips to help students do their best when taking exams.

B's & A's in 30 Days
$9.95, Canada *$13.95*
(0-8120-9582-0)
Here's a sure-fire student success system for better grades, less stress, and greater self confidence. The book is divided into thirty short entertaining, instructive chapters—one for each day of the program. Students will learn how to set goals they can reach, study better in less time, take better classroom notes, and more. Amusing cartoon illustrations keep the mood appropriately light.

Barron's Educational Series, Inc.
250 Wireless Boulevard
Hauppauge, New York 11788

In Canada:
Georgetown Book Warehouse
34 Armstrong Avenue
Georgetown, Ontario L7G 4R9

Prices subject to change without notice. Books may be purchased at your bookstore, or by mail from Barron's. Enclose check or money order for total amount plus sales tax where applicable and 18% for postage and handling (minimum charge $5.95). All books are paperback editions.

Visit our website at: barronseduc.com

(#9) R 1/03

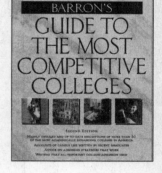